Green Economics

An Introduction to Theory, Policy and Practice

Molly Scott Cato

D0082627

publishing for a sustainable future

London • Sterling, VA

First published by Earthscan in the UK and USA in 2009

ISBN: 978-1-84407-571-3 (pb)
         978-1-84407-570-6 (hb)

Typeset by MapSet Ltd, Gateshead, UK
Printed and bound in the UK by TJ International Ltd, Padstow
Cover design by Rob Watts

For a full list of publications please contact:

Earthscan
Dunstan House
14a St Cross Street
London EC1N 8XA, UK
Tel: +44 (0)20 7841 1930
Fax: +44 (0)20 7242 1474
Email: earthinfo@earthscan.co.uk
Web: **www.earthscan.co.uk**

22883 Quicksilver Drive, Sterling, VA 20166-2012, USA

Earthscan publishes in association with the International Institute
for Environment and Development

A catalogue record for this book is available from the British Library

Library of Congress Cataloging-in-Publication Data has been applied for

  Green economics : An introduction to theory, policy and practice / Molly Scott
  Cato.
       p. cm.
    Includes bibliographical references and index.
    ISBN 978-1-84407-570-6 (hardback) – ISBN 978-1-84407-571-3 (paperback)
    1. Environmental economics. 2. Economics–Sociological aspects. 3. Sustainable
  living. 4. Economic policy. 5. Social policy I. Title.
    HC79.E5C383 2008
    333.7–dc22

                                                              2008036287

For James Robertson,

The Grandfather of Green Economics

A map of the world that does not include Utopia is not worth even glancing at, for it leaves out the one country at which Humanity is always landing. And when Humanity lands there, it looks out, and, seeing a better country, sets sail.

Oscar Wilde

Contents

PART III POLICIES FOR A GREEN ECONOMY

List of Photographs, Figures, Tables and Boxes

PHOTOGRAPHS

FIGURES

TABLES

BOXES

Acknowledgements

My first and deepest gratitude must be for all those, named and unnamed, who have taxed their minds and spirits to clear the path towards a way of living more comfortably within our environment. I am also extremely grateful to those who have put aside time in their busy lives to support me by reading drafts of various chapters: John Barry, David Fleming, Steve Harris, Chris Hart, Brian Heatley, Colin Hines, Nadia Johanisova, Martin Large, Mary Mellor, Barbara Panvel and Jane Serraillier. John Barry, in particular, has helped me at every stage of the writing and supported my conviction that green economics is an academic discipline in its own right, and one that needs to be taught as such in the universities.

Others who have supported and helped me in the writing of this book are too numerous to mention. A few who spring immediately to mind are Len Arthur, Richard Bickle, Rebecca Boden, Richard Douthwaite, Debbie Epstein, Rob Hopkins, Pete North, James Robertson, Helen Royall, Diana Schumacher and Tony Weekes, and from the Green Party, Caroline Lucas, Fi Macmillan, John Marjoram, Philip Booth, Rupert Read and Martin Whiteside.

Special thanks to my gifted and talented daughter, Rosa, who has loaned me her laptop at times when she heartily wished to be watching *The Mighty Boosh*.

And finally thanks to the Stroudies, for welcoming me so warmly into their community and for putting a green economist to good use.

Preface

As I have been writing I have come to think of this book as a scrapbook – or perhaps, in a book that concerns itself with a whole range of ways of provisioning and is particularly interested in those that do not involve the market, I should say that I have become a hunter and a gatherer. I have had to hunt down obscure books and writers who have been neglected by the mainstream. I have gathered up their insights and offer them here for your consumption. Of course all books draw widely on other sources in presenting a case, but this book is more like a collection of ideas and evidence drawn from the many writers who have contributed to this developing field – often without identifying themselves as green economists. I have been responsible for the selection and for the thread that runs through the work, but this is not a work of original or creative writing.

What has inspired me during the writing has been the growing admiration for the huge oeuvre that has gone unnoticed by policy makers and the general public. This is partly our own responsibility as green economists. We are a somewhat media-shy and gnomic bunch, lurking in dark corners burnishing our gems but not exposing them to enough light. Many of the people whose work I cite in the following chapters are colleagues; many are also friends. While it has been an enjoyably cosy adventure thus far, I think it is time that this work was taken beyond the charmed circle. I hope the following chapters will give you a taste for what green economics is all about; however, there is not enough space to do more than that. In Chapter 13 I provide a summary and lists of resources for taking your interest further.

The book begins with some history of green economics ideas to give a grounding to the discipline. For me it is important to know where we have come from, but if your concerns are more with the proposition and policies we are offering, you could go straight to Chapter 4. You will notice that there are contributions from politicians and campaigners as well as academics throughout the book. In Chapter 1 I discuss the way that green economics has grown up from the grassroots in response to identifiable social and environmental problems. This is why the nascent discipline is enriched by the contributions of those outside the academy.

There is little doubt that we face a major environmental crisis for which traditional solutions appear useless. I am so glad to be able to share with you the fruits of the labours of so many dedicated men and women over the past 30 years or so. It seems to me that most of the answers we need are here. Please share them, build on them and, most importantly, act on them.

Molly Scott Cato
Stroud
June 2008

1
Green Economics: Economics for People and the Planet

Economic man is fit, mobile, able-bodied, unencumbered by domestic or other responsibilities. The goods he consumes appear to him as finished products or services and disappear from his view on disposal or dismissal. He has no responsibility for the life-cycle of those goods or services any more than he questions the source of the air he breathes or the disposal of his excreta... Like Oscar Wilde's Dorian Gray, economic man appears to exist in a smoothly functioning world, while the portrait in the attic represents his real social, biological and ecological condition.

Mary Mellor, 'Challenging Economic Boundaries: Ecofeminist Political Economy', 2006

Over the past five years or so the issue of climate change has moved from a peripheral concern of scientists and environmentalists to being a central issue in global policy making. It was the realization that the way our economy operates is causing pollution on a scale that threatens our very survival that first motivated the development of a green approach to the economy. We are in an era of declining oil supplies and increased competition for those that remain. This raises concerns about the future of an economy that is entirely dependent on oil and a wider recognition of the importance of using our limited resources wisely. This was the other motivation for the development of green economics. In addition, green economists have been concerned about the way an economic system based on competition has led to widening inequalities between rich and poor on a global as well as a national scale, and the inevitable tension and conflict this inequality generates.

At last, these three issues are reaching the mainstream of political debate. This increased attention is being driven mainly by public opinion and by campaigners such as in the Make Poverty History campaign or the Climate Chaos Campaign. Politicians appear to have been caught on the hop and their responses seem both half-hearted and inadequate. In this context, green economics has for the past 30 years been developing policy based on a recognition of planetary limits and the importance of using resources wisely and justly; these insights are of crucial importance.

Why green economics?

I have called this chapter 'Economics for People and the Planet', and that is a glib phrase which green economists frequently use to describe how their proposal for the world's economy is different. It is really shorthand for expressing a need to move beyond the narrow view of the economy as it is currently organized. So many perspectives are never considered by a system of economics that privileges white, wealthy, Western men. The way the global economy is organized can be seen as an extension of a colonial system, whereby the resources and people of most of the planet are harnessed to improve the living standards of the minority of people who live in the privileged West. On the one hand, the rights of people living in the global South to an equal share in the planet's resources should be respected. On the other, their approach to economics, especially that of indigenous societies that have managed to survive within their environments for thousands of years, has much to recommend it and much we may learn from.

Even within Western societies there are gross inequalities between people. As the data in Box 1.1 show, inequality is growing steadily in the UK, and this is mirrored in other countries, including the rapidly developing economies in the South.[1] The system of patriarchy has ensured that the majority of resources are controlled by men. Most of the world's poor are women. The male dominance of the economy has resulted in a situation where women form 70 per cent of the world's poor and own only 1 per cent of the world's assets (Amnesty International). According to the United Nations Population Fund (UNFPA) (2005), on a global basis women earn only 50 per cent of what men earn. And in spite of equal pay legislation in the UK and US the pay gap between the genders persists.

Policy makers are happy to use the word 'exploit' when talking about resources such as oil or minerals. Yet for green economists exploitation of the planet's resources is as unacceptable as exploitation of the people who live on it. The failure to respect the planet has led to problems as diverse as climate change and desertification. In order to address these problems green economists suggest that we need a completely different attitude towards meeting our needs, one which involves respecting ecology and living in balance with the planet.

Another short phrase that encapsulates something important about green economics is 'beyond supply and demand to meeting people's needs.' This contains an explicit criticism of the discipline of economics for its obsession with graphs and mathematics and its inability to look out of the window and see what is really happening in the world. Green economics begins with people and their concerns rather than with theories or mathematical constructions of

---

BOX 1.1 INEQUALITY IN THE UK, 1994–2004

- Since 1997, the richest have continued to get richer. The richest 1 per cent of the population has increased its share of national income from around 6 per cent in 1980 to 13 per cent in 1999.
- Wealth distribution is more unequal than income distribution, and has continued to get more unequal in the last decade. Between 1990 and 2000 the percentage of wealth held by the wealthiest 10 per cent of the population increased from 47 per cent to 54 per cent.
- Although the gender pay gap has narrowed, only very slow progress has been made since 1994. In 1994 women in full-time work earned on average 79.5 per cent of what men earned; by 2003 this had only increased to 82 per cent.
- Deprived communities suffer the worst effects of environmental degradation. Industrial sites are disproportionately located in deprived areas: in 2003, there were five times as many sites in the wards containing the most deprived 10 per cent of the population, and seven times as many emission sources, than in wards with the least deprived 10 per cent.

Source: 'State of the Nation', Institute for Public Policy Research, 2004.

---

reality. Conventional economics will provide a graph with two straight lines representing 'supply' and 'demand' and then apply this to the complex relationships entailed by the production and exchange of goods. Green economics calls for a richer and deeper understanding of people, their relationships, and how they behave and are motivated. The 'needs' we are concerned about are not merely physical needs but also psychological and spiritual needs.

The word 'holism' sums up the way in which we have to learn to see the big picture when making economic decisions. The absence of holistic thinking is clear in modern policy making, where crime is punished by incarceration without attempting to understand how an economic system that dangles tempting baubles in front of those who cannot afford them, and deprives them of the means of meeting their deeper needs, is simply generating this crime. A similar comment can be made in the case of health, where pollution creates ill health which is then cured by producing pharmaceuticals, the production of which generates more pollution. From a green perspective we need to see the whole picture before we can solve any of these problems.

Green economics also extends the circle of concern beyond our single species to consider the whole system of planet Earth with all its complex ecology and its diverse species. As an illustration of the narrowness of the current approach to policy making we can use the thought experiment of the Parliament of All Beings. We begin by considering a national parliament in the UK or the US, which is made up of representatives of a significant number of people in those countries, only excluding those who could not or will not vote or whose votes do not translate into seats. Now we imagine a world parliament, where each country sends a number of representatives so that all countries' interests are equally represented. We now have a much broader-based and democratic way of deciding whether the solutions to Iraq's problems will be solved by a US invasion, or about policies to tackle climate change. But

Photo 1.1 *The men who devised the existing financial system: US Secretary of the Treasury Morgenthau addressing the opening meeting of the Bretton Woods Conference, 8 July 1944*

Source: Photo from the US National Archives made available via the IMF website

now we need to extend this further, to include all the other species with whom we share this planet in our decision making. We need a representative from the deep-sea fish, the deciduous trees, the Arctic mammals, and so on. If we imagine putting to the vote in such a parliament the issue of our human wish to increase the number of nuclear power stations, we begin to see how narrow our current decision making structures are. In the case of most of what we do for economic reasons we would have just one vote against the collected votes of all the other species of planet Earth.

The lesson of ecology is that, as species of the planet, we are all connected in a web of life. A Buddhist parable brings to life this rather stark and scientific lesson from ecology. During his meditation a devotee fantasizes that he is eating a leg of lamb, an act proscribed by Buddhism where a strict adherence to vegetarianism is required. His spiritual master suggests that when this fantasy comes to him he draws a cross on the leg of lamb. The devotee follows the advice and, on returning to self-consciousness, is amazed to find the cross on his own arm. A more prosaic way of reaching the same sense of connection is to think about a time when you might have hit an animal or bird when driving your car. The sense of shock and horror that you have destroyed something so precious is the same, no matter how insignificant the animal appears.

This is the first lesson that green economics draws from ecology: that we cannot please ourselves without considering the consequences of what we are doing for the rest of our ecosystem. The other lesson is about adapting to the environment we find ourselves in, rather than trying to force the environment to adapt to us. It is a sense that forcing the planet as a whole to accept an impossibly high burden because of our excessive consumption that is making the lessons of ecology increasingly pressing. The solution proposed by green economics is bioregionalism. At a conference organized by Land for People in 1999, Robin Harper, the Green Party's first Scottish MP said 'We need to move towards the idea of ecological development: the economy should be seen as a subset of the ecosystem, not the other way around.' This sentence sums up what a bioregional economy would entail.

Figure 1.1 illustrates how green economics views the formal economy as embedded within a system of social structures and only a very small part of economic activity. For mainstream economists the only part of the diagram that matters is the 'formal economy' which they call the 'circular flow'. They ignore the social and environmental setting within which these exchanges between households and business take place. But in reality these transactions are embedded within social relationships, and these in turn are enclosed within the planet, which is itself a closed system. It is when we fail to recognize these complex interreactions that things go off course. The diagram also illustrates the injustice inherent in the allocation of rewards within a capitalist economy, which only values what is exchanged in the monetary economy. As Mary Mellor has written, 'The valued economy is a transcendent social form that has gained its power and ascendancy through the marginalisation and exploitation of women, colonised peoples, waged labour and the natural world increasingly on a global scale.' It is clear from this sort of understanding that green economics is also raising difficult and radical political questions.

What is green economics?

Green economics is distinct from the dominant economic paradigm as practised by politicians and taught in the universities in three main ways:

1   It is inherently concerned with social justice. For mainstream economics 'welfare economics' is an add-on, a minor part of the discipline which is only considered peripherally. For a green economist equality and justice are at the heart of what we do and take precedence over considerations such as efficiency. Many of the contributors to green economics have a history of work in development economics, and those who do not are equally concerned to forge an international economy that addresses the concerns of all the world's peoples equally.
2   Green economics has emerged from environmental campaigners and green politicians because of their need for it. It has grown from the bottom up and from those who are building a sustainable economy in practice rather than from abstract theories.
3   Green economics is not, as yet, an academic discipline with a major place in the universities. In fact, this is the first book which has attempted to pull

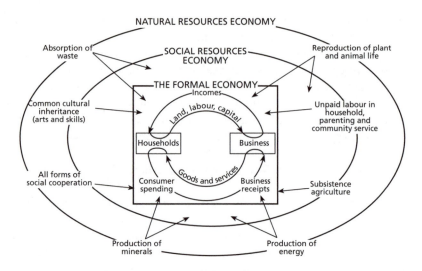

Figure 1.1 *Widening the consideration of economics beyond the classical economists' 'circular flow'*

Source: F. Hutchinson, M. Mellor and W. Olsen (2002) *The Politics of Money: Towards Sustainability and Economic Democracy*, London: Pluto.

together the various contributions to this field into a coherent whole. The explanation for this is not that green economics has little to offer (as I hope the following pages will show); rather it is that academic debate around economics and, some would argue, the role of the university itself, has been captured by the globalized economic system, whose dominance is a threat to the environment. The motivations of this system are incompatible with the message of green economics – hence the tension.

The obvious problems being caused by economic growth have not been ignored by academics: they were noticed by some in the economics profession, who then attempted to incorporate these concerns into their discipline. This led to the development of environmental economics, and also the related study of natural-resource economics. Conventional economics considers environmental impact to be an 'externality', something outside its concern. Environmental economists were keen to bring these negative impacts back within the discipline. However, they still approached the subject in a scientific and measurement-based way, for example using shadow pricing to measure how much people were concerned about noise pollution or the loss of habitat. In other words, the way in which economics traditionally marginalizes or ignores something that cannot be priced was still adhered to, but the response was to attempt to evaluate in some way aspects of life which economics had ignored. Green economists would consider this to be a category error; in other words, they believe it is important to accept that some aspects of life have social or spiritual worth that simply cannot be measured.

In fact many green economists go so far as to suggest that the counting itself is part of the problem. To take one example, in order to count anything we must divide the world into separate categories, say part-time or full-time workers, men or women, and so on. This challenges the principle of holism that lies at the heart of a green approach to the economy and society. Another example: while considering the economy, we can celebrate rising rates of productivity and higher percentages of labour-force participation, while ignoring the fact that those who measure social changes are reporting increasing levels of stress and mental disease among children. It is the nature of the process of measurement itself to compartmentalize our experience so that the left hand cannot see the damage the right hand is doing. While this sort of 'accounting for the environment' can be beneficial, it remains within the paradigm of placing quantity before quality (these measurement issues are discussed in more depth in Chapter 7).

While environmental economics has achieved much in putting the social and environmental impact of economic activity much more firmly on the agenda, it continues to take a hierarchical approach to solving these problems, which again runs counter to a green approach. The title of one of the most prominent environmental economics books makes this clear. *Blueprint for a Green Economy* was published in 1989 at the height of the first wave of environmental concern following Chernobyl and the Bhopal disaster. It takes an explicitly numerical approach, proposing valuation and accounting methods. For a green economist such a concept of a generalized 'blueprint' is problematic, since the nature of ecology suggests adaptation to the local environment, a diversity of solutions to economic problems that reflect the conditions in the locality. When it comes to understanding a philosophical position there is always a lot in a name. Environmental economists are likely to discuss the environment; green economists are much more likely to talk about the planet or the Earth. This is an indication that it is a grounded philosophy, rather than an exclusively intellectual or academic one.

Ecological economics attempts to bridge the gap between the two separate disciplines of ecology and economics. It is thus firmly rooted in ecology, which is also the basis for green economics. However, it still places considerable emphasis on measurement and valuation, and considers itself a scientific discipline, drawing many concepts and techniques from mainstream economics. The following quotation helps to clarify the distinction:

> *A broad distinction can be made between environmental and ecological economics, although nomenclature is often very loosely used. Environmental economics in general addressed the ecological issue from within a framework of conventional economies, whereas ecological economists take a more critical position. However, Herman Daly, founding editor of the journal* Ecological Economics, *who criticises mainstream economic*

Table 1.1 *Comparison of different strands of economics with a concern for the environment*

Type of economics	Difference from green economics
Environmental economics	Based in conventional economics paradigm: exaltation of measurement and numerical approach; lesser importance of values
Ecological economics	Attempt to unite the disciplines of ecology and economics; less importance accorded to spiritual dimension
Ecosocialism	Shares emphasis on equality but defends materialism and anthropocentrism
Ecofeminism	Shares principles and values but covers a more limited area; theoretical rather than policy-driven

theories of circular flow and growth, still uses terms such as 'natural capital' drawn from mainstream economic rhetoric.[2]

This is not to decry the important contribution of ecological economics; it is merely that green economists have a different orientation. They have, for example, taken much from the work of those in other areas of heterodox economics, particularly ecofeminist and ecosocialist economists, as well as development economists, as already mentioned. Table 1.1 makes clear the links between these different strands of economics that prioritize environmental concerns in their different ways.

When green economists do engage in measurement they try to do it in a more human and accessible way. This is partly based on a belief that in the past economics has been the province of those with PhDs and preferably in mathematics. This has limited the discussion and reduced the economic choices available in areas that are crucially important to our democracy. An example of a measure that might be useful to a green economist is the 'ecological footprint', the area of land and water that is required to support indefinitely the material standard of living of a given human population using prevailing technology. This allows us to make straightforward comparisons between the land available and the demands we make on it, such as that the ecological footprint of London is 120 times the area of the city itself. The concept actually grew up within the ecological economics discipline, but it has been valuable in developing awareness of the climate change impact of our economic behaviour. However, a green economist might go a step further and seek a simpler, more human-scale economic indicator – perhaps the average distance food travels between site of cultivation and site of consumption. Table 1.2 helps to compare two ways of measuring the environmental impact of economic activity: ecological footprinting and shadow pricing.

Shadow pricing is a way of attempting to include non-measurable aspects of life (such as the value of a songbird) in economic calculations by asking people what they would be prepared to pay, for example, to stop a species from becoming extinct. Ecofootprinting is a way of measuring human demands on the available resources of the planet in terms of an area of productive land.

Table 1.2 *Ecological footprinting and shadow pricing compared*

Ecological footprinting	Shadow pricing
Human scale and accessible	Academic
Maths limited to simple arithmetic	Complex formulae can exclude the uninitiated
Organizations and individuals can immediately use the measure as a tool for change	Expensive and complicated research is necessary before the measure is usable
The measure can be illustrated graphically in an attractive way	The concept is somewhat diffuse and difficult to grasp
Empowering	Disempowering: relies on experts

While the measurements can never be accurate, and productive land is not uniform, the idea of the footprint is human and accessible and has thus become a popular way of discussing individuals' environmental impact. It is possible to draw conclusions, such as the number of planets it would take if everybody's lifestyle were the same as that of the average US citizen; hence the development of the idea of 'one-planet living.'

From economic growth to a balanced economy

The major objective of the economy as it works now is to grow, and the more it grows, the happier the politicians are. Green economists would have more sympathy with the view of the radical US environmentalist Edward Abbey that 'Growth for the sake of growth is the ideology of the cancer cell.' In the capitalist ideology it does not matter that economic growth is destructive and does not increase human well-being; it only matters that there is more money changing hands in the global market. There is too much emphasis on standard of living, usually measured in purely material terms, and not enough on quality of life. For green economists growth is the major problem, not only because it is usually bought at the expense of the planet, but also because it is actually reducing our quality of life. The lifestyles we expect in the 21st century have caused the extinction of species on a massive scale, and by causing climate change are actually threatening our future as a species. Yet they have not even improved our lives. Richard Douthwaite makes this case forcefully in his book, *The Growth Illusion*. Table 1.3 lists some of the examples he gives of ways in which economic growth has reduced our quality of life.

Conventional economics focuses almost exclusively on quantity, whereas green economists are more concerned with the quality of human life. The prime motivator of economic activity is growth, but this is measured in a very narrow way, purely in terms of economic activity. So long as people are busy and money is changing hands, then the economy is successful. Herman Daly parodied this approach to measuring success when he said that if all the virgin forests of the US were cut down and turned into gambling chips, this would constitute an economic improvement in terms of conventional measures. Another story popular among green economists makes a similar point in a less

Table 1.3 *The negative consequences of economic growth for quality of life*

Indicator	Negative impact on quality of life
Technology	Reduced skill in work, lower wage levels, increased stress
Health	Pollution and inequality cause physical and mental disease
Crime	Growth generates envy and higher crime levels
Community	Intensified work patterns undermine relationships
Inequality	The proceeds of growth are unfairly distributed

Source: R. Douthwaite (1992) *The Growth Illusion*, Totnes: Green Books.

elevated way. Two men are walking along a street when they see some dog mess on the pavement. The first man says to the other, 'I'll pay you £10,000 if you eat that.' The other is initially disgusted but then thinks about the money and agrees. They carry on walking and they come upon another pile of dog mess, at which point the second man says to the first, 'OK, if you will eat that dog mess I'll pay you £10,000.' The first man is similarly affronted but realizes that he is now £10,000 short and so agrees. The two men continue their walk in thoughtful and nauseated frame for a while. Eventually the first says to the second: 'What did we really achieve?' The second replies, 'Well, not a lot, but we have added £20,000 to GDP.'

The narrow focus on quantity at the cost of quality has brought us to a situation where we are able to accumulate more and more things and yet these fail to bring us satisfaction. Green economics critiques the concept of consumption. Wants are created and manipulated to become needs by an advertising industry whose raison d'être is to create and extend profitable markets. A few years ago mobile phones and DVD players had not even been invented and yet now we all feel that they are necessities of life. Goods are produced that wear out easily, and what is fashionable is frequently something that will not last. This process began with built-in obsolescence and goods such as fridges that would cease to function almost on the day their guarantee expired. Now fashion dictates that we should have a cream carpet for the sole reason that this will become dirty more rapidly than any other colour and so we will need to buy a new carpet. Goods that last or have a quality that transcends the mercurial demands of the fashion industry cannot generate profits at the rate that the stock market demands.

Green economics proposes a move away from a focus on economic growth and towards a 'steady-state economy', which is the only type of economy that can be sustainable in the long term. In the steady-state economy, the planetary frontier is respected and the Earth is therefore the most scarce resource. This leads us to conclude that we should use it as wisely as possible, maximizing its productivity while at the same time minimizing our use of it. We should therefore focus more on quality and less on quantity. In order to achieve the steady state we need to pay attention both to the number of people who are sharing the Earth's resources, and to their level of consumption. We should also be aware of the regenerative capacity of the planet, our only basic resource, so that non-renewable resources should not be removed at a rate faster than renewable substitutes can be developed, and our outputs of waste, including pollution, should be limited to the level where they do not exceed the planet's carrying capacity.

The issue of resources is crucial. Economics is defined as the study of how resources are or should be distributed. Green economics suggests a whole change of perspective in our attitude to resource use, one that can be portrayed as a shift from the perspective of the cowboy to the perspective of the space-man. The cowboy views his world as infinite and lives without a frontier in an environment where there are endless resources to meet his needs and a vast empty area to absorb his wastes. The attitude of the spaceman could not be more different. He is aware that his environment is very limited indeed. He has available only the resources that can be fitted into his small capsule, and he is only too familiar with his own wastes.

Green economists suggest that we need to leave behind the attitude of the cowboy and move towards that of the spaceman. Nowhere is this more neces-sary than in the world of business, where the gunslinger stills rules supreme but where viewing the Earth as our only available spaceship would be a better guarantee of our survival as a species:

> *A businessman would not consider a firm to have solved its production problem and to have achieved viability if he saw that it was rapidly consuming its capital. How, then, could we overlook this vital fact when it comes to that very big firm, the economy of Spaceship Earth and, in particular, the economies of its rich passengers?*[3]

Why green economics now?

For too long discussions of politics and economics have been trapped inside an artificial dichotomy between capitalism and communism, and since commu-nism is no longer seen as a viable competitor, capitalism has been touted as the only way of organizing our economic life. Even environmentalists are not immune from this narrow-minded thinking:

> *Like it or not (and the vast majority of people do), capitalism is now the only economic game in town. The drive to extend the reach of markets into every aspect of every economy is an irresistible force, and the benefits of today's globalization process still outweigh the costs – however substantive those costs may be, as we shall see. The adaptability and inherent strengths of market-based, for-profit economic systems have proved themselves time after time, and there will be few reading this book who are not the direct beneficiaries of those systems.*[4]

This sort of comment demonstrates a sad lack of imagination – as though human beings, with all our creativity and resourcefulness, could only think of at most two, and probably only one way of arranging our economic affairs! In reality the 'end of history' thesis is nothing more than an intellectual play by the hegemonic forces of neoliberalism, and almost as soon as it emerged it was drowned out by the voices from the global South, as well as those campaigning against the environmental and social problems associated with this economic system. But the advantage of the end of communism and the breaking down of the dualist system of the post-war years is that there is considerably more intellectual freedom to discuss different systems of economic organization. Green economics is one alternative to market economics.

It follows from the fact that greens recognize the limits to growth that we must be particularly concerned about the way the existing resources are distributed. For this reason concerns with equity are as central to green economics as concerns for the planet. For many greens, an interest in economics grew out of a concern for poverty either in the richer economies of the West or in the context of the South. A good example is Caroline Lucas, Green MEP since 1999, who began her career working for Oxfam. She has now become a leading critic of globalization, pouring scorn on the ability of conventional economics and global trade to solve the problems of global poverty. Green economics sees globalization as a system for entrenching an unfair global distribution of resources, in fact a system that takes resources from the poor and gives them to the rich.

The situation is complicated by the fact that a green lifestyle, including such items as hybrid vehicles and organic food, is significantly more expensive than a conventional lifestyle. For many greens their practical response to the environmental crisis that they recognize around them has been to buy a green lifestyle off the shelf, what has been referred to as 'deep pocket ecology' because it is only available to those with the income to support this choice. Those with larger bank balances can also insulate themselves from the worst effects of pollution or environmental stress generally, since the worst environmental conditions are found in poorer countries or poorer areas within countries. On the other hand, greens would question what precisely it means to have a good life. In conventional economics consumption is encouraged and is fuelled by the creation of needs and wants by the advertising industry. In many ways we feel less satisfied than more 'primitive' societies whose people have not learned to want so much. Green economics argues that we should count our blessings and learn to adopt the 'ethic of plenty' and the 'wealth without measure' that is offered by nature, rather than desiring ever more consumer goods.

The real impetus pushing green economics towards the centre of political debate is climate change. In the past couple of years the reality of the situation with regard to our impact on the very life-support system of the planet has begun to dawn on politicians. They have also realized that it is the economy that is creating the problem of climate change, hence the establishment of investigations such as the Stern Review of the Economics of Climate Change in the UK, whose remit was 'a major review of the economics of climate change, to understand more comprehensively the nature of the economic challenges and how they can be met, in the UK and globally'. There is a real opportunity for green economics to suggest a balanced, holistic and ecologically grounded approach to economics which has been developed over the past 30 years.

Where do we go from here?

Like all systems of thought, green economics has its intellectual antecedents. In the case of green economics they are a rather eclectic bunch, ranging from Aristotle to Rosa Luxemburg and from William Morris to E. F. Schumacher. The following chapter discusses some of these individual contributions to our discipline and illustrates how the threads are woven together. We also discover that green economists have found both support and inspiration in a range of spiritual traditions. The chapter then considers the seminal contributions of a few of the leading green economists of the past 100 years or so, concluding with a brief account of challenges to the economics discipline in the contemporary academic world. The first part of the book is then completed by Chapter 3, which explores the guiding values and vision of green economics. It offers further detail of issues that form the identity of green economics, including the importance of reconnecting with the land, revaluing our human relationships, and the absolute need to put a limit on economic growth and create instead a balanced economic system. It ends by considering how the principles of permaculture might be applied to an economic analysis.

Part II consists of three chapters offering different aspects of the green vision for the future of our economy. Chapter 4 focuses on work, which from a green perspective should be a fulfilling and community-building activity, not just a means of earning money for survival. Schumacher's idea of 'right livelihood' and James Robertson's thinking about 'ownwork' are explained. Chapter 5 explores how money shapes and controls the global economy, beginning with the establishment of the current monetary system at Bretton Woods at the end of the Second World War and moving on to consider empowering local alternatives. To round off this part, Chapter 6 offers a green perspective on economic development. How would local economies look within a green vision? Which economic sectors would thrive in the low-carbon world of the future? And where would we find the resources we need in a bioregional world?

Part III moves on from the vision to deal with the reality, and presents green policies in action across today's world. GDP is an easy target for critics of economic growth, but what would greens use to replace it? Tools we would use to move our development towards a sustainable future are presented in Chapter 7, which begins with a discussion of the policy tussle over how deep reforms required by the environmental crisis will run. Chapter 8 sets the international context with a consideration of the consequences of globalization and trade for the environment and the impact on them of climate change. Green ideas about trade subsidiarity and the sufficiency economy are proposed as alternatives, as well as proposals for greening the international trade regime. A green economy will be a more locally based economy: Chapter 9 outlines green policies to make this a reality using a system of bioregional economics, thereby ensuring greater resilience and better human relationships. Many greens are already implementing policies in their own localities, and these means for strengthening and supporting local economies are presented in Chapter 9. Chapters 10 and 11 deal with tax and welfare, offering policies such as the Citizen's Income as a solution to the poverty trap, and ecotaxes as a means of both raising revenue and encouraging economic behaviour that is beneficial for the planet. Just as a green approach to taxation will seek different sources of revenue, so a green approach to welfare will take a wider perspective than repairing the damage caused by a destructive economy. Chapter 12 offers policies to ensure that land, our most basic resource, is more fairly shared and more respectfully used in the future than at present. As well as questioning the nature of our relationship with land, and how this influences our treatment of the 'environment', the chapter covers the issues of land taxation, green agriculture and sustainable construction. Finally, Chapter 13 provides a brief summary of the content of the twelve preceding chapters, as well as some ideas for further reading.

Notes

1 A. Pettifor (ed) (2003) *Real World Economic Outlook*, Basingstoke: Macmillan.
2 F. Hutchinson, M. Mellor and W. Olsen (2002) *The Politics of Money: Towards Sustainability and Economic Democracy*, London: Pluto, p. 161.
3 E. F. Schumacher (1973) *Small is Beautiful*, London: Abacus, p. 12.
4 J. Porritt (2006) *Capitalism as if the World Mattered*, London: Earthscan, p. xiv.

PART 1
Theory

2
Where Did It All Start?

Get Greek melodies from a piano? As well get beauty from economics!

Ivan Illich

Greens are practical people, focused on creating change and haunted by the sense of urgency that the environmental crisis brings. As an academic who is also involved in the green movement, I share a prevalent impatience with theorizing about what we are doing, rather than just doing it. However, it is crucially important that we know where we are coming from, that we understand our intellectual heritage, that – in the words of the Transition Towns movement – we respect the ancestors. This chapter is a distressingly brief attempt to provide a preliminary grounding in the lore and learning that informs green economics. It is one of the distinguishing features of this new way of approaching economics that space must be found in a book like this to include this perspective. However, that space is limited and in this chapter, more than any other, I am aware of my inability to do justice to the vast territory that could be covered. I hope readers can approach this chapter as a series of pointers towards further reading for those who are inclined to delve more deeply into the historical underpinning of green economics.

The chapter ranges widely, finding possible sources of inspiration in spiritual teachings and the wisdom of ancient Greece as well as in the writing of pioneering green economists. I make no claim that today's green economists are aware of the intellectual traditions included, and very few make explicit reference to them. However, ours is an eclectic and diverse discipline; the following sections present some of the authors and philosophies we draw on. First I consider our intellectual roots going back to ancient Greek philosophy and then the contribution of various spiritual traditions and of socialism broadly defined. We then move on to consider some of the seminal figures: the pioneering green economists who have built the foundations for the discipline. The final section briefly considers possibilities for change within academic economics.

Intellectual roots: Greeks, socialists and anarchists

All intellectual movements wish to trace their origins back to the ancient Greeks, who seem to have been the first to think of everything, and green economics is no exception. Aristotle drew a distinction between the economy focused on social and natural resources (*oikonomia*), and an economy where consideration of property, wealth and currency dominated (*chrematistics*).[1] Although our word economics derives from 'oikonomia', as a result of our disconnection from the land, and especially with the expansion of capitalism, we have drifted away from a focus on managing resources towards a focus on money and property. It can be argued that, as a result of the mortgaging of land and the creation of money primarily through debt (see Chapter 5), the chrematistics economy has all but displaced the household economy. According to John Barry, 'It is clear that what sustainable development requires is integrating the "management of the household" with the "economy of the household": that is, integrating economy and ecology.'[2]

Aristotelian philosophy also encompassed a consideration of trade, which was considered 'natural' so long as it provided for sufficiency needs and that the prices of exchange were 'just', i.e. based on the time invested in the production, rather than a surplus value for gain by middlemen. Aristotle acknowledged the key green principle of a limit to human desires, balanced against a cornucopian perception of the bounty of nature:

> *Aristotle rejected the idea that human needs are boundless and that there is a scarcity of subsistence in nature. If there was a perception of scarcity, it must be attributed to a misconception equating the 'good life' with a desire for greater abundance of physical goods and enjoyments.*[3]

Consistent with the convivial account of human well-being discussed in later chapters, Aristotle identified civic virtues and communal leisure pursuits as the source of 'eudaimonia' – the good, or satisfying, life.

The Greek philosophers Plato and Aristotle again have something to offer in terms of an ethical theory that helps to underpin green approaches to economics. The moral system known as 'virtue ethics' is derived from their philosophical focus on what is required of the individual in order to live a good life – morality then consists in the habits and behaviours that lead to this good life. In the environmental sphere this can be framed in terms of ecological virtue, the demonstration and practice of which can enable a good life lived comfortably within one's ecosystem. The antithesis is that behaving in an environmentally destructive way is likely to lead to a lack of virtue, and a less fulfilling existence.[4] In political terms – and perhaps in economic terms also – it is our responsibility as citizens to show 'ecological virtue': 'the practice of "ecological virtues" is constitutive of this green conception of citizenship.'[5] Extending Aristotle's arguments about what is required to live a 'good life', green social theorists have also argued that an appreciation of the natural world is a prerequisite of living the fully human life.[6]

The problem with any consideration of the socialist intellectual tradition[7] is that it has been ideologically hijacked. Many, if not most, green economists would find much of value in the Marxist critique of economics and we tend not to be queasy about making reference to his work to support our case. However, as the discussions of autonomy and scale in other chapters will make clear, nothing could be further from the green vision for a sustainable economy than the centralized, bureaucratic, materialist and overweening state that practical applications of Marxist philosophy tend to produce. Some powerful contributions to green economics have been produced by writers such as Brian Milani, Mary Mellor and Derek Wall, who would identify themselves as socialists. While Wall highlights green opposition to accumulation[8] – a key concern of Marxist economists – Milani focuses instead on the importance of maintaining an awareness of the rights of workers as well as those of the planet.[9]

However, this is just one of the socialist traditions. Green economics would find more affinity with the lost tradition of socialism represented by such figures as William Morris and Robert Owen (the so-called utopian socialists) and the related economic thinking of the anarchist Peter Kropotkin. Their idealization of small-scale, self-sufficient human communities, based on craft work, has influenced green economists' attitudes towards localization (see Chapter 9) and work in general (see Chapter 4). This was revived later by the guild socialists, whose work has been rediscovered and championed by Frances Hutchinson. It also expresses itself through emphasis on cooperative business and the social economy, which is discussed in Chapter 6.

Spiritual dimensions

It may be unexpected in a book on economics to include a discussion of spirituality, but a spiritual grounding, broadly defined, has been important to many if not most of those who have built the discipline that is the focus for this book. A colleague reported a remark by Teddy Goldsmith, that every recipient of the Right Livelihood Award (the alternative, green Nobel Prize) had had some sort of spiritual faith which helped to ground and guide their work. For those who eschew this sort of thinking, it may be sufficient to consider the ethical dimension of green economics, but many of the words green economists use in their writing – words such as reverence and awe – come from a realm of human existence which is neglected in our predominantly materialist culture. For many green economists this is a source we need to draw on when reorienting our economic life. In this section I cover very briefly the links between green economics and some spiritual traditions.

The most well recognized spiritual grounding is probably the worship of the Earth as practised by indigenous peoples and our own ancestors. The following quotation attributed to Chief Seattle, who is also well loved by greens for having pointed out that we cannot eat money, sums up this perspective:

> *This Earth is precious. Teach your children what we taught our children. The Earth is our Mother. The Earth does not belong to man; man belongs to the Earth. Every part of this Earth is sacred because everything is connected, like the blood which unites one body. Trees, air, water, animals, grass, Earth are like many fine strands that weave the web of life; men are merely a strand of it. Respect your Mother because whatever befalls the Earth soon befalls the sons of the Earth.*[10]

This type of relationship with the Earth, which is still the source of everything that allows us to live, was intrinsic to human life for many thousands of years. It is still predominant in many areas of the world today, interestingly in some that have been least successful in the more exploitative type of economy that flourishes in the early 21st century. Perhaps the most pungent attempt to bring this sort of thinking into modern economic debates has been achieved by US writer Kirkpatrick Sale. His bioregionalism is an attempt to link ecological science with the spiritual reverence for the Earth mother. Such a philosophy requires us to become 'dwellers in the land'.[11]

One of the guiding figures of our discipline, E. F. Schumacher, wrote that 'It is inherent in the methodology of economics to ignore man's dependence on the natural world.' Schumacher also famously wrote an essay called 'Buddhist Economics' in which he considered various economic questions from the perspective of a Western academic economist compared with that of a Buddhist economist. His argument was built on the fact that 'right livelihood' is one of the requirements of the Noble Eightfold Path Buddhists are required to follow. What, he asked, would this imply in terms of how we organize our economy? As just one example, he extrapolates from Buddhist teachings in order to suggest the role of work within the economy: 'to give man a chance to utilise and develop his faculties; to enable him to overcome his ego-centredness by joining with other people in a common task; and to bring forth the goods and services needed for a becoming existence'.[12] The centrality in Buddhist teaching of striving to sever one's attachment to the material world has serious implications for the existing economy, and can support the move towards a more convivial economy – 'more fun; less stuff' – that sustainability will require.

The Quakers play an immanent, although often invisible, role in the green movement (Kenneth Boulding, whose contribution is discussed later, was a Quaker). The Quaker way of acceptance and deep respect seems to offer a spiritual basis for a revision of the way we deal with our planet. Quakers are also untroubled by the need for significant political upheaval and have the useful phrase of 'speaking truth to power' to describe the need for acting according to one's conscience in the world. The faith is not heavily textually based, the most useful reference being the Advices and Queries that have been produced by Quakers themselves over the centuries. Of these, no. 42 is most pertinent to the theme of this book:

> *We do not own the world, and its riches are not ours to dispose of at will. Show a loving consideration for all creatures, and seek to maintain the beauty and variety of the world. Work to ensure that our increasing power over nature is used responsibly, with reverence for life. Rejoice in the splendour of God's continuing creation.*[13]

Just as many in the anti-poverty campaign have drawn inspiration from a Christian faith, so Jesus' mission to the poor (as later revived by the Liberation Theologians of Latin America) has provided a spiritual grounding for some green economists. Ideas from the wider Judaeo-Christian tradition – particularly that of the Jubilee, the reallocation of land and forgiveness of debt every 50 years to prevent the concentration of wealth – have also been important. In the UK context, the Christian Council for Monetary Justice has been a prominent campaign body for monetary reform, as Christian groups have been at the forefront of campaigns for fair trade.

Other green economists have drawn inspiration from an eclectic range of spiritual sources. Derek Wall, for example, has used the Rastafarian principle of *ital*, a kind of sacred injunction to consume locally. Those calling for monetary reform have sought support in the prohibition of *riba*, the Koranic injunction against usury or the charging of interest on loaned money. Meanwhile, the Celtic pagan religion has inspired others with its rejection of the dualism of mind–body or male–female, its embedding of human life within nature, and its celebration of the annual cycle. While this may appear something of a spiritual ragbag, that is in a sense unsurprising if we take seriously the suggestion that we are moving into a new phase of human development that seeks to better balance the material and immaterial, reacting against the strongly Sensate (in Sorokin's terms) phase of the Enlightenment.[14]

Key figures and ideas

James Robertson

James Robertson was born in 1928 and brought up in Yorkshire and Scotland; he studied at Balliol College, Oxford. He worked on decolonization policy for the British government and then in the Cabinet Office and the Ministry of Defence. In the 1970s he worked as a consultant while developing his green economics ideas. In 1978 he published *The Sane Alternative* with his partner, Alison Pritchard, and in 1983 they helped found The Other Economic Summit and later the New Economics Foundation, a think tank that has been fundamental in developing the new economics and giving it a sound empirical base. He has been a fellow at Green College, Oxford and worked with the Oxford Centre for Environment, Ethics and Society, as well as working for the World

Photo 2.1 *James Robertson with his wife and co-worker Alison Pritchard; together they helped establish TOES (the other economic summit) in the early 1980s*

Note: The picture was taken in Edmonton, Canada in 1977 during a lecture tour that James and Hazel Henderson were to have shared with Fritz Schumacher, who sadly died unexpectedly shortly beforehand.
Source: Thanks to James Robertson for permission to reproduce this photo.

Health Organization, the European Commission and the OECD. His work is influenced by the rise of feminist and ecological consciousness and particularly by the work of Schumacher and Illich.

Unlike the other green economists mentioned in this section, Robertson cannot be identified with any particular aspect of economics: his contribution has been to provide a wide-ranging vision of a 'sane alternative' to the existing economic paradigm. In the book of that title he argued for a holistic approach to change rather than a focus on any particular crisis:

> *First, our approach was comprehensive ... I suggested that, by applying principles of 'enable and conserve' to almost every sphere of human life and organization, we could create inter-active support for benign change between them all. Instead of combined system collapse, we could achieve combined system renewal.*[15]

In 1985 he published *Future Work*, which argues for a revolution in the organization of work with more focus on self-provisioning and what Robertson calls 'ownwork' (this aspect of his writing is discussed in more detail in Chapter 4).

Future Wealth, published in 1990, has been called by the author 'one of my more important books'. It is another holistic and visionary book, dealing with the need for rethinking our economic paradigm, a new approach to work, localization, global poverty, trade and global finance, the role of corporations, money and taxation. Apart from work, the other central focus of Robertson's study has been money – the manner of its creation and the impact that has on the economy as a whole. In *Creating New Money* (published with Joseph Huber in 2000), Robertson argues that the creation of money, and the value gained from this, should revert from commercial banks to governments:

> *The proposed method of creating new money will be simpler, more straightforward and easier to understand than the present one. It will be markedly beneficial from the viewpoint of public spending, borrowing and taxation. Subject to one proviso, it will almost certainly provide a more effective and practical instrument of monetary control. The proviso is that the creation of new money by commercial banks shall stop.*[16]

Robertson's other major contribution is in the area of fiscal policy, where he has argued for the taxation of commons, primarily land, and a range of green taxes, enabling the reduction of taxes on incomes and the funding of a Citizen's Income scheme.

This book is dedicated to James Robertson whom I have called 'the grandfather of green economics'. His contribution is monumental and indispensable. He is probably the only contributor to green economics who is referred to in every chapter of the book and his contribution to all the themes covered is insightful, authoritative and compassionate.

Schumacher on scale and appropriateness

Ernst Friedrich (E. F.) Schumacher was born in Germany in 1911, studied at Oxford and then, to avoid Nazism in his homeland, returned to the UK, where he continued his studies under J. M. Keynes and wrote academic and journalistic articles. Following the end of the war he worked with the British government to rebuild the German economy and was then an economist and statistician for the British Coal Board. Hence he began as a fairly conventional, though brilliant, economist, and through his career developed a growing concern for the environment and the profligate way in which the economy uses resources. His development of 'Buddhist economics' following a consultancy visit to Burma in 1955 has been discussed in an earlier section.

Leopold Kohr[17] – whose work is less well-known but arguably just as important as a basis for green economics and certainly highly influential on his student Schumacher – wrote that Schumacher's central message was that 'Instead of concentrating on mending the sides of the overgrown hull of the ship', he suggested, 'get out of it. Save yourself in a fleet of small lifeboats.'[18] Schumacher's work had two themes of crucial importance to green economics:

the importance of scale, to which his attitude is summed up in the mantra of environmentalists, Small is Beautiful; and the value of intermediate technology. Like Kohr, Schumacher questioned the concepts of 'progress' and 'development' so prevalent among economists and particularly the onward march of organizations and nations into larger units. For him there was an appropriate scale, which related to the geography and culture of a locality.[19] This type of organization makes possible the choice of an appropriate level of technology, meeting human needs without ever-more sophisticated machinery, using up increasing quantities of energy and resources.

Schumacher challenged some of the most powerful assumptions of economic theory:

> He saw the need to provide his colleagues and audiences with philosophical maps related to actual reality. In the process, his life was one of constant challenges and questioning, including most of the basic assumptions on which Western economic and academic theory had been based. What are the 'laws' that govern the 'science' of economics? What is the true value of money? What is the relationship between time and money? What is the real worth of work? And of development?[20]

This questioning of the motivation and organization of the economy was fundamental and extremely radical for its time; its influence on later green thinking on economics has been profound. In many ways Schumacher set the agenda for the subdiscipline of green economics, as identified by Diana Schumacher in her introduction to a posthumous collection of essays:

> fundamental prerequisites for sustainability – namely the transcendence of moral values; the equality and dignity of all people in the eyes of God; the integrity of human work as the resource base of any economy; the value of local communities; and the need for decentralized decision-making and self-sufficiency wherever practicable.

Kenneth Boulding and limits to growth

Kenneth Boulding was born in Liverpool, UK in 1910 and studied at Oxford, Harvard and Chicago; he taught economics at Michigan and Boulder, Colorado. He began his career in a fairly conventional economic vein, and achieved an impressive academic reputation for publishing and teaching. However, after the war he changed tack, attempting to fuse biology and economics in the book *Evolutionary Economics*, published in 1944. This was the first attempt to synthesize the scientific aspects of economics and ecology and thus an important precursor to green economics. Boulding argued for a more interdisciplinary approach and also for the importance of the normative aspects that economics often sidelines. Among green economists Boulding is perhaps best known for his comment that 'Anyone who believes that exponential growth can go on forever in a finite world is either a madman or an economist.'

As an early proponent of the need to move towards a non-growth or 'steady-state' economy, Boulding used the contrasted images of the cowboy and the spaceman to explore our attitude to the environment. The cowboy, who finds his apotheosis in American capitalism, is always pushing outwards, expanding his available resources, finding ever new frontiers to exploit. The spaceman, by contrast, is forced to recognize the limits of what he has brought on his small ship:

> Earth has become a single spaceship, without unlimited reservoirs of anything, either for extraction or for pollution, and in which, therefore, man must find his place in a cyclical ecological system which is capable of continuous reproduction of materials even though it cannot escape having inputs of energy.[21]

This image provides a stark illustration of two of the key principles of green economics: the importance of the circular flow of materials around the planet and the need to handle wastes positively. It is an interesting ironic development of this contrast that, with the NASA project to put a human being on the surface of Mars now itself using up a large quantity of Earth's resources, the cowboy will meet the astronaut at the final frontier: space.

Boulding was also critical of the straight-line thinking inherent in mainstream economics; this he described as 'a linear economy ... which extracts fossil fuels and ores at one end and transforms them into commodities and ultimately into waste products which are spewed out the other end into pollutable reservoirs'.[22] This way of organizing an economy was, he declared, 'inherently suicidal'. His alternative was a prototype for Spaceship Earth which he thought he had identified in the traditional village economy of Asia. Rather than a linear form this had a circularity built in – 'a high-level cyclical economy'. This was written nearly 40 years ago and laid the groundwork for the closed-loop economy and the principles of permaculture which will be discussed in the next chapter.

Nicholas Georgescu-Roegen and the entropy law

Nicholas Georgescu-Roegen was a Romanian born in 1906 who studied mathematical statistics in Bucharest and at the Sorbonne before moving on to Harvard to learn economics from Schumpeter. Following the communist takeover of post-war Romania he settled permanently in the US, with an academic job at Vanderbilt University. As a teacher he had an important influence on a generation of economists, of whom the most important for the purposes of this book is probably Herman Daly, whose writings on the steady-state economy will be discussed in the next chapter. Georgescu-Roegen made various important theoretical contributions to mainstream economics, but from the 1960s onwards turned his attention towards the interaction of the economy with the environment.

Georgescu-Roegen shared with Boulding an interest in an evolutionary approach to economic theory and in the creative potential of combining traditional science disciplines with economics. In Georgescu-Roegen's case his focus was physics and his application of the second law of thermodynamics to economic processes was a revolutionary step in terms of green economics. This law states that 'In nature there is a constant tendency for order to turn into disorder',[23] or that there is an inherent tendency in the universe towards chaos. As Boulding put it, there is 'no way of turning pots back into clay'[24] and this has important implications for the use of energy within an economy. Although it seems shocking to us that economists should be so neglectful in their consideration of energy, Georgescu-Roegen points out that economics as a discipline developed before the theory of thermodynamics had been devised: economics began in around 1770 but thermodynamics had its origins some 50 years later.

The importance of the second law of thermodynamics *to the economy* now underpins the thinking of those whose objective is a sustainable economy:

> *Trying to buck the laws of thermodynamics is not sensible... The second law of thermodynamics ... is sometimes called the law of entropy – entropy being a measure of the amount of energy no longer capable of further conversions to perform useful work. Entropy within any closed system inevitably increases over time; it is only the fact that our system is open to incoming solar radiation that prevents an inexorable decline into chaos.*[25]

It is important to note that the law applies *in a closed system* (meaning that no energy enters or leaves) and that Georgescu-Roegen's argument therefore assumes that nature is such a closed system – a precursor to the 'limits to growth' thesis that will be discussed in the next chapter. The implications of this for the economy are wide-ranging: energy can be used once only and while materials can be reused and recycled this is a process which faces diminishing returns. The law also implies that creating order through human activity must lead to disorder elsewhere and this process is accumulative and increasingly chaotic.

Hazel Henderson and the love economy

Hazel Henderson was born in Bristol, UK in 1933 and has worked at the University of California as well as advising the US government and being elected a member of the British Royal Academy of Arts. She styles herself as an 'evolutionary economist and futurist' and has been a stringent critic of existing economic theories which she dismisses as 'flat-earth economics': 'The word is out that economics, never a science, has always been politics in disguise. I have

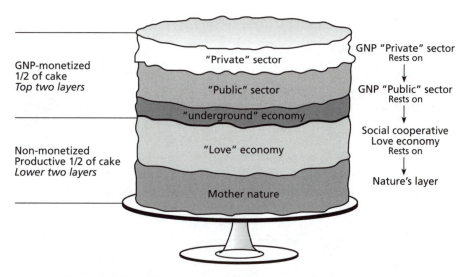

Figure 2.1 *Hazel Henderson's illustration of the love economy*

Source: Thanks to Hazel Henderson for permission to reproduce this illustration.

explored how the economics profession grew to dominate public policy and trump so many other academic disciplines and values in our daily lives.'[26]

Her magnum opus is *The Politics of the Solar Age: Alternatives to Economics*, first published in 1988. The book perfectly exemplifies the way in which green economics unites concerns for sustainability and social justice, indeed how these are inextricably joined:

> *An economy based on renewable resources carefully managed for sustained yield and long-term productivity of all its resources can provide useful, satisfying work and richly rewarding life-styles for all its participants. However, it simply cannot provide support for enormous pyramided capital structures and huge overheads, large pay differentials, windfall returns on investments, and capital gains to investors.*[27]

Her illustration of the global economy as a cake (see Figure 2.1), of which conventional economic measures ignore the most significant aspects, exemplifies her approach to economics. GDP is a narrow, economistic, patriarchal measure of the economy that fails to take into account the most important aspects of productive life, such as caring and the environment itself. Henderson has engaged with the key topics of concern to green economists: land ownership, ethical consumption, money creation and control, the absence of freedom in the 'free market', the need for smaller scale, revitalized local economies, and she has also worked tirelessly to create viable alternatives in her own local community.

Photo 2.2 *Richard Douthwaite*

Source: Photograph copyright belongs to Richard Douthwaite.

Richard Douthwaite and the growth illusion

Richard Douthwaite was born in Yorkshire, UK in 1942 and studied at Leeds and Essex universities. He worked as a government economist in the West Indies before moving to Ireland to become a freelance economist and writer with a special interest in climate and energy issues and local economic development. Taking forward the concern of both Boulding and Schumacher with the growth addiction of capitalist economics, Douthwaite anatomized its negative consequences in his first book, *The Growth Illusion: How Economic Growth Enriched the Few, Impoverished the Many and Endangered the Planet*, which was published in 1992.[28] He followed this up in 1996 with a more practical reflection of his experiences with attempts to build stronger local economies, especially in Ireland. *Short Circuit* (1996) gives examples of currency, banking, energy and food production systems which communities can use to make themselves less dependent on an increasingly unstable world economy.

Douthwaite has also engaged in political activity – both through lobbying work by the Dublin-based FEASTA organization he co-founded, and by working with the Irish Green Party. His focus in recent years has been particularly on energy and climate change issues, including the editing of *Before the Wells Run Dry* (2003), a study of the transition to renewable energy in the light of climate change and oil and gas depletion and the development of the Cap and Share model for limiting CO_2 emissions and sharing the value from

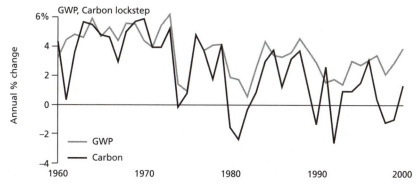

Figure 2.2 *The relationship between economic activity and CO$_2$ emissions*

Source: GCI 2001. Thanks to Aubrey Mayer and Tim Helweg-Larsen of the Global Commons Institution.

their trade on an equal basis. Douthwaite also acted as economic adviser to the Global Commons Institute (London) from 1993 to 2005 during which time GCI developed the Contraction and Convergence approach to dealing with greenhouse gas emissions. Figure 2.2 illustrates the 'lockstep' relationship between economic growth and CO$_2$ emissions that is the impetus behind Douthwaite's work and that of the Global Commons Institute.

Learning from the South

It is noticeable that, in spite of my contention in Chapter 1 that green economics is keen to bring multiple perspectives to bear on the analysis of our economy, the economists profiled here have been predominately white, Western males. The contribution of ecofeminists to the development of green economics is covered in the next chapter, but it is important to note here the contribution of economists and other thinking from the global South, as well as the influence of life in the colonial and post-colonial countries on many green economists, including some of those included by name in this chapter.

Manfred Max-Neef is a Chilean self-styled 'barefoot economist',[29] who links poverty and ecological devastation with the inappropriateness of neoclassical models of economic development. He describes his work, based on his study of poor communities in Latin America, as 'economics as if people matter'. He was awarded the Right Livelihood Award in 1983 for his work on 'human scale development'. Martin Khor, the Malaysian economist, has been influential in critiquing the present global trade system and in proposing the World Social Forum as a means of re-empowering the poor world. The insights of the Liberation Theologians of Latin America have also been important in developing the concept of the 'solidarity economy', as has Paolo Freire's 'pedagogy of the oppressed' in developing a teaching style for green economics.

India has provided much inspiration for green economists, primarily based on the work of Gandhi and his followers. Gandhi's concept of *Swadeshi* or self-reliance and his idealization of the life of the rural community in India have supported the development of ideas about re-localizing the economy.[30] Vandana Shiva has indicated the value of India's traditional Vedic beliefs in building a response to the ecological devastation wrought by global capitalism. Writing with Maria Mies, she, like Gandhi before her, confirms the point made earlier about the need for a spiritual grounding to economics:

> 'Mati Devata, Dharam Devata – The soil is our Goddess; it is our religion.' These are the words of adivasi women of the Save Gandmardhan movement as they embraced the earth while being dragged away by the police from the blockade sites in the Gandmardhan hills in Orissa. Dhanmati, a 70-year-old woman of the movement had said, 'We will sacrifice our lives, but not Gandmardhan. We want to save this hill which gives us all we need.'[31]

Challenging economics in the academy

The quotation from Hazel Henderson given earlier indicates the scepticism green economists have towards the academic discipline of economics – elsewhere she dismisses its contribution as 'three hundred years of snake oil' and calls for 'defrocking the economics priesthood'. Although the green economists profiled in this chapter have studied within the academy there is a historical drift away from the universities in the development of economic responses to the environmental crisis. This is unsurprising as the university is hostile territory for any except those economists wedded to the neoclassical paradigm and equipped with an advanced degree in mathematics. Economics journals are stuffed with mathematical models and peer reviewers are likely to reject papers that omit mathematical formulae, no matter how urgent the topics they address. Because of this power structure, that critics have likened to a pseudo-theological control of the discipline, many important insights that have contributed to the development of green economics – as outlined in the next chapter – have emerged either in other academic disciplines, such as geography, development studies, politics and so on, or outside the academic world altogether. Green economists are as likely to work for pressure groups or as freelance consultants as in universities.

For Henderson this political control of economics is no accident. The discipline has been used as a fig leaf to excuse and justify a political project designed to bring about an unequal sharing of the Earth's resources. As described by Henderson this procedure was calculated and well-funded, including such masterstrokes as the creation of an apparent 'Nobel Prize' for economics, which is in fact a prize funded by the Bank of Sweden and invented in 1968 to attempt to enhance the status of the discipline. In his introduction to *Small is Beautiful*, Theodore Roszak quotes Professor Erik Lundberg of the Nobel Committee justifying the new award thus: 'Economic science is developed increasingly in the direction of a mathematical specification and a statistical quantification of economic contexts... These techniques have proved successful and have left far behind the vague, more literary type of economics.'[32] This has become a self-fulfilling prophecy as the list of prizewinners over the past 40 years attests. Even former winners of the prize are rebelling, as in Joseph Stiglitz's statement that '[Economics as taught] in America's graduate schools ... bears testimony to a triumph of ideology over science.'

The hegemony of the neoclassical paradigm within the university has been challenged in recent years. There has been a call for a paradigm shift in the methods and approach of economics, an abandonment of what has been called 'physics envy' – the desire for accurate measurement and objectivity in a discipline whose subject matter is primarily that unmanageable species, the human being.[33] The Association of Heterodox Economists supports those who champion alternative ways of considering the economy, and green economics is a recognized strand within the Association. A more robust challenge has come from the Post-Autistic Economics network, an organization set up by a group of students from the Sorbonne in Paris who were tired of the narrow nature of the economics they were being taught. While there has been criticism of their use of a medical term, they have justified the name on the basis that it describes the closed-minded and self-absorbed nature of contemporary economics. The following example illustrates this incestuousness:

> *A glance through the 2003 edition of Penguin's* Dictionary of Economics *illustrates the accentuated continuation of this tiny all-powerful closed shop. The dictionary has entries for 29 living economists. Of these, 26, 89.7 percent, are from the US or have had all or the most important part of their careers there. Think about that: 26 for one country and 3 for the rest of world. And that is in a British publication by a team of three British authors. And what are the affiliations of the 26 US economists? 100 per cent of them have either taught at or received their PhD from one of the Big Eight [US universities].*[34]

So there are rumblings in the academy and this is an interesting time to work as an economist. Green economics is one response – a positive proposition for a study of the sharing of resources based in a respect for the planet and a commitment to the equal treatment of human beings and the species we share this planet with. Unlike economics as it has been practised over the past 60 years or so, this is an approach which does not limit itself to the management of the economy but asks searching questions about power structures as well.

Notes

1   F. Hutchinson, M. Mellor and W. Olsen (2002) *The Politics of Money: Towards Sustainability and Economic Democracy*, London: Pluto.
2   J. Barry (1999) *Environment and Social Theory*, London: Routledge, p. 166.
3   H. Henderson (1988) *The Politics of the Solar Age: Alternatives to Economics*, Indianapolis, IN: Knowledge Systems Inc., p. 161.
4   A. Dobson (1995) *Green Political Thought*, London: Routledge; T. Hayward (2006) 'Ecological citizenship: Justice, rights and the virtue of resourcefulness', *Environmental Politics*, 15/3: 435–46.
5   Barry, *Environment*, p. 65.
6   J. O'Neill (1993) *Ecology, Policy and Politics*, London: Routledge.
7   For more on the link between anti-capitalism and the green movement, see M. S. Cato (2004) 'The watermelon myth exploded: Greens and anti-capitalism', in J. Carter and D. Morland (eds) *Anti-Capitalist Britain*, Gretton: New Clarion Press.
8   D. Wall (2006) 'Green economics: An introduction and research agenda', *International Journal of Green Economics*, 1/1–2: 210–14.
9   B. Milani (2001) *Designing the Green Economy: The Postindustrial Alternative to Corporate Globalization*, Lanham, MD: Rowman & Littlefield.
10 The origin of this quotation is in fact obscure and Arts in Seattle informed me that it was in fact written by screenwriter Ted Perry for an environmental film in 1972. I decided to include it none the less because it is so popular in green circles and has become a touchstone for environmentalists, whatever its origin.
11 K. Sale (1983) 'Mother of all: An introduction to bioregionalism', Third Annual E. F. Schumacher Lecture, Mount Holyoake College, South Hadley, MA, October; available online: www.smallisbeautiful.org/publications/sale_83.html; K. Sale (2006) 'Economics of scale vs. the scale of economics: Towards basic principles of a bioregional economy', *Vermont Commons*, February.
12 E. F. Schumacher (1968) 'Buddhist economics', *Resurgence*, 1/11; the essay is available online at: www.smallisbeautiful.org.
13 Yearly Meeting of the Religious Society of Friends (Quakers) in Britain (1995) Advices and Queries no. 42, London: Friends' House.
14 Henderson, *Solar Age*, p. 158.
15 From Robertson's preface to the 2008 edition of *The Sane Alternative: Signposts to a Self-Fulfilling Future*, London: private publication, 1978.
16 J. Robertson and J. Huber (2000) *Creating New Money: A Monetary Reform for the Information Age*, London: New Economics Foundation, p. 8.
17 See I. Illich (1994) 'The Wisdom of Leopold Kohr', Fourteenth Annual E. F. Schumacher Lecture, Great Barrington, MA: E. F. Schumacher Society; L. Kohr (1957) *The Breakdown of Nations*, London: Routledge and Kegan Paul.
18 L. Kohr, 'A Tribute to E. F. Schumacher', published by the Schumacher Society: www.schumacher.org.uk.
19 E. F. Schumacher (1973) *Small is Beautiful*, London: Abacus.
20 D. Schumacher (1998) 'Introduction' to E. F. Schumacher, *This I Believe*, Totnes: Green Books.
21 K. E. Boulding (1966) 'The economics of the coming spaceship Earth', in H. Jarrett (ed) *Environmental Quality in a Growing Economy*, Washington, DC: Johns Hopkins University Press, p. 303.
22 K. E. Boulding (1970) *Economics as a Science*, New York: McGraw-Hill, p. 147; later quotation from p. 148.

23 N. Georgescu-Roegen (1971) *The Entropy Law and the Economic Process*, Cambridge, MA: Harvard University Press, 1971.

24 K. E. Boulding (1981) *Evolutionary Economics*, London: Sage.

25 J. Porritt (2006) *Capitalism as if the World Mattered*, London: Earthscan, p. 47.

26 H. Henderson (2006) 'The politics of money', *The Vermont Commons*, January.

27 Henderson, *Solar Age*, pp. 101–2.

28 For a summary see R. Douthwaite (1999) 'The need to end economic growth', in M. S. Cato and M. Kennett (eds) *Green Economics: Beyond Supply and Demand to Meeting Human Needs*, Aberystwyth: Green Audit.

29 M. Max-Neef (1981) *From the Outside Looking In: Experiences in Barefoot Economics*, Uppsala: Dag Hammarskjöld Foundation.

30 See the brief description of Gandhi's contribution to economics in M. S. Cato (2006) *Market, Schmarket: Building the Post-Capitalist Economy*, Gretton: New Clarion Press, pp. 173–5.

31 M. Mies and V. Shiva (1993) *Ecofeminism*, London: Zed, p. 100.

32 Quoted in Henderson, *Solar Age*, p. 175.

33 Henderson, *Solar Age*, p. 184.

34 Information about the AHE and PAE can be found via their websites: www.open.ac.uk/socialsciences/hetecon/ for the Association of Heterodox Economics and www.paecon.net/ for the Post-Autistic Economics network.

3
Economics and Identity

Even today, it is heretical to suggest that economic growth, of which international trade is an increasing part, is constrained by any fundamental limits like the management of the natural capital of the atmosphere.

Andrew Simms in *Collision Course*, 2000, p. 4

Sustainability values, not monetary value

Economics is conventionally focused on one sort of value: monetary value. One of the guiding principles of green economics is to extend the remit of economics to include a wider vision and deeper values. The US ecofeminist Starhawk has described three principles of ecofeminism which I have applied to economic analysis: these are unity-in-diversity, interconnectedness and immanence. The first of these principles describes the need to respect difference and to value the whole as requiring all its different parts. In the economic sphere this requires diversity of organizational and operational forms rather than the constrained business model our economy is based on today. The second, interconnectedness, is a belief in the inevitable relationship between all the aspects of the planet, a principle which is closely supported by ecology. It is this principle that leads to the holistic policy making that will be described in Part II of the book. Without it we see an economy where the needs and wants of some peoples and species lead to the suffering and death of others, an arrangement that results in conflict and war. The principle of 'immanence' is inevitably somewhat nebulous and is best illustrated by the following quotation, where James Lovelock describes how he realized his Gaia hypothesis:

Suddenly, as a revelation, I saw the Earth as a living planet. The quest to know and understand our planet as one that behaves like something alive, and which has kept a home for us, has been the Grail that beckoned me ever since. It came to me suddenly, just like a flash of enlightenment, that to persist and keep stable, something must be regulating the atmosphere... My mind was

*well prepared emotionally and scientifically and it dawned on me
that somehow life was regulating climate as well as chemistry.
Suddenly the image of the Earth as a living organism ... emerged
in my mind. At such moments, there is no time or place for such
niceties as the qualification 'of course it is not alive – it merely
behaves as if it were'.*[1]

We are only beginning to think through what it might mean to perceive our
planet in this way, as something sacred rather than a larder we can raid at will.
Some indigenous peoples find mining for oil or coal to be blasphemous because
it violates the body of the Earth. This kind of respect would mean taking our
economic decisions about extraction and use of the Earth's resources very
much more seriously than we do now.

Others who are equally committed to creating an economy that respects
the planet and all the creatures who make up life on Earth would feel intensely
uncomfortable with this sort of writing. They tend to focus more on a rational
discussion about which sort of values such an economy would be based on.
According to Lawson's 'axiomatic basis of green economics': it is impossible to
expand for ever into a finite space; it is impossible to take for ever from finite
resources; and everything is interconnected.[2] In his view, applying these axioms
would allow a harmonious balance between economics and the ecosystem. The
values that we will need to build a sustainable economy as viewed by Jonathan
Porritt are reproduced in Box 3.1.

The three circles model (Figure 3.1) helps to explain the different view of
the economy that results from taking sustainability seriously. In the conventional view (on the left of the graphic), the economy, environment and society
interact but are not interdependent. They are drawn as of equal size and therefore importance, although in reality the economy carries much more sway in
decision making, with society bearing the cost and the environment paying the
highest price of all. This figure makes clear why economists refer to the
negative consequences of production processes – say, pollution from a nuclear
power station – as an 'externality', because in their view of the world what

---

BOX 3.1 SUSTAINABILITY VALUES

Recognition of interdependence
Self-determination
Diversity and tolerance
Compassion for others
Upholding the principle of equity
Recognition of the rights and interests of non-humans
Respect for the integrity of natural systems
Respect for the interests of future generations

Source: J. Porritt (2006) *Capitalism as if the World Mattered*, London: Earthscan, p. 289.

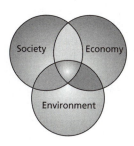

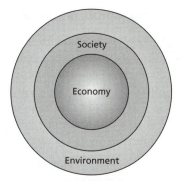

The conventional economic view of the interaction betwen economy, society and environment

The green economics paradigm: economy operates within social relationships and the whole of society is embedded within the natural world

Figure 3.1 *Three is a magic number: Re-imaging the relationship between society, economy and environment*

Source: I owe this idea to Jenneth Parker.

happens to the environment and the people who live in it happens somewhere else. It can be pushed outside the 'economy' circle and dealt with elsewhere. Once you realize that there is no 'elsewhere' you have to consider the wastes you produce in all your economic activities differently. This is illustrated on the right-hand side of the graphic, where society nestles inside the environment and the economy is a part of society. In this view, both society and economy are dependent on the environment. It also implies that economic activity takes place within a network of social relationships – an insight whose implications we will return to later. This is the world as viewed by green economics:

> *The economy is, in the first instance, a subsystem of human society ... which is itself, in the second instance, a subsystem of the totality of life on Earth (the biosphere). And no subsystem can expand beyond the capacity of the total system of which it is a part.*[3]

If you bear in mind this image of where the economy fits, it helps to make sense of the interpretations of different economic issues and the policies proposed throughout the rest of the book. The next section explains why the outer circle, the environment, is fixed and therefore the inner circle, the economy, must be also. Then I move on to consider the link between economy and society before considering, in the following section, the implications of regrounding the economy within the environment. The final section considers the practical implications of this understanding through a brief exploration of permaculture.

The guiding vision: Balance not growth

If you only take away one idea from an introduction to green economics such as this it should be that green economics is opposed to continuing economic growth. Even those environmentalists who mingle in exalted political circles, such as Jonathon Porritt, are clear that 'sustainable growth' is a 'self-evident oxymoron'.[4] If you say this to a conventional economist he will throw up his hands in horror and consider you a lunatic – or perhaps a blasphemer. As Richard Douthwaite has pointed out, growth is the sanctum sanctorum of conventional economics:

> *It is not the results of growth that are important to the people who make it happen. What matters is the process itself; and the more of that process there is, the better politicians and business people like it. Growth means change. More rapid growth means even more change; more change means more market opportunities to be turned into profits. And more profits are not only the system's motivating force but the source of the financial resources needed for it to grow faster still. For a company director, corporate growth creates a virtuous circle with increased profits leading to increased investment leading to more growth, more profit and more investment still.[5]*

However, as Douthwaite makes clear, growth is necessary to a capitalist economy, not to any economy.

So in the closed worldview of the neoclassical economist growth may appear unproblematic, but since it lies at the heart of the existing economic system, economic growth touches on many other aspects of our life – and our world. For example, we measure our economy in terms of GDP, a measure which is based on a narrow range of economic activity, so that what is growing may not be something that increases even human well-being, not to mention the well-being of the planet. The limitation of this method of measurement, and the consequences it has for the economy in general, are discussed further in Chapter 7. Growth is often argued to be necessary for the 'creation of jobs', another key objective of our present economy which is questioned by green economics. The most fundamental reason why we need economic growth is because of the way our money is created – this system, why we need to change it, and how we could make sustainable money form the themes of Chapter 5.

But now we shall spend some time exploring the call for an end to economic growth itself. It may seem fairly obvious to the uninitiated that we share one small planet, and that, since our environment is limited, so should our economy be. But to an economist this is not obvious at all. Human ingenuity can find ways of using resources in infinitely more efficient ways, allowing us to expand for ever. We saw in Chapter 2 that Georgescu-Roegen was the first economist to apply the principles of thermodynamics to economic thinking – a science that was only developed 50 years after economics itself. The second law, also known as the entropy law, defeats the economists' optimism. The reality is that the apparent efficiency is only exporting the problem to somewhere else within the system, and the longer it takes us to face up to the reality of the limits within which we live, the more serious the problem we are storing up for ourselves.

This change in thinking emerged first in the environmental movement in the 1960s and came to public attention towards the end of the decade with the publication of the Report to the Club of Rome, *Limits to Growth*.[6] This report drew attention to the exponentially increasing exploitation of resources and argued that this, or the parallel increase in waste generated, would destroy the environment unless it were halted: the limits it identified were those of resource depletion and waste overload, linked to a concern for the rising population and the need for a parallel increase in food growing. The report was, as would be expected, lambasted by the political and economic establishment, but it set the scene for the rise of environmental concern and its link with economic activity. The authors of the report produced an update in 2004, including a useful summary of their argument:

> *Our analysis did not foresee abrupt limits – absent one day, totally binding the next. In our scenarios the expansion of population and physical capital gradually forces humanity to divert more and more capital to cope with the problems arising from a combination of constraints. Eventually, so much capital is diverted to solving these problems that it becomes impossible to*

*sustain further growth in industrial output. When industry
declines, society can no longer sustain greater and greater output
in the other economic sectors: food, services and other consumption. When those sectors quit growing, population growth also
ceases.*[7]

Because of the addiction to growth demonstrated by globalized capitalism the
rejection of it is somewhat rhetorical. We can, of course, accept that there will
be a need for more economic activity in the world's poorer countries to enable
an acceptable standard of living. Even in the developed economies of the West,
we can enjoy more of certain types of activities; it is the ones that are profit-
driven and fuelled by fossil fuels that will have to be curtailed. Douthwaite has
produced a list of the types of growth that are compatible with a sustainable
economy and these are reproduced in Box 3.2.

BOX 3.2 DOUTHWAITE'S CRITERIA FOR 'GREEN' GROWTH

Growth is acceptable if it can be achieved without:

- reducing the number of people employed;
- increasing the amount of energy and raw materials used;
- using more transport;
- shifting the distribution of income in favour of the better off;
- releasing genetically engineered organisms into the environment;
- patenting life forms;
- using technologies that make working less interesting and fulfilling;
- increasing the amount of waste that goes into landfill or into the environment;
- driving smaller firms out of business or damaging local economies;
- allowing chemicals which are not quickly and harmlessly broken down into safe and stable
  constituents to leave factories;
- purchasing from parts of the world where prices are subsidized because environmental,
  social or working conditions are significantly inferior to those in the countries they are
  supplying;
- increasing human, animal or plant exposure to nuclear or electromagnetic radiation;
- making production and supply systems less sustainable.

Source: R. Douthwaite (1999) 'The need to end economic growth,' in M. S. Cato, and M. Kennett (eds)
Green Economics: Beyond Supply and Demand to Meeting Human Needs, Aberystwyth: Green Audit.

So what do greens want instead of relentless growth? The answer is a balanced
economy, what is usually referred to as the steady-state economy. This was the
call of Herman Daly, a student of Georgescu-Roegen who launched the ecological economics movement. Daly used the phrase 'uneconomic growth' to
describe growth which increases costs to human well-being faster than it
increases benefits. His alternative was the steady-state economy with constant
population and stock of capital and a lower rate of throughput (compared with
today) that did not exceed the planet's ability to regenerate itself. This view has

Table 3.1 *Comparison between the HE (hyper-expansionist) and*
SHE (sane, humane, ecological) possible futures

HE	SHE
Quantitative values and goals	Qualitative values and goals
Economic growth	Human development
Organizational values and goals	Personal and interpersonal values and goals
Money values	Real needs and aspirations
Contractual relationships	Mutual exchange relationships
Intellectual, rational, detached	Intuitive, experiential, empathetic
Masculine priorities	Feminine priorities
Specialization/helplessness	All-round competence
Technocracy/dependency	Self-reliance
Centralizing	Local
Urban	Country-wide
European	Planetary
Anthropocentric	Ecological

Source: J. Robertson (1985) *Future Work: Jobs, Self-employment and Leisure after the Industrial Age*, London: Temple Smith/Gower.

been taken up by those seeking to influence businesses to work in a more sustainable way (discussed further in Chapter 6).

The popularity of such a call among the orthodox economists can be guessed from the following quotation from Adam Smith: 'The progressive state is in reality the cheerful and the hearty state to all the different orders of society. The stationary is dull; the declining melancholy.' In fact, from the perspective of green economics it is anything but. As discussed in the final section of this chapter, within a limited planet and without the optimistic assumption of conventional economics that technology can act as a substitute for natural capital, we are required to show ingenuity and creativity in developing new systems that mimic nature and live in balance with the ecosystem. This 'circular metabolism' to replace the linear, progressive economy 'aims to re-use and re-circulate resources'.[8]

More than 20 years ago James Robertson made a distinction between the HE-economy which was hyper-expansionist and the SHE-economy which was sane, humane and ecological.[9] The contrasting characteristics of the two are presented in Table 3.1.

Economics and relationship

So far in this chapter we have had principles and axioms and visions; we have not heard very much about people. This is fairly typical of writing on economics – and in fact most economics writing is much more cold and technical than this. Academic economics is stuffed full of formulas and arcane mathematics and in universities at the start of the 21st-century economics is more often found in business schools, rather than in the social sciences faculty. But economics is fundamentally about people: how they work, what motivates them, what they enjoy spending their time doing. These are social questions which it is artificial and misguided to consider in the scientistic way that most economists do. One of the key differences about green economics is that it puts people back at the heart of what economics should be about. And when it comes to everyday economics – the sorts of transactions we engage in every day – green economists encourage a system based more on relationship.

One aspect of this approach is to question both the spread of the market, and what we mean by the market. In an earlier book called *Market, Schmarket* I cast a sceptical eye over the claims of the neoclassical economists that the market is the most efficient way to organize our economic lives, not to mention other areas of our life such as care and even relationships and voting.[10] Other theorists of the green economy are keen to draw a distinction between 'capitalism' and the 'market': economics relates to the organization of relationships between the state, the market and community, whereas the green worldview sees the state and the market as mechanisms to achieve what people want, rather than people being subject to market dictates. The French proponents of *decroissance* or 'degrowth', for example, talk about 'putting the economy back in its place'.[11] Green economists differ in their view of how much of our economic life would be mediated by the market, although for most entrepreneurialism will still play a role.

Although most green economists would see the sustainable economy as involving considerably less trade and the revival of local economies, green economics is not about cutting ourselves off from each other, either within nation states or globally. Only the most extreme would seek the eco-anarchist vision of tiny, rural self-sufficient communities. Rather we are calling for a humanizing of economic relationships. It can be argued that the late capitalist economy has reduced human beings to their economic function – we are merely production and consumption units.[12] In a green economy people would relate to each other first and trade with each other second. Drawing on studies of markets in Africa, as well as the *agora* of ancient Greece, markets are seen as places of sociality and joyful companionship,[13] where news and political views are exchanged as well as goods and money: 'The *agora* is first and foremost a place of public life and civil society.'[14]

I recently made a purchase which seems appropriate for this kind of convivial economy. I spent a weekend on a basket-making course with a local craftswoman. As well as working with willow from the Somerset levels and hedgerow materials that she grows herself, she also makes an annual trip to the river some 50 miles north of where we live to cut rushes. These she dries, prepares and uses for seat covering and weaving into hats. My mass-produced, charity-shop straw hat wore out last year so I needed a new one and was able to buy one of hers. The sense of relationship with that hat, its connection to my local environment, knowing the person who made the hat, and admiring her skill are all side benefits of the purchase that cannot be counted in monetary value. The delight I feel when wearing the hat cannot be expressed in words. It does so much more than protect me from sunstroke!

Photo 3.1 *The author modelling a 'bioregional hat'*

Source: Rosa Cato

Such an account is so distant from the culture, methodology and ideology of neoclassical economics that I hesitated to include it in this book for fear of undermining its authority. However, as Douthwaite makes clear, the fact that economics uses a narrow lens when focusing on the world is only because of its wish to achieve scientific accuracy, not because that is the best means of explaining how economic relationships actually work:

> *Economists are forced to ignore the possibility that irrationality, prejudice, love, community solidarity, idealism, upbringing, and even enlightened self-interest might help explain the way people behave because, if they abandoned their twin simplifying assumptions of rationality and pure self-interest and let some or all of these other possible factors stay in the picture, the world would remain so complicated that they would not be able to say anything definite – and they hope, useful – about it. In many cases, of course, their simplifications seem to work in that they enable them to predict what will happen with reasonable accuracy. However, it is a grossly unwarranted step to go on to say, as most economists do, that the real world ought to be modelled on their simplified theoretical one in order to be efficient and that any actual system, action or outcome which does not accord with what they would have advised under their assumptions is sub-optimal.[15]*

Photo 3.2 *The convivial economy: Stroud farmers' market*

Source: Rosa Cato

The aspects of economic life that are excluded from a conventional analysis are just those aspects which would come to the foreground in a green economy.

The three properties identified by David Fleming as essential to a sustainable (he would say 'lean') economy are 'self-distance, play and accomplishment'.[16] 'Self-distance' is a concept taken from Richard Sennett. It refers to the way that successful communities have rules about how much self-revelation is appropriate. It is a sign of our culture's incapacity for genuine closeness in social relationships that we feel the need for confessional TV and sometimes excessively confessional relationships with friends too. The concept of 'play' picks up the slogan of the Transition Towns about 'living experimentally', not being too afraid of making mistakes or getting things wrong. With his notion of 'accomplishment' Fleming is suggesting that being a successful citizen requires practice and takes determination and will, an expenditure of energy that is merited by the reward of living in a thriving community. 'Without it, forget the solar panels and local food. If the local economy, the community, can produce accomplished music, dance, celebration, it will have a chance.' He argues that for the achievement of these qualities the public sphere is central: 'It is the place where a community's culture happens.'

Such a convivial economy can only be possible if the market is relocalized since personal relationships cannot be maintained across the globe. More importantly, the relationships we do have with the manufacturers of products in China and Bangladesh are exploitative, since wages in those countries are at

Table 3.2 *Indicators of consumption and population in different regions of the world (2004–05)*

	USA	Europe	China	India	Asia	Africa	Latin & Central America	World
Passenger cars per 100 people	750	240	7	6	20	9	56	91
Annual petrol and diesel consumption (litres per person)	1624	286	33	9	47	36	169	174
Energy consumption p.a. (kg/oil equivalent)	8520	3546	896	515	892	580	1190	1640
Annual CO_2 emissions per person (tonnes)	20.3	8–12	2.7	0.99	<1	<1	<1	3.85
Annual meat consumption (kg per person)	125	74	52	5	28	13	58	40
Daily water consumption (litres per person)	430	159	135	174	172	47	147	173
Population	293	730	1306	1080	3667	887	518	6500
Children born per woman	2.08	1.56	1.72	2.78	3.1	4.82	2.75	2.55

Source: J. Pretty (2007) *The Earth Only Endures: On Reconnecting with Nature and our Place in It*, London: Earthscan.

a level that would be illegal within our own societies. While green economics is not ideologically opposed to all global trade, and welcomes cultural and personal exchange, we need to ask searching questions about the justice of those relationships. The imbalance is reflected not only in vastly different levels of wages but also in terms of resource use, as illustrated in Table 3.2.

Re-embedding economics in nature

As we saw at the beginning of this chapter, from the perspective of mainstream economics, economy and environment are separate spheres; they overlap when environmental resources are 'exploited' to produce goods that can be sold, but they are not mutually dependent. From a green economics perspective this separation is the heart of the problem. Recent human history has been a story of increasing disconnection from our environment or from 'nature' – both in the sense of the beautiful planet which we share and in the sense of our own intrinsic nature as an integral part of the complex web of life on that planet. This sort of thinking might find space within a book on ecology, but never within a book on economics. This distance from the natural world is the source of the environmental crisis:

> *What a terrible indictment, to have a culture that prides itself on its distance from the natural world and the natural cycles and rhythms, that regards its mission as needing (in Francis Bacon's words) to conquer and subdue nature with its indomitable technology, and that is built on the idea that nature has value*

only if it is harnessed and exploited for economic purpose:
'Nature, Mr Allnutt,' says the spinster on the African Queen, *'is*
what we have been put in this world precisely to rise above.'[17]

In his book *Soil and Soul* Alistair McIntosh presents a lyrical account of the dislocation of humanity from nature and of the consequences this has for politics and economics.[18] Jules Pretty goes further, providing an appealing vision of a reconnected human community, which has relearned its 'agri-culture' and found again its place in the landscape.[19]

For the ecofeminists, this disconnection between people and their planet is directly related to the economics of the 'rational economic man' which they consider to 'be written by men about men, ignoring women's work and women's issues'. This is not only unjust, but also dangerous:

> *The core argument of ecofeminist political economy is that the*
> *marginalisation of women's work is ecologically dangerous*
> *because women's lives as reflected in domestic and caring work*
> *represent the embodiedness of humanity, the link of humanity*
> *with its natural being... Ecofeminist political economy argues*
> *that the capitalist market is disembodied and disembedded,*
> *carved out of the totality of human existence within the natural*
> *world. Through the analysis of women's work it shows how the*
> *dualist 'economy' fails to acknowledge its true resource base and*
> *the way it is parasitical upon sustaining systems, including the*
> *environment. As a result these are exploited and damaged.*[20]

The ecofeminists argue a link between the way in which men deny their depen-dence on women through patriarchy and the way the economy denies its dependence on nature. In the individual case this is represented by our denial of our bodily existence, which leads to physical ill health just as the denial of dependence on nature leads to environmental ill health. In the words of Teresa Brennan: 'nature is the source of all value, and ultimately of all energy, but the inherent dynamic of capital is to diminish this value and this energy in favour

Table 3.3 *Valuation of activities and functions within the patriarchal economy*

Highly valued	Low/no value
Economic 'Man'	Women's work
Market value	Subsistence
Personal wealth	Social reciprocity
Labour/Intellect	Body
Skills/Tradable Knowledge	Feelings, emotions, wisdom
Able-bodied workers	Sick, needy, old, young
Exploitable resources	Ecosystems, wild nature
Unlimited growth, consumption	Sufficiency

Source: M. Mellor (2006) 'Ecofeminist Political Economy', *International Journal of Green Economics*, 1/1–2: 139–50.

of time and technology'.[21] It is not that women have an essential link with nature but more that their work, such as domestic and caring work, in Mary Mellor's words, 'represents the embodiedness of humanity, the link of humanity with its natural being'. Maria Mies and Vandana Shiva go further still, arguing that there is a specific link 'between patriarchal violence against women, other people and nature'.[22] The value system of conventional economics specifically denies the value of the body, the planet and female aspects of life, as illustrated in Table 3.3.

Permaculture Flower

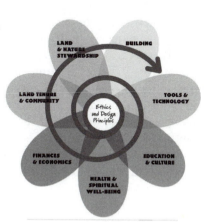

The permaculture journey begins with the Ethics and Design Principles and moves through the key domains required to create a sustainable culture. The spiral evolutionary path joins together these domains, initially at a personal and local level, and then proceeding to the collective and global level.

Some of the specific fields, design systems and solutions that have been associated with the wider view of permaculture are listed below.

Land & Nature Stewardship

Bio-intensive gardening	Holistic Rangeland Management
Forest gardening	Natural Sequence Farming
Seed saving	Agroforestry
Organic agriculture	Nature-based forestry
Biodynamics	Integrated aquaculture
Natural Farming	Wild harvesting & hunting
Keyline water harvesting	Gleaning

Building

Passive solar design	Earth sheltered construction
Natural construction materials	Natural disaster resistant construction
Water harvesting & Waste Reuse	Owner building
Biotechture	Pattern Language

Tools & Technology

Reuse & creative recycling	Bio-char from forest wastes
Hand Tools	Co-generation
Bicycles and electric bikes	Micro-hydro & small scale wind
Efficient & low pollution wood stoves	Grid-tied renewable power generation
Fuels from organic wastes	Energy storage
Wood Gasification	Transition engineering

Education & Culture

Home Schooling	Social ecology
Waldorf education	Action Research
Participatory arts and music	Transition culture

Health & Spiritual Well-Being

Home birth & Breast feeding	Spirit of place, indigenous
Complementary & holistic Medicine	cultural revival
Yoga, Tai Chi & other	Dying with dignity
body/mind/spirit disciplines	

Finances & Economics

Local and regional currencies	WWOOFing & similar networks
Carpooling, Ride sharing & Car share	Tradable Energy Quotas
Ethical Investment & Fair Trade	Life Cycle Analysis & Energy
Farmers markets & Community	accounting
Supported Agriculture (CSA)	

Land Tenure & Community

Cooperatives & Body Corporates	Open Space Technology &
Cohousing & Ecovillages	Consensus Decision Making
Native Title and traditional use rights	

 permacultureprinciples.com   **HOLMGREN DESIGN SERVICES** www.holmgren.com.au

Figure 3.2 *Permaculture flower*

Source: The illustration was drawn by Richard Telford based on the ideas of David Holmgren (www.holmgren.com.au). Thanks to them for permission to reproduce this free of charge.

Not squaring the circle but closing the loop

Sometimes, as when you hear the phrase 'sustainable development', you can question whether the attempt to achieve sustainability within the existing paradigm is possible at all. It does feel like trying to square the circle, trying to build something different and better with existing tools and within the existing mindset. The system of thinking that grows out of permaculture is a route out of this impasse. Permaculture arises from a recognition of the Earth as a limited system; although it began as a system of sustainable agriculture that respected ecology, its way of looking at the world has relevance to the economy as well. It relies on a sequence of design principles that can be applied with local varia-tions to generate sustainable, self-sufficient communities. According to the Permaculture Research Institute of Australia website, 'The philosophy behind permaculture is one of working with, rather than against, nature; of protracted and thoughtful observation rather than protracted and thoughtless action; of looking at systems in all their functions, rather than asking only one yield of them; and allowing systems to demonstrate their own evolutions.'

The most important principle from permaculture that can be applied to the economy is the closed loop, or closed system:

> *Closed systems. It is here that the solution lies. And closed systems will take the form of local organization, local economies. There will be no alternative. They will not be able to buy-in their needs, to import their way out of trouble. Local lean economies will not simply be a good idea; they will be the only option.*[23]

Let's take the example of biofuels. As soon as biofuels were seen as a solution to climate change they became a promising investment opportunity for venture capital. Farmers, too, moved rapidly into this new market as a means of maximizing profit from their land. The movement of vast areas of the Earth's fertile soils from food to fuel production has – when combined with reduced crops consequent upon climate change and an increasing population with more land-intensive demands – led to rapid increases in global food prices. The consequences of biofuel production for the environment, especially the remnants of rainforest, have also been stark. This is the result of an open-loop economy, where all productive land is a piece in a global monopoly game. By contrast, if my local community decides that some of its land should be trans-ferred to the growing of oilseed rape for the production of diesel to drive our tractor we will have to consider the consequences of that for our food produc-tion. We might well decide to use the tractor less. We will be experiencing the consequences of that decision within our own system. Similarly, if the only diesel available were that produced within our community we would be careful to recycle all used vegetable fat into biodiesel – a process that is rarely profitable on the scale at which it is feasible.

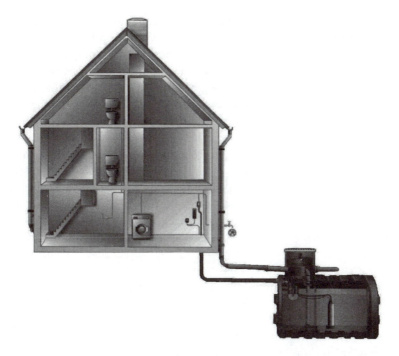

Figure 3.3 *Rainwater harvesting system for a domestic property*

Note: Rain from the roof drains into an underground tank and is then pumped back into the house to feed domestic appliances and sewerage. Only drinking water is piped into the house.

Source: Image provided free of charge by UK Rainwater Harvesting Association.

Rainwater harvesting is another example of a closed loop. In 2007 the UK experienced some of the worst floods in living memory; they were largely the result of poor water management, combined with the increased intensity of rainfall caused by climate change. Gardens and open spaces had been paved and tarmacked, allowing no possibility for the rain to be absorbed. The irony was that, because water pumping stations are located close to rivers, a large one in Gloucester was flooded and had to be shut down for fear of electrical explosion. This meant that in my village and surrounding areas some 300,000 people were left without water while the heavens continued to provide it in abundance. We were instructed not to use bottled water to flush toilets, which led many to realize that is exactly what we do every day – purify water to drinking quality and then send it down the sewer. This is the linear economy approach to domestic water supply. Experts estimate that 90 per cent of the water being piped into homes and sent out via sewerage is unnecessary.[24] We could instead circulate water from roofs into underground storage tanks and around our domestic systems, which would also reduce the pressure on drains in times of heavy rainfall. The problem with this is for the water companies, who make their profits by charging us for delivery and removal of water.

In the years since the Second World War in the more developed economies of the world the exploitation of land for growing food has gradually been organized more along the lines of a capitalist business, demonstrated by the use of the term 'agribusiness' to describe it. The culture of competitiveness, profit maximization and short-term thinking has replaced the traditional values of land management.[25] This has had horrendous consequences for the natural world that we are part of: species have become extinct, soil fertility has declined, and the landscape has been turned into a monocultural wilderness that fails to feed us both literally and figuratively.[26] A green economist might suggest that we reverse the process – not only should we relearn the culture of care for the land, but we might also use an approach of care and protection for our industries. If we really wanted to 'green business', adopting the culture and thought processes of permaculture might be a good way to start. The use of the phrase 'rainwater harvesting' gives us a clue that we might already be moving in that direction.

In these two brief chapters I have done my best to give you a sense of the antecedents of green economics. It has an eclectic range of influences and styles, which is consistent with the diversity it would seek to restore to our economic life. The three chapters that follow address three key economic themes – work, money and business – and offer guidance as to how green economists are rethinking these issues in ways which offer us a vision of a sustainable future.

Notes

1   J. Lovelock (2000) *Homage to Gaia: The Life of an Independent Scientist*, Oxford: Oxford University Press.
2   R. Lawson (2007) 'An overview of green economics', *International Journal of Green Economics*, 1/1–2: 23–36: 23.
3   J. Porritt (2006) *Capitalism as if the World Mattered*, London: Earthscan, p. 46.
4   Porritt, *Capitalism*, p. 58.
5   R. Douthwaite (1992) *The Growth Illusion: How Economic Growth Has Enriched the Few, Impoverished the Many and Endangered the Planet*, Totnes: Green Books, p. 27.
6   D. H. Meadows, D. L. Meadows, J. Randers and W. W. Behrens (1972) *The Limits to Growth: A Report for the Club of Rome's Project on the Predicament of Mankind*, New York: Universe Books.
7   D. H. Meadows, D. L. Meadows and J. Randers (2004) *Limits to Growth: The 30-Year Update*, White River Junction, VT: Chelsea Green.
8   F. Hutchinson, M. Mellor and W. Olsen (2002) *The Politics of Money: Towards Sustainability and Economic Democracy*, London: Pluto, p. 160.
9   J. Robertson (1985) *Future Work: Jobs, Self-Employment and Leisure after the Industrial Age*, London: Gower.
10 M. S. Cato (2006) *Market, Schmarket: Building the Post-Capitalist Economy*, Gretton: New Clarion Press.
11 V. Fournier (2007) 'Escaping from the economy: The politics of degrowth', paper presented to the research seminar of Cardiff School of Management, February.
12 P. Aries (2005) *Décroissance ou Barbarie?*, Lyon: Golias.

13 S. Latouche (2003) 'Le Marché, l'agora et l'acropole: Se rapproprier le marché', *Refractions*, 9: 17–26.

14 Fournier, 'Escaping', p. 13.

15 R. Douthwaite (1996) *Short Circuit*, Totnes: Green Books, ch. 7.

16 D. Fleming (2004) 'The lean economy: A vision of civility for a world in trouble', in *Feasta Review 2: Growth: The Celtic Cancer*, Dublin: Feasta, pp. 69–81, p. 79. This is a fascinating account which is available via the FEASTA website and which I have had to abridge painfully to fit into the limited space available in this chapter.

17 K. Sale (2006) *After Eden: The Evolution of Human Domination*, Durham, NC: Duke University Press, p. 127.

18 A. McIntosh (2001) *Soil and Soul: People Versus Corporate Power*, London: Aurum.

19 J. Pretty (2007) *The Earth Only Endures: On Reconnecting with Nature and our Place in It*, London: Earthscan.

20 M. Mellor (2006) 'Ecofeminist political economy', *International Journal of Green Economics*, 1/1–2: 139–50.

21 T. Brennan (1997) 'Economy for the Earth: The labour theory of value without the subject-object distinction', *Ecological Economics*, 20/2: 175–85: 179.

22 M. Mies and V. Shiva (1993) *Ecofeminism*, London: Zed.

23 Fleming, 'Lean Economy', p. 74.

24 Personal communication, Paul Munns of The Green Shop, The Camp, near Stroud.

25 J. Pretty (2002) *Agri-culture: Reconnecting People, Land and Nature*, London: Earthscan.

26 C. Tudge (2003) *So Shall We Reap: What's Gone Wrong with the World's Food – And How to Fix It*, Harmondsworth: Penguin.

PART 2

Vision for the Future

4
Work

O, dear me, the world is ill-divided
Them that works the hardest are the least provided
                    from the 'Jute Mill Song' *by Mary Brookbank*

From the perspective of contemporary capitalism, work is a necessary requirement for survival. Work is something you perform, generally under the
instruction of another, in return for money with which you buy the necessities
and the luxuries which the economy provides. As we have already seen in
Chapter 3, green economists ask searching questions about the consequences
of an economy which has growth and consumption at its heart, and this
inevitably influences their approach to work. The essence of work within a
capitalist economy is to turn primary resources into more complex goods or to
use resources to create services, both goods and services being sold in a marketplace. Greens question this view at every point. How can we be sure that this is
the best use of the planet's resources? How should the process of transformation be organized? What is the experience of the human beings employed in the
transformation and how does this relate to the way their work is managed?
And, perhaps most importantly of all, is it right that the ability to provide for
one's basic needs without entering into an employment relationship has been
continually eroded as the industrial economy has developed and spread?

Many modern democracies have a sometime governing party which represents the interests of labour; in the UK this party is even called the Labour
Party. It has become the historic role of this party to fight for jobs, defend jobs
and organize marches for jobs; one of the proudest boast of such governments
is that there are higher rates of employment than ever before. However, from a
green perspective the issue of quality is more important than that of quantity
when we come to consider work. We should ask not only how the job affects
the person who is required to carry it out, but also what its benefit is to the
wider human community and the planet itself. As I have written elsewhere:

> *We should not see work as an end in itself, and should do our*
> *best to minimize the work needed, rather than creating work.*

Only somebody who was set to benefit from the work of others would want to do something that would seem so insane to the members of a society we might label primitive.[1]

Since one of the key demands of a green economist is an end to economic growth there has been much discussion about how this is compatible with full employment, and whether there is a dichotomy between jobs and protecting the environment. This debate is the subject of the first section in this chapter. The following section begins to ask deeper questions about what work is and how it forms both the individual and our society. Then we move on to consider recent tangible developments in the world of work, especially the impact of globalization on the way work is shared between different countries with different levels of wealth – the so-called 'international division of labour hypothesis'. The final section looks at green alternatives to the present work system including lessons we might learn from the guild system, the organization of production and distribution, and a green approach to organizing business within the economy.

Will a green economy mean more work or less?

The issue of the quantity of work that there will be in a sustainable economy is a contentious one for green economists. Many in the green movement have come from more conventional left-wing parties and bring socialist attitudes towards labour and its organization. From this perspective, the status of a person as a 'working man' (and only latterly working woman) is paramount and the aim of much political activity is to use industrial muscle to maximize the wages of this employed worker and defend or improve his/her terms and conditions. Milani calls on organized labour to play its role in the Green Industrial Revolution that is needed to move rapidly towards a sustainable economy:

> Organized labour *is unlikely to be a pacesetter in a green trans-formation. Nevertheless, the role of unions is particularly important in the conversion process. To play an effective role, labor must relinquish its status as 'cog in the machine'. It must move proactively to redefine and reorient wealth production and to revive traditions of worker-control and self-management, while extending its long-time concern with the fair distribution of wealth.*[2]

However, for other green thinkers, it is work itself that is the problem – or at least work as organized in a capitalist economy. Since it is the nature of the economic system that is problematic, no amount of negotiation and agitation can solve this. A complete structural overhaul is required, a reclaiming of the economy and the planet's resources for meeting human needs directly. This clearly has significant implications for land ownership (as discussed in Chapter

12). This strand of green thinking has much in common with the utopian and guild socialists, who argued for a return to the land, small self-sustaining communities and self-provisioning rather than employment. While green economists can be sympathetic to both positions in theory, it is important to recognize that they are alternative visions. The vision of those who favour self-provisioning and self-reliant local communities would create an economy quite different to that in Milani's vision of worker control and self-management, which is intended to achieve collective democratic control of the economy, an economy that would still remain structured around larger economic and industrial units. This is a debate that is ongoing within the green movement.

When the ideas of green economics, particularly those about reduced consumption and an end to economic growth, entered the public debate, opponents from left and right responded with the suggestion that a green economy would mean high levels of unemployment. Green economists such as Frances Hutchinson responded positively, welcoming the reduced amount of work required in a green economy as the dawning of the leisure age that had been promised with the advent of technological production processes in the 1960s.[3] Much is made of the cultural transition to wage slavery from the Middle Ages onwards, as first the bell and then the clock replaced natural rhythms based on the movement of the sun, and as festivals and 'holy days' were gradually eroded as we moved towards today's 24/7 work pattern.[4] Others maintained a strong commitment to the quality of working life, suggesting that we should not be forced to choose between 'jobs and beauty'.[5]

However, some greens have suggested that we are in fact on the brink of a time when we shall be called upon to be very busy indeed, repairing the damage caused by 200 years of industrialism: a million extra jobs may need to be created as a consequence of a Green Industrial Revolution (see Box 4.1). From this perspective we need to shift into a higher gear, to something like a war economy in order to build all the wind turbines and to adapt vehicles and homes to a low-carbon future, as well as to produce whole new areas of employment in sectors such as the mending of goods and the repair of machinery and equipment. In response to a political debate taking place, at least in the UK, against a backdrop of high levels of unemployment, as long ago as 1994, Friends of the Earth argued that 'the UK economy could gain in the order of 33,000 to 78,000 additional jobs directly through environmental policy by 2005'.[6] The sectors they considered included renewable energy, recycling, public transport and organic farming.

Among politicians, this argument now appears to have been concluded by the understanding that greening the economy will be a labour-intensive process, at least in the short run. Evidence of this shift in official thinking includes the Green Jobs Strategy for Scotland that was first raised by Green MSP Robin Harper in 2002 and has since been taken up by Scottish Executive.[7] Their consultation report produced last year estimated a growth in offshore wind production of 185MW in the UK by 2007 and a near doubling in the waste and recycling sector by 2010. Similar arguments are made in

---

BOX 4.1 CREATING A MILLION EXTRA JOBS THROUGH A GREEN INDUSTRIAL REVOLUTION

- 30,000 UK jobs in wind energy leading to a trebling of employment in the energy sector
- Unsustainable farming practices have cut farming jobs by two-thirds in 50 years – while devastating the environment.
- Organic food production employs 20–30 per cent more people per hectare than chemical- and mechanical-intensive farming.
- Sustainable agricultural practices could create 40,000 new jobs.
- Banning throwaway containers for beer and fizzy drinks would create up to 4000 jobs.
- More UK jobs in repair of cars and white goods would lead to more skilled jobs tied to the UK.
- Recycling offers to create 14,000 extra jobs in London alone.

Source: S. Fitz-Gibbon (2004) *Best of Both Worlds: Green Policies for Job Creation and Sustainability*, London: Green Party

---

response to the recession following on the global financial crisis as in the Green New Deal.[8]

Where there is agreement it is on the issue of what work will be necessary in the sustainable economy. Much of the work carried out today is soul-destroying and wasteful of resources, creating gadgets than can be sold to make a profit for the corporation which controls the brand they are sold under, but offering little in terms of real satisfaction to the purchaser, and equally little in terms of job satisfaction to the producer. The use of resources and energy by workers in this sort of employment is indefensible within a green economy. Some green economists seek to make a distinction between 'work', which is useful, sustainable and a valid investment of resources, and 'employment', which is undertaken within a destructive economic system driven solely by profit.[9]

Green parties have engaged forthrightly in the debate about work. The French greens, for example, were prime movers in the debate which led to the mandatory 35-hour week in France. This is a typical contrast to socialist parties, most of which are still arguing for an increase in the number of jobs and concerning themselves with rates of pay and conditions; greens would sooner raise questions about the structure of the economy and the meaning of work: 'Ultimately, and in the long term, from a green perspective, informal, non-cash modes of economic activity and work ought to be seen as at least equally important as remunerated formal employment (if not more).'[10] This suggestion is supported by a quotation from green economist Frances Hutchinson:

> It is possible to argue that the primary purpose served by paid employment is financial, to meet the need to obtain a money income. The financial function of paid work is its only function. The personal function of work – its emotional, intellectual,

psychological and even spiritual purposes – can be equally well served where there is no financial reward. All that is required is that basic needs are met. Each task undertaken as a paid form of work can also be undertaken as a voluntary or leisure pursuit.[11]

Whose work is it anyway?

Several of the proto-greens identified in Chapter 2 were censorious in their criticism of the nature of work within a capitalist economy. Here is William Morris on the subject towards the end of the 19th century:

> *Most of those who are well-to-do cheer on the happy worker with congratulations and praises, if he is only 'industrious' enough and deprives himself of all pleasure and holidays in the sacred cause of labour. In short, it has become an article of the creed of modern morality that all labour is good in itself – a convenient belief to those who live on the labour of others. But as to those on whom they live, I recommend them not to take it on trust, but to look into the matter a little deeper.*[12]

While only some green economists reserve a place of special esteem for Marx, most would acknowledge the importance of his concept of alienation in any discussion about work. Marx considered that work fulfils a peculiar and essential role within human society; when people work for others in situations beyond their control and without enjoying ownership and control over the production process this is psychologically damaging and results in a state of mind for which he coined the word 'alienation'. Labour becomes 'objectified' and not only does the worker lose a sense of the value of his work, his whole concept of reality is distorted. Marx related alienation to our relationship with nature: 'Estranged labour not only (1) estranges nature from man and (2) estranges man from himself, from his own active function, from his vital activity; but because of this it also estranges man from his species. It turns his species-life into a means for his individual life.'[13]

Socialist green economists maintain this critique, pointing out how Marx's concept of commodification is increasingly relevant in today's economy, where more and more goods and services are provided by the market with people losing their ability to perform even the most basic functions, such as cooking and rearing children, for themselves. For some this is a deliberate strategy from an economic system which seeks to encroach into every area of life and open it up for business and profit: 'Capitalism is the first economic system in history that does not give access to resources as of right to the citizens of a country. Resources, goods and services are available only to those who have money, not to those who live within the boundary of a national economy.'[14]

This sentiment echoes that of Thompson in his history of the growth of the working class in England and links to green views of land as a basic means for

subsistence from which people have been excluded, in the case of the UK by the enclosure movement from the 17th century onwards. The sentiment was also shared by Ivan Illich, who considered the degradation of work to be the primary cause of a society without meaning, 'where individuals, throughout their lives, live only through dependence on education, health services, transportation and other packages provided through the multiple mechanical feeders of industrial institutions'.[15] Without access to land and basic resources to provide for themselves, citizens living in a late capitalist economy are in fact less empowered than many farmers in poorer countries or than their own ancestors.

Many green economists share the philosophical and sometimes spiritual values associated with privileging work as a social, humanizing process and not merely an instrumental necessity. Illich considered that economic conditions, foremost among these being those in the employment situation, undermined 'the conditions necessary for a convivial life'.[16] Partly in response to this critique, Robertson develops a concept he calls 'ownwork' – 'activity which is purposeful and important, and which people organize and control for themselves' – only part of which is in the formal economy.[17] He argues for the revival of the informal economy and the encouragement of 'home-grown' local economies, along with local self-reliance and the expansion of the third sector. 'Ownwork' is explained by reference to a quotation from Khalil Gibran, 'You work that you may keep pace with the earth and the soul of the earth. For to be idle is to become a stranger unto the seasons, and to step out of life's procession that marches in majesty towards the infinite.'[18] Robertson's argument for moving from employment to ownwork is partly economic – 'because the development of productive and useful work in the local and household sectors will reduce the present dependency of localities and households on jobs provided by the large-scale manufacturing and service sectors of the economy, as well as on goods and services purchased from these sectors or provided by them at public expense' – and partly psychological. He interprets the employment relationship as one of dependency where 'employees lose control of their working time by selling it to their employers, and employers gain control of their employees' time by buying it from them'.[19] In a system of 'ownwork' people take control of their own time.

Robertson's arguments in turn owe much to the thinking of Schumacher, whose own objections to the system of employment under capitalism also had a spiritual dimension. Schumacher took issue with the Calvinist–capitalist interpretation of work as something that must be a sacrifice made in return for the reward of heaven and/or wages for survival. He used the Buddhist concept of 'right livelihood' – a means of achieving subsistence without causing offence to one's own values, to other people or to one's environment – as a substitute for the exploitative work maximizing output that characterizes our economy. Schumacher drew a contrast between bad work – the repetitive, mindless and soulless work on an industrial production line – to good work, which fulfilled the requirements of right livelihood. Such good work should meet three criteria: what it produces should be useful and necessary; it should allow the worker to fulfil his/her potential; and it should be within a cooperative workplace to allow us to make unselfish relationships. Schumacher considered that 'this threefold function makes work so central to human life that it is truly impossible to conceive of life at the human level without work'.[20]

Deskilling and reskilling

As long ago as 1974, Braverman discussed the way in which, in the industrialized economies, an increasing number of jobs were being 'deskilled', that is to say, craft and specialist knowledge was no longer required to perform them.[21]

His was a Marxist analysis, and hence he couched his thesis in terms of the 'proletarianization' of labour, and its consequent reduced power for negotiating a fair share of the exchange value of the product. Globalization has accelerated this process, as many workers in Western societies have been required to use a limited range of skills and work has become homogenized. In what is called the 'international division of labour', corporations are able to maximize their returns from different national economies by honing an appropriate role for their citizens: workers in lower-paid economies are responsible for manual production, especially in China; Indian workers, with higher levels of computer skills and the advantage of the English language, specialize in call-centre and software roles; while the workers in Western societies are increasingly important in their consumer rather than their producer role.

For a green economist this admittedly simplified picture arouses several concerns. The globalized economy with its extended supply chains, linking producers in low-wage economies to consumers in high-wage economies, relies on international transport of goods on a huge scale (see the further discussion of the trade system in Chapter 11); this is one of the fastest growing sources of carbon dioxide emissions. These long supply chains also leave us highly dependent for even our most basic necessities, in an era when both financial and climatic instability would suggest the importance of sufficiency rather than vulnerability. The UK now imports the majority of its food: food imports into the UK increased by 24.6 per cent between 1992 and 2002 while the balance of payments deficit in food moved from £4.7 billion to £9.8 billion during the same period.[22] Figures from Eurostat indicate that both imports and exports of food by the EU-25 increased by around 16 per cent during the period 1999 to 2004. A Defra report on food miles identified a large-scale increase in transport of food. It estimated the annual cost of this transport, in social, environmental and economic terms, as more than £9 billion, the largest proportion of that being road congestion. This represents a full 34 per cent of the total value of the UK food and drinks industry.

At a deeper level, the international division of labour leaves us disempowered and useless, what Milani refers to as 'cog-labour', subject to decisions made by corporations about what we should consume and how it should be made.[23] Within the globalized economy the process of deskilling has continued, with complex operations now performed by computers and more routine work outsourced or performed by low-paid, part-time staff. The quality of these jobs in the traditional sense of pay rates and terms and conditions of employment has declined radically; but so has their quality in terms of nurture of the human spirit. For reasons of security as well as dignity, green economists call for reskilling and the rediscovery of craft in work: 'In the era of quality, work must recover its craft dimension.' In the UK 'reskilling' is one of the aims of the Transition Towns movement – a community response to economic life in the era of climate change and peak oil. The Transition Towns offer training in skills such as vegetable growing, darning and mending, preservation of surplus crops, spinning and weaving – the skills that will be needed in a sufficient

CONSUMERISM FOR BEGINNERS

Look honey, I bought something today!

Oh darling, I'm so proud of you!

Sidewalk Bubblegum ©1993 Clay Butler

Source: Cartoon by Clay Butler; for more visit www.sidewalkbubblegum.com

economy. This approach is in tune with the emphasis on sufficiency and self-provisioning that is an underlying principle of green economics:

> *Who is richer? (1) The person who must pay money out to somebody else to fix the lawnmower, or buy another when the lawnmower has become obsolete? Or (2) the person who is capable of fixing the lawnmower or digging up the lawn to grow safe organic vegetables for their children?*[24]

The concern for operating as a rounded person in one's work, and for developing craft and skill, is also addressed by the cooperative form of industrial organization, where skills are shared and workers take responsibility for all tasks, rather than using a narrow range of skills within a structure dictated by the division of labour. Empowerment is a key concept. The cooperative enables workers to maintain power over their own work, a central requirement for green economists. A cooperative requires a pooling of skills and that everybody within the cooperative be prepared to involve themselves in all the tasks required. Cooperatives also provide a structure for maintaining all the value of work within the group of workers. As Henderson argues, a sustainable economy requires 'the rise of worker-owned, self-managed enterprises, and of bartering, self-help, and mutual aid'.[25] Such an economy can provide satisfying work and rewarding lifestyles but 'simply cannot provide support for [the] enormous pyramided capital structures and huge overheads' associated with the late capitalist economy.

Greening production and distribution

One of the lessons of green economics is that much of what we use in our everyday lives need not have come from a production process of the formal economy at all. Robertson coined the term 'informal' economy to describe the work we have traditionally done, unpaid, to provide for our needs and those of others close to us. This economic sector is increasingly squeezed as the market takes over more areas of our lives, so that children are sent to nurseries rather than being looked after by their grandmothers or neighbours, and we eat ready meals rather than cooking for our families or sharing meals with friends. This pressure for all adults to be included in a formal employment relationship has been linked to the breakdown of communities, as people who traditionally provided voluntary service to the vulnerable in their communities no longer have time for this.[26] Boyle and colleagues make a number of proposals (see Box 4.2) which would revalue unpaid but socially valuable work.

The time-banking movement offers a structure to help to formalize exchange within the informal or co-production economy.[27] To address the issue of alienation and the poor quality of working roles within the employment situation, several green economists have called for an increase in the proportion of workplaces owned and controlled by their own employees by virtue of being cooperatives. Richard Douthwaite argues for the priority of such a business structure within a green economy, citing studies which show

---

BOX 4.2 POLICIES TO ENCOURAGE VOLUNTARISM AND SELF-HELP

- Focus on volunteering and participation as a vital role that is important for its own sake, rather than just a step towards paid work, and encourage informal, self-help activity.
- Develop an acceptable way of allowing people on benefits to be recompensed for their effort in the community, so that those outside paid work are given incentives to become active contributors to the community – but funnelled as far as possible through local institutions that may be affiliated to or funded by public services, but are independent of central government.
- Reform Incapacity Benefit regulations so that they stop discriminating against rehabilitation.
- Develop ways for people outside paid work who are doing useful activity in their neighbourhoods to have sufficient income to maintain some quality of life.
- In the long term, this may form some kind of Citizen's Income available to all [for more detail on this proposal see Chapter 9].

Source: D. Boyle, S. Clark and S. Burns (2006) *Hidden Work: Co-Production by People Outside Paid Employment*, York: Joseph Rowntree Foundation.

BOX 4.3 THE EXPANSION OF WORKER COOPERATIVES IN ARGENTINA

Towards the end of 2001 the developed, sophisticated economy of Argentina entered a devastating financial crisis – a result of tying its currency to the dollar rather than any problem with its own real productive capacity. None the less, because the value of money had eroded and money had been sucked out of the country, the real economy was affected, with wages remaining unpaid, and no ability to buy new inputs to production processes. Although the factories had usable machinery, markets for their products, skilled workers, and in many cases raw materials in stock, their owners walked away and abandoned the enterprises because conditions of trade were so poor. In response the workers took over their own factories, running them as worker cooperatives or *empresas recuperadas* (reclaimed firms). The reclaiming of factories is taking place on a large scale and in a wide variety of sectors. Some 1800 enterprises are in the process of being reclaimed, with 150 already operating under this system, providing for the livelihoods of over 12,000 workers. Around three-quarters are in manufacturing with the other quarter being in the services sector. Workers found different meanings in the takeovers: 60 per cent considered it as a source of labour, while more than 30 per cent asserted their moral right to ownership based on previous work for the company; slightly less than 10 per cent considered the takeover justified in order to continue production.

Source: M. Howarth (2006) *Worker Co-operatives and the Phenomenon of* Empresas Recuperadas *in Argentina: An Analysis of their Potential for Replication*, Manchester: Co-operative College.

---

that work satisfaction is highest when a firm is owned and controlled by those working in it.[28] The emphasis on maintaining one's power in the work environment relates back to the work of James Robertson:

> *The direct way to enlarge people's freedom to change the kinds of paid work they regard as valuable and to organize it for themselves under their own control is to alter the conditions in which paid work is done ... The creation of many more co-operatives and community businesses, the conversion of existing companies and other organizations into these forms, and their acceptance as normal parts of the mainstream economy, will bring wider opportunities for people to work together in pursuit of their own shared aims and values.*[29]

In seeking ways of restructuring the post-capitalist economy, green economists have found inspiration in medieval economics,[30] specifically the idea of the 'just price'[31] and the guild system. The idea of the just price was defined by St Thomas Aquinas in terms of the labour and costs of the producer. This outlawed the gaining of profits by middlemen, since only remuneration in return for just labour was acceptable, and prices should be sufficient only to allow the craftsman or trader to enjoy a standard of life suitable to his station. The prices of the most significant goods and services were fixed by public officials. Richard Douthwaite cites a statute from Kilkenny in 1376 that required the mayor to call forward two 'discreet men' to negotiate with a merchant arriving in the town the prices he should charge based on his statement, made on oath, of his costs and expenses.[32]

Operating within a strictly religious ideology, the medieval craft guilds controlled trade in a particular product, regulating not only standards of production but prices, as just discussed. They also played an important social role, supporting community life, as well as providing representatives to the governing bodies of their cities and supervising apprenticeships in their particular trade or craft. The operation of the guilds was at the heart of the medieval community, involving educational, social and religious dimensions:

> *Apprentices and journeymen were taught the craft and all its secrets, being brought to live in the same house as the master, as one of the family, without class distinction. The only distinction was in age and skill... Apprentices were trained to progress in their skills in order to become master in their own right, able to set up their own household.*[33]

Much of what is common practice in the contemporary economy would have been designated as profiteering and banned by the guilds: 'For example, London had a regulation to prevent anyone buying up cargoes of essential goods in order to corner the market. Thus when a shipment of coal arrived it had to be sold retail for the first eight days, each family being limited to fifty basketfuls.[34] Only then, in order to empty the boat, could any remaining coal be sold wholesale. And naturally, the shipper's retail margin was determined on a just price basis.' The guilds helped to hold the community together both by ensuring fair economic exchange but also through deeper cultural and spiritual functions:

> *Belonging to a guild was connected with a complex of emotions which a man shared with other members: pride in his guild whose reputation and authority he would jealously defend, participation in meetings and general decisions, assertion of his dignity as a fully-fledged burgher vis-a-vis the town patricians and the nobles, and a feeling of superiority vis-a-vis the unorganised craftsmen, the apprentices, pupils, servants – the common people of the town. A master craftsman sought and found in his work not simply a source of material prosperity: his work gave him satisfaction in itself. Hence his work and his product could be a means of achieving artistic pleasure. Perfection in a craft was handed down from generation to generation, forming a tradition of excellence and pushing the productive and the artistic possibilities of the craft to their utmost limits. A craft was a skill, and a skill was artistry. The free work of a master craftsman within a guild was a means of asserting his human personality and heightening his social awareness.*[35]

1 The Mercers (1394)
exported cloth

3 The Drapers (1364)
sold cloth on the domestic market

6/7 The Merchant Taylors (1327)
made cloth into garments

8 The Haberdashers (1371)
made cloth worn beneath armour and sold accessories

12 The Clothworkers (1528)
fulled, sheared and packed the cloth

13 The Dyers (1471)
dyed the wool or cloth

42 The Weavers (1155)
wove the cloth

43 The Woolmen (1522)
bought and sold raw wool

48 The Broderers (1561)
embroidered

49 The Upholders (1626)
upholstered

63 The Feltmakers (1604)
made felt, hats and headwear

64 The Framework Knitters (1657)
made knitted cloth

London Livery Companies involved in textiles with their precedence number and date of incorporation

Photo 4.1 *Crests of the London livery companies associated with textiles with dates of their funding*

Source: Thanks to the Clothworkers Company of London for pointing out this illustration.

While none of these economists is arguing for a return to a medieval system, which was anyway deeply embedded in a religious worldview and socially static culture which have since disappeared, it does give a pre-market perspective on the nature of the sharing of the spoils of economic activity. Bearing this in mind, a green economist might argue for a form of community business, recognizing that every business is in reality a collective endeavour and that profits made by businesses with the support of the community do not belong to the business alone but rather to the whole community. In such a business system risks could be shared along with profits; there would be a much stronger commitment to the locality; and a vocation to serve would predominate over the profit motive, leading to a different, more rounded, type of satisfaction. Considerations about standards of service and quality of goods would re-enter economic life. We might see evidence for the emergence of such business forms in some green sectors, such as renewable energy and organic foods, where there is a preponderance of community-owned and cooperatively organized businesses.

Green approaches to business have yet to apply the idea about limits to growth to individual businesses, where it is likely to conflict with the conventional idea about the importance of economies of scale. Small businesses, grounded in the local community, tend to show higher levels of responsibility and accountability.[36] As firms expand they are in a position to accumulate capital, which they can use to build new businesses or for other investment. They have also probably acquired specific and general skills and networks of customers and goodwill. If we consider the expansion of a sole trader or self-employed business person, how should they respond to the pressure to expand? A first step might be to take on an apprentice, to share skills and respond to the growing demand. Another mechanism might be to form a consortium or secondary cooperative, so that work can be shared between those with similar skills, while also allowing those in a similar trade to learn from each other. From a green perspective, these means of expansion are more just than simply taking on more workers and extracting some of the value of their labour as profits for the business.

Notes

1   M. S. Cato (2006) *Market, Schmarket: Building the Post-Capitalist Economy*, Gretton: New Clarion Press, p. 159

2   B. Milani (2001) *Designing the Green Economy: The Postindustrial Alternative to Corporate Globalization*, Lanham, MD: Rowman & Littlefield, p. 203.

3   F. Hutchinson (1998) *What Everybody Really Wants to Know About Money*, Charlbury: John Carpenter.

4   For example in J. Robertson (1985) *Future Work: Jobs, Self-Employment and Leisure after the Industrial Age*, London: Temple Smith/Gower.

5   E. Goldsmith, R. Allen, M. Allaby, J. Davoli and S. Lawrence (1972) *A Blueprint for Survival*, Harmondsworth: Penguin.

6   Friends of the Earth (1994) *Working Future? Jobs and the Environment*, London: FoE.

7   Scottish Executive (2005) *Going for Growth: A Green Jobs Strategy for Scotland*, Edinburgh: Scottish Parliament.

8   A Green New Deal, published by the New Economics Foundation on behalf of the Green New Deal Group, downloadable from www.neweconomics.org, last accessed 8 October 2008.

9   J. Barry and B. Doherty (2001) 'The greens and social policy: Movements, politics and practice?', *Social Policy and Administration*, 35/5: 587–607.

10 Barry and Doherty, 'Greens and social policy', p. 600.

11 Hutchinson, *What Everybody*, p. 145.

12 W. Morris (1885) 'Useful work vs. useless toil', in A. L. Morton (ed) *Political Writings of William Morris*, London: Lawrence & Wishart, 1973, p. 86.

13 T. Eagleton (1997) *Marx and Freedom*, London: Phoenix.

14 M. Mellor (1992) *Breaking the Boundaries: Towards a Feminist Green Socialism*, London: Virago.

15 I. Illich (1981) *Shadow Work*, London: Marion Boyars, p. 21.

16 I. Illich (1977) *The Right to Useful Unemployment and its Professional Enemies*, London: Marion Boyars.

17 J. Robertson (1985) *Future Work: Jobs, Self-Employment and Leisure after the Industrial Age*, London: Temple Smith/Gower, p. x.

18 J. Robertson (1989) *Future Wealth: New Economics for the 21st Century*, London: Cassell, p. 65.

19 Robertson, *Future Work*, pp. 26–7.

20 E. F. Schumacher (1973) *Small is Beautiful: A Study of Economics as if People Mattered*, London: Abacus.

21 H. Braverman (1974) *Labor and Monopoly Capital: The Degradation of Work in the Twentieth Century*, New York: Monthly Review Press.

22 M. S. Cato (2007) 'Climate change and the bioregional economy', in A. Cumbers and G. Whittam (eds) *Reclaiming the Economy: Alternatives to Market Fundamentalism in Scotland and Beyond*, Glasgow: Scottish Left Review Press.

23 Milani, *Designing*, p. 113.

24 Hutchinson, *What Everybody*, p. 168.

25 H. Henderson (1988) *The Politics of the Solar Age: Alternatives to Economics*, Indianapolis, IN: Knowledge Systems, p. 101.

26 D. Boyle, S. Clark and S. Burns (2006) *Hidden Work: Co-Production by People Outside Paid Employment*, York: Joseph Rowntree Foundation.

27 www.timebanks.co.uk.

28 R. Douthwaite (1996) *Short Circuit: Strengthening Local Economies for Security in an Unstable World*, Totnes: Green Books.

29 Robertson, *Future Wealth*, pp. 31–2.

30 M. S. Cato (2006) *Market, Schmarket: Building the Post-Capitalist Economy*, Gretton: New Clarion Press.

31 Robertson, *Future Work*.

32 Douthwaite, *Short Circuit*, p. 344.

33 Hutchinson, *What Everybody*, p. 83.

34 Douthwaite, *Short Circuit*, p. 344.

35 A. Gurevich (1985) *Categories of Medieval Culture*, London: Routledge, p. 277.

36 M. S. Cato, L. Arthur, R. Smith and T. Keenoy (2007) 'CSR in your own backyard', *Corporate Responsibility Journal*, 3/2: 32–8.

5
Money

Money makes the world go round – but in ever-diminishing circles
Frances Hutchinson

Green economists have differed in their approach to money and its role in a sustainable economy. There is overwhelming agreement that the existing money system is destructive and particular revulsion at the 'casino economy', which is how the international financial system is frequently labelled. However, on deeper issues of monetary reform and the social and economic roles of money there is some divergence of views.

James Robertson has again been a pioneer in linking the broader agenda of financial and monetary reform to the central concerns of green economics. His view is that the money system is perverse because of its responsibility:

- for the systematic transfer of wealth from poor people and countries to rich ones;
- for the money-must-grow imperative that compels people to make money in socially and environmentally damaging ways;
- for the diversion of economic effort and enterprise *towards* making money out of money and *away* from providing useful goods and services.[1]

We can draw from this succinct critique a structure for this chapter. The following section explores the way the money system creates inequality between rich and poor within nations and this is followed by a section discussing how a similar process operates at the international scale. The following section describes the direct link between the nature of money creation within a capitalist economy and the growth imperative that leads to ecological destruction. The penultimate section explores the negative impacts of the financial system in its diversion of energy away from useful ends and towards the accumulation of wealth, and discusses the impact this system has on all our livelihoods. The last section then discusses positive responses to this critique in terms of community currency systems that have grown up around the world, many of them the result of work by environmental activists.

The politics of money

Long before there was concern for the survival of humankind as a species there was criticism of the money system and the way it was linked to the work system, causing inequality and poverty. Both Robert Owen and Karl Marx subscribed to the labour theory of value, which identifies how capital is accumulated from the difference between the use value of a product and its exchange value. The use value is effectively the value of the inputs plus the labour expended to make the item; the exchange value includes the profit from trade. During the 19th and early 20th centuries this explanation was given for the existence of poverty during a time of economic boom. This was a moral critique but an ecological critique along similar lines could be made, since the surplus value extracted puts unnecessary pressure on the planet. In Gandhi's famous phrase: 'The Earth has enough to satisfy the need of all the people, but not for satisfying the greed of some.'[2]

Owen's solution to the labour theory of value had two sides: one was the cooperative system which enabled the balancing of production and consumption; the other was the abolition of the existing money system and the substitution of a system of monetary exchange based on labour value. Rather than an arbitrary currency, whose creation and value were determined by rentiers and bankers, working people should exchange with each other by valuing their goods in terms of the labour invested in producing them. Owen's National Equitable Labour Exchange, established in London in 1830, first at Gray's Inn Road but soon after moved to Charlotte Street, facilitated exchange by working people of the fruits of their labour. The scheme was an instant success among producers, and it has been estimated that perhaps a thousand artisans were involved in the Exchange.[3] The medium of exchange was the 'labour note', which related directly to time, so that people were trading in terms of the time they spent making items, equating use value and exchange value.

The work of two economists has been crucial in updating and propagating this critique: Michael Rowbotham and Frances Hutchinson. Hutchinson explores the relationship between the growth of trade and the growth of the modern, debt-based money system which 'placed production of goods for the market onto a production-for-profit basis, revolutionizing the relationship between manufacturer, worker and consumer'.[4] She links this system of bank money directly to the falling share of production going to labour throughout the following two centuries and to the displacement of all other values including 'socially and ecologically useful work like tilling the soil, preparing the food, making clothes and tending the sick' which are 'undervalued and poorly paid'.

This is an argument shared by most green economists and one which links with the critique of the money system on the basis of inefficiency, i.e. wasting productive labour, outlined below. As made by Mellor, Hutchinson and Olsen, however, it is an argument about provisioning which relates to the green

Photo 5.1 *Labour note as used at Owen's Equitable Labour Exchange in 1933*

Source: Thanks to Gillian Lonergen archivist of the Co-operative College for permission to reproduce the scan of this note, which forms part of the Robert Owen collection.

attitude towards work outlined in Chapter 4. As they argue, the capitalist economic system is peculiarly dedicated to translating all values into monetary values:

> *The temptation to convert the human relationship with the land and its people into a money relationship is not new, dating from at least biblical times (see, for example, Amos 8: 4–7). However, capitalism has successfully overcome dissent to its extermination of all but money values by devaluing local and home production of the basic necessities of all aspects of life.*[5]

This narrow method of valuation pressurizes activities not included in the market economy, primarily caring activities, but it also eliminates the possibility of preserving all aspects of life which cannot be monetized, especially the value of the planet itself.

Rowbotham's work also focuses on debt, especially mortgage debt which is the 'grip of death' in the title of his 1998 book. From his perspective this debt is the cause of the most pressing ills of modern society, from the failure of public services and forced economic growth to the ever-increasing emphasis on competition and the poor quality of consumer goods. Rowbotham identifies the inflation of house prices in the economies with the highest levels of capital accumulation as a mechanism for facilitating debt-based money creation. He shares the common green critique of a money system based on debt, i.e. that it causes personal and planetary servitude:

The creation and circulation of money requires permanent debt. And so long as we are in debt, so are we bound to paid employment. No matter how much we produce, no matter how efficiently and cheaply; no matter how much mass-production and cost-cutting is undertaken, overall we must be in debt. The money supply demands it.[6]

In terms of practical responses to the inadequate and unjust monetary system they have criticized, green economists are fairly consensual in their call for a political solution. The most resounding call is for the democratization of the money system. Why should something so fundamental to economic life as money be left under the control of unaccountable banks? Should it not be the case rather that money, as a social construct, be under social and political control?

In a democratic age one would expect money, created in official currencies as part of a national or supranational money supply backed by governments, to be created by professionally independent central monetary authorities (like the European Central Bank) and given to governments or international government agencies to spend into circulation on public purposes.[7]

Money and global injustice

While at the national level the consequences of the existing money system are focused on the way it generates private and public debt, its instability, and the way it creates a squeeze on the social aspects of the economy, in an international context green economists criticize the money system for its role in stimulating conflict and creating massive inequality between nations.

The international financial system is complex and closely interrelated with the system of global trade. The relationship revolves around the system of reserve currencies – the dollar, euro, yen and pound sterling – which countries are prepared to accept from one another, or from third countries outside the charmed circle, in settlement of external trade balances.[8] This system clearly gives the countries that control these currencies a huge advantage in trade terms, especially the US, which negotiated that its currency should have the supreme advantage of being acceptable alongside gold as the international reserve asset during the Bretton Woods negotiations that established this system at the end of the Second World War. Although the US then undertook to maintain gold reserves to support the dollar, this agreement was unilaterally suspended by President Nixon during the Vietnam War in 1971. So since that time the US has been in a situation where it can print dollars and then exchange them for imported goods at virtually no cost.

This system has not worked entirely to the advantage of the US, since it is

the explanation for that country's vast and growing debt. However, for US consumers it has been a bonanza. This is one side of the critique shared by green economists, since the ability to draw in consumer goods has led to unprecedented levels of consumption at huge environmental cost – a level of consumption that has then been adopted by other countries. The other side of the critique is the poverty generated in those countries forced to sell their labour and their resources to support this consumption by the citizens of the

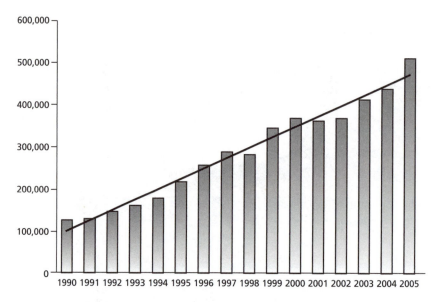

Figure 5.1 *Total debt service of low- and middle-income countries, 1990–2005 (US$ million, current)*

Source: Data from the Word Resources Institute environmental information portal *Earth Trends*, which is licensed under a creative commons licence.

countries with global financial power. The only way they can finance their own development is through borrowing from Western institutions and then repaying these loans, increasing yet further the gap between rich and poor countries (see Figure 5.1). Green economists would argue that we can never 'make poverty history' without renegotiating the terms of the Bretton Woods settlement. It is for this reason that writers such as Ann Pettifor have turned their attention from campaigns like Jubilee 2000 to an intellectual critique of the global money system: 'IMG and creditor-led policies ... encourage low-income debtor nations to export raw materials, undermine subsistence agriculture and local businesses, and turn their societies into markets for imported food and irrelevant consumer goods.'[9]

Why should this matter to green economists? There are three reasons: first it is unjust and immoral that a politically constructed money system should cause death and suffering to the majority of the world's population while those who control this system live in luxury. Second, because the system is based on competition between nations rather than cooperation it is a major source of international tension and war. Third, the need to generate money to repay debts caused by the global system, just as in the case of national economies, forces the poorer nations of the world to over-exploit their natural resources to earn export revenue.

Rowbotham calls for a return to the policy of the Bancor, proposed by J. M. Keynes on behalf of the British government at Bretton Woods.[10] Such a system would create a new non-aligned currency (Keynes called it banc-or bank-gold) to be used for settling external debts. The trade system should be established with the aim of achieving balance between nations, with fines for those displaying trade balances or trade surpluses. Modern developments of this proposal include the suggestion that the international currency be linked to land[11] or be created as an EBCU (environment-backed currency unit) and issued in combination with a system to limit CO_2 emissions.[12] More pragmatically, many countries are now switching their foreign reserves out of the dollar and are choosing to trade, especially in oil, using euros. Countries such as Iran and Venezuela have arranged alternative systems for settling their external trade balances. The countries of Latin America are rapidly repaying their debts to the IMF and World Bank, threatening to bankrupt those organizations which rely on debt repayments for their survival. However, it appears unlikely that these problems can be solved without an international conference to renegotiate the Bretton Woods agreement.

Money creation: Financially and ecologically unstable

In these first two sections we have seen green economists providing vehement critiques of the consequences of the existing monetary system. It seems appropriate now to delve a little deeper into the theory of money creation. At the time of writing the global financial system was suffering the most serious upheaval since the Wall Street Crash, with well-established banks and financial intermediaries collapsing almost on a daily basis. This has made apparent the system by which money is created by banks, a system which, as rapidly became apparent, was only hazily understood – including by politicians and financial journalists. This is an area where green economists have been ahead of public debate, at least in terms of asking how money is created and how this relates to the growing level of debt, and the pressure this creates to continue economic growth.

The clearest account is provided by Richard Douthwaite, whose short

---

Box 5.1 Traditional money in Vanuatu

Inhabitants of the Pacific island of Vanuatu are spurning the global economy and returning to traditional means of monetary exchange including pigs, pig tusks, woven grass mats and sea shells. The move began in 2005 when the National Council of Chiefs decreed that the 'bride price' paid by young men on marriage had to be made in goods rather than in cash. The country's Prime Minister Ham Lini declared 2007 the Year of the Traditional Economy, supporting the 80 per cent of the country's 210,000 people who grow their own food. The campaign to revive the traditional economy takes place in the face of climate chaos (Vanuatu is low-lying and threatened by inundation) matched by threats to the social fabric created by the lure of material wealth and the globalized economy. The turn towards a simple life was part of the reason that Vanuatu was nominated the world's happiest country in the New Economics Foundation's Happy Planet Index for 2006.

Source: N. Squires 'Content islanders reject capitalism for traditional trade', *New Zealand Herald*, 12 December 2007.

volume *The Ecology of Money* explores the history of money creation and makes clear the instability of the present money system, where commercial banks are permitted to lend money to the public, which then accrues value to the banking system as a whole. Here is Porritt's description of the way that banks create money, and the advantages this gives them:

> *For instance, about 97 per cent of the UK's money supply is created by commercial banks more or less out of thin air as interest-bearing (profit-making) loans . . . The banks in the UK make about £20 billion a year in interest from this arrangement. ... The money supply created in this way is not linked to real resource use or to the amount of goods and services in the national economy – it is based entirely upon the banks' commercial judgement about the ability of an individual or an enterprise to pay their loans. The more money there is, the more debt there is; as the money supply increases, so does a nation's indebtedness.*[13]

Such a system is clearly unstable, since the failure of one of the forms of 'financial instrument' held as collateral, such as mortgages granted to those without the ability to make their repayments, can threaten to bring down the whole global financial system like a house of cards.

But green economists have an additional concern with the unbalanced nature of the debt–money system. They argue that a system which creates money by creating parallel debts is necessarily imposing a pressure to increase economic activity, since the holders of debt need to work more hours to generate cash to repay it: 'The growth imperative imposed by the debt-money system is a positive feedback mechanism – a vicious spiral.'[14] A steady-state economy, by contrast, would require that the amount of money in circulation had a relationship with the amount of economic activity. For conventional economists this is not a problem, since they understand monetary creation as a mechanism to encourage economic growth, which they favour. The reality is that growth in money is vastly outstripping growth in the real economy (see the illustration of the relationship between these two in the UK in recent years in

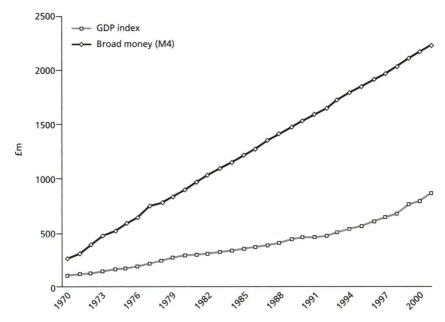

Figure 5.2 *Growth in broad money (M4) compared with growth in the economy (GDP), UK*

Source: GDP data from UK Office for National Statistics; M4 data from Bank of England.

Figure 5.2). Even were this not the case, the positive attitude towards growth shown by neoclassical economists is only possible because their theories exclude from their model of the economic world 'externalities' such as pollution and resource depletion.

A third concern is with the unaccountable nature of banks and loss of control over the money system, which is a fundamental function within a complex democratic economy. For most green economists money should be spent into circulation by democratically elected governments, rather than being loaned into existence by private businesses known as banks. This would also address social issues, since it would enable governments to pay for public services directly, rather than having to find this money indirectly through taxation of incomes or businesses.[15]

How money wastes people

A standard critique of the capitalist money system shared by most green economists is that the available money tends to be sucked into areas of the economy with little social value, leaving some of the most important aspects of life marginalized and underfunded. Harmer refers to areas of the economy where money accumulates as 'upper circuits'.[16] They include specialist consumption backwaters, such as the markets for yachts or fine art, as well as a whole range of speculative investment markets, which these days swallow up the majority of financial transactions. This explains the weak relationship between monetary growth and growth in the real economy, as illustrated in Figure 5.2; it also explains why money is scarce for many individuals within national economies, as well as for governments seeking to invest in goods and services on behalf of the public.

Edgar Cahn goes back to the Greek word *oikonomia*, meaning 'household', to draw attention to the importance of what he calls the 'core economy' as opposed to market-based economic activities that dominate most people's lives as a result of the distortion caused by the money system. Cahn argues that the core economy is more efficient than the market economy in some of the most important areas of life: caring for children and old people and building a strong community. It relies on self-sufficiency rather than specialization; bases distribution on need rather than market power; and rewards psychologically rather than in money. The core economy suffers the impact of 'externalities' generated by the market economy, which undervalues environmental costs and social benefits; restoring and nurturing the core economy will reduce this environmental impact. For Cahn the solution is a cooperative form of economic organization he calls 'co-production':

> *Co-Production economics necessitates a kind of ecological awakening about the non-market [or core] economy. It illuminates externalities that are as critical as those that threaten biodiversity, deplete the ozone layer, pollute the air we breathe, and contaminate the water we drink.*[17]

A solution proposed by Cahn and shared by other green economists is that of time banking. Using the concept developed by Robert Owen nearly 200 years ago – although with no apparent intellectual link – time banking automatically equates the value of everybody's work and allows the exchange of labour and skills without having the exchange distorted by the dominant money system.[18] Time banks have developed in numerous communities in the UK and US, although to some extent they remain trapped in the 'core economy' as defined by Cahn, which is the marginal economy within capitalism. Thus, while it is possible for those within communities to build up supportive networks by exchanging services, and this has unquestionably greatly improved their quality of life, for most this is peripheral to their main livelihood.

LETS is another time-based local exchange system that was particularly popular in the UK in the 1980s and 1990s.[19] Many of the UK's cities and towns developed computer-based systems for exchange of services and some goods, each of which took on a name with local resonance – bobbins in Manchester, beacons in Brecon, and so on. Research carried out by LETS-link UK in 1996 found over 450 schemes in the UK involving some 40,000 individual members. By 2007 the number had shrunk to around 300 schemes with LETS having passed its peak. The weakness of many of these schemes was that certain services were readily available, aromatherapy and dog-walking are the

---

Box 5.2 The parable of the South African talents

Cometh the hour, cometh the complementary currency. When apparently logical man-made systems create obviously unnecessary suffering, humans can sometimes take a step back, spot the defect and correct it, starting at local level. So it is with the money system. Currently it is clearly cruel and dangerous, leaving millions of people out while trillions of money is hoarded and unstable bubbles of 'derived' money, debt and 'passive income' streams abound.

South Africa has one of the most sophisticated systems of trading through complementary currencies in the world, including widespread LETS systems. A nationwide alternative currency, based in Cape Town, is the Talent Exchange. Talents are traded in Cape Town between some 2000 members. Talents are valued roughly equivalent to the national currency. Since 2003, when the system was set up, about 2.5 million talents have been traded – equivalent to R2,500,000.

The talent exchange operates like a bank but more rationally – and more transparently, since everyone's account can be seen by everyone. You can 'borrow' from it by going into deficit in your account; and you can hold reserves in it by going into credit. In neither case is interest involved. If your deficit gets too deep, other members will not sell to you until you recover; if you stay in credit for too long you are asked to start spending to keep the system lively.

On the Talent Exchange you can get a holiday cottage, your car serviced, compost, any number of health services, staff training of all kinds, office and home furniture, books, accountancy and computer services, gardening, home cleaning and repairs … you name it. Regular monthly trading days enable display of wares and communal activities. A network of talent depots is being established. There is also an overlap into the rand economy. Rand-rich but time-poor members can help rand-poor members with rands in exchange for talents.

Written by Margaret Legum, at SANE (South African New Economics Network).

Source: www.CES.org.za.

---

examples usually cited (!), while it was notoriously difficult to find solicitors or plumbers prepared to work for LETS money. In areas such as Stroud, where a wide range of business and professional services became traded through the LETS, interest from the Inland Revenue hastened the collapse of the system. LETS' major achievement in the UK context is to educate people in the nature of money and work; this is the central reason for the interest in such schemes on the part of green activists as well as green economists.

Local currencies for a localized world

The justification for the creation of money by fractional reserve banking, i.e. more money than there are real assets to support it, is that it stimulates economic activity. While green economists are concerned to link this to a level of economic activity that the planet can sustain, they are frequently in favour of the creation of money on a local basis to stimulate local production and exchange. In fact many of the accounts of historical examples of money creation in response to shortages of cash are given by green-leaning as well as other radical economists.

The most recent flourishing of locally created currencies occurred, unsurprisingly, during the years of economic recession that occurred across the industrialized world between the two world wars in the 20th century. In

---

BOX 5.3 THE CHIEMGAUER LOCAL CURRENCY IN CHIEMGAU, GERMANY

Photo 5.2 *An example of a Chiemgauer note, showing the stamps that have to be added to preserve its value over time*

Source: Thanks to Christian Gelleri for permission to reproduce this image.

The Chiemgauer was launched in the Salzburg town of Chiemgau in 2003 and is accepted by around 150 shops and service providers including the optician and pizzeria. Chiemgauers to the value of 60,000 euros were spent in the first year of the scheme, which was started by a local economics teacher. To add credibility the currency is backed one-for-one by euros, which are deposited in a local bank before Chiemgauers are issued. They can be exchanged back for a 5 per cent fee. The Chiemgauer uses Silvio Gesell's concept of demurrage to increase its velocity of circulation. Gesell observed that part of the reason for German deflation was that money was not circulating rapidly enough, because people believed it would increase in value if they held on to because of its role as a store of value as well as a circulating medium. His concept of demurrage is like negative interest, so that money slowly loses its value over time, thus increasing the number of times it is spent in a fixed period of time. This is achieved by effecting a staged reduction in its face value: it has an initial validity of three months, after which its value can only be extended by purchasing a stamp costing 2 per cent of its value. Since it earns no interest there is no incentive to hoard or invest, meaning that the currency will instead be spent, increasing economic activity. Money generated from the extension and exchange charges is used to fund local social projects.

Europe the leading inspiration for the issue of such local money was the German economist Silvio Gesell. German and Austrian local authorities issued money to the local unemployed to create employment on public works programmes. Due to a general shortage of cash this money passed into general circulation and ensured local economic booms amid generalized depression. Gesell introduced the concept of *demurrage* that is still popular among proponents of community currencies. It is a form of anti-interest, meaning that the money deteriorated rather than accumulating value over time, and had to be spent and validated in order to keep its value. Gesell's idea was to increase the velocity of circulation of the local money. The Chiemgauer is a contemporary money system that uses demurrage to ensure its rapid circulation (see the details in Box 5.3).

Similar systems of local money creation grew up in various states of the US during the Great Depression of the 1930s and were known as 'scrip issue'.[20] Estimates of the amount of money created in this way have risen as high as one billion dollars with some one million people involved in the schemes. In desperation at the complete halt brought to the real economy as a consequence of the financial collapse on Wall Street, local authorities in Cleveland, Minneapolis and Oklahoma City, among others, issued circulating notes backed by their political credibility.

There appears to be a paradox generated by the interest on the part of green economists in creating local currencies when the purpose of those currencies is to generate more economic activity and yet at the same time one of the central axioms of green economics is the need to halt economic growth. The resolution of the paradox is in understanding that only growth for the purposes of profit-making and capital accumulation is being criticized. National money systems are pernicious not only because the growth they generate puts pressure on the planet but also because they generate economic activity with questionable social benefit – for example, the creation of an ever-expanding range of short-lived consumer products – while marginalizing economic activities valued more highly by society as a whole, such as childcare or nursing. If local currency systems generate beneficial economic activity, and especially if they substitute local economic activity for products made and transported in the unsustainable global economy, then they are a useful part of the green economist's toolkit.

Disillusion with the environmental consequences of the existing money system, as well as concern for its inequitable social consequences, has led community activists to devise a multitude of alternative systems of monetary or pseudo-monetary exchange:

> *Drawing from the early history of human civilization, and from recent developments, many communities are beginning to introduce new economic systems to enhance trade in local areas... Parallel currency systems attempt to balance the influence of an 'efficiency based' global monetary system with an 'equity-based' community economy, by issuing an interest-free currency with a value agreed to by the members as the medium of exchange.*[21]

Peter North describes a range of 'green currencies',[22] meaning alternative money systems which are inspired to a greater or lesser extent by the prerogative of changing the way we interact with our environment. He gives the example of Kor (circles) from Hungary, which enabled ecological and social activists to extend the country's tradition of mutual aid or *kalaka* during the transition from state socialism to capitalism. (A brief account of New Zealand's green dollars is presented in Box 5.4.) From the UK, North cites the example of LETS, which was frequently supported by environmentalists who saw it as a way of achieving social justice objectives as well as reinforcing local economic links. This connection has been strengthened recently by the Transition Towns movement, whose local groups in Totnes and Lewes have launched currencies to emphasize the importance of building strong resilient local economies as a bulwark against the insecurities brought by climate change. Seyfang makes the point in her more academic account of local currencies:

> *A key characteristic of resilience and adaptability is diversity. The challenges facing us across the globe demand action both to mitigate, and adapt to environmental, social and economic change. Arguably, a diverse range of systems of provision, extending beyond the confines of current mainstream institutions and into increasingly self-reliant and empowered communities, will prove the best defence against external shocks.*[23]

One of the most exciting examples of a community currency flourishing occurred in Argentina between 1995 and 2001;[24] it was known as the Red Global de Trueque (RGT) or global barter network. The scheme was first set up in Buenos Aires by a small group of environmentalists, whose intention, as is the case with many involved in the community response to peak oil and

---

BOX 5.4 NEW ZEALAND'S COMPLEMENTARY CURRENCIES

New Zealand has a widespread system of complementary currencies similar in design to LETS schemes. They differ in that the value of these 'green dollars' is linked to the NZ dollar rather than to an hour of time and that they are exchangeable one with another via the Green Dollar Connections. The first systems were established in 1986/7 and by 1993 there were around 55 in existence. This suggests a membership at that time of around 5900 people; in 1996 the largest scheme – Auckland Green Dollar Exchange – had 2040 members and was the largest alternative currency network in the world. Some of the systems were dominated by green activists; others were versed in theories of social credit or based on religious motivation. The most successful provided 'observable material and psychic benefits' and 'worked for those whose livelihood strategy or philosophical, political or moral orientation was strengthened through membership of the network'. As in other countries, the New Zealand systems struggled with the amount of time spent in administration and some also faced problems with local tax offices, concerned that economic activity diverted from the national currency was leading to a fall in tax revenue. Much of the success of the New Zealand complementary currencies can be explained on the basis of the fierce economic pressures resulting from the rapid change to neoliberal economic policies in the late 1990s. In addition, their strong identification with green campaigns and the Green Party resulted in a politicized debate around their usefulness as well as their morality.

Source: P. North (2007), *Money and Liberation: The Micropolitics of Alternative Currency Movements*, Minneapolis: University of Minnesota Press.

climate change, was to stimulate local production and trade. However, following Argentina's financial collapse and the disappearance of money from the country, the community currency, which was now being issued as small notes called *arboles* (trees), became the main medium of exchange in the city. This led to an explosive growth of the currency and the loss of control over its issue by the founding group. The currency also spread throughout the country, supported by local politicians desperate for a response to the economic crisis. Without control or regulation, forgery was rife, people lost confidence in the currency, and it collapsed. It provides a fascinating example of how a currency issued by people for their own use and without support of any reserves, can provide a means of facilitating exchange and, in fact, of underpinning a whole economy.

Conclusion

Green economists have shown a strong interest in all aspects of monetary reform, from concern for the way a reserve currency system creates geopolitical instability and global poverty, to a critical stance on the distorting and inefficient nature of national money creation. Many of the most prominent green economists have also been involved as pioneers of their own local currency systems. In conclusion it is worth mentioning the ongoing division within green economics concerning the focus of effort in the arena of monetary reform. While the critique is fairly consensual, proposals for change differ.

Mary Mellor, Frances Hutchinson, James Robertson and Richard Douthwaite agree that the target for policy effort should be the system of money creation itself. While they all support complementary currencies in the interim, they see them as just that: complementary currencies which should be replaced by a democratized and stable system of money creation. This is in contrast to other commentators, foremost among them being Bernard Lietaer, who portrays the monetary arena as a natural balance between bank money and community money, which he likens to the yin and yang of the financial system. Lietaer's target is not the nature of capitalist money; indeed he sees a role for complementary currencies because of their 'capacity to transform resources into capital',[25] a capacity which would be problematic to more radical green economists. Mellor is critical of this approach which, to her and her co-authors, 'seems as if once more, as in many of the yin–yang analogies, the feminine is left to pick up the pieces'. As they continue:

> *The limitations of such auxiliary currency proposals is that they are not framed within a fundamental criticism of mainstream economic theory and practice. While problems are identified, the global economy is seen as in need of reform rather than reconstruction. The capitalist market economy is not perceived as a mechanism that actually exists to destroy utility by converting it*

to worthless money. Also auxiliary money systems do not address the need for democratic control of property and resource access.[26]

As greens move into government in an increasing number of countries this policy difference may become more pressing. For now, the focus of green activists, both in the world's ecovillages and the Transition Towns that are springing up as a community response to climate change, is on creating alternative currencies, both as a means of facilitating the expansion of local economic activity and as a possible shadow currency in the event of the failure of the unstable global monetary system.

Notes

1   J. Robertson (1989) *Future Wealth: New Economics for the 21st Century*, London: Cassell, p. 142.
2   P. Sheth, (n.d.) 'The Eco-Gandhi and ecological movements': www.mkgandhi.org/environment/ecogandhi.htm.
3   I. Donnachie (2000) *Robert Owen: Owen of New Lanark and New Harmony*, East Linton: Tuckwell Press. See also R. Bickle and M. S. Cato (2008) *New Views of Society: Robert Owen for the Twenty-First Century*, Glasgow: Scottish Left Review Press.
4   F. Hutchinson (1998) *What Everybody Really Wants to Know About Money*, Charlbury: Jon Carpenter, p. 106.
5   F. Hutchinson, M. Mellor and W. Olsen (2002) *The Politics of Money: Towards Sustainability and Economic Democracy*, London: Pluto, p. 167.
6   M. Rowbotham (1998) *The Grip of Death: A Study of Modern Money, Debt Slavery and Destructive Economics*, Charlbury: Jon Carpenter, p. 73.
7   J. Robertson (2004) 'Using common resources to solve common problems', *Feasta Review 2: Growth: The Celtic Cancer*, Dublin: Feasta.
8   For a detailed account see M. Rowbotham (2000) *Goodbye America! Globalisation, Debt and the Dollar Empire*, Charlbury: Jon Carpenter; A. Pettifor (2006) *The Coming First World Debt Crisis*, Basingstoke: Macmillan.
9   Pettifor, *The Coming*, p. 118.
10 Rowbotham, *Goodbye America!*
11 B. Lietaer (2001) *The Future of Money*, London: Century.
12 R. Douthwaite (1999) *The Ecology of Money*, Schumacher Briefing no. 4, Totnes: Green Books.
13 J. Porritt (2006) *Capitalism as if the World Matters*, London: Earthscan, p. 191.
14 R. Madron and J. Jopling (2003) *Gaian Democracies: Redefining Globalisation and People-Power*, Totnes: Green Books, pp. 70–71; for a full account of this process, see Mellor et al, *Politics of Money*.
15 J. Huber and J. Robertson (2000) *Creating New Money: A Monetary Reform for the Information Age*, London: New Economics Foundation.
16 M. Harmer (1999) 'A green look at money', in M. S. Cato and M. Kennett (eds) *Green Economics: Beyond Supply and Demand to Meeting People's Needs*, Aberystwyth: Green Audit, pp. 128–42.
17 E. S. Cahn (2004) *No More Throw-Away People: The Co-Production Imperative*, Washington, DC: Essential Books, p. 44.

18 For a full description of Owen's work in this area, see M. S. Cato (2008) 'Emancipation from monetary exploitation', in Cato and Bickle *New Views*; more details of contemporary time banking in the UK are available at: www.timebanks.co.uk/The_History_of_Time_Banking.asp).

19 P. North (2007) *Money and Liberation: The Micropolitics of Alternative Currency Movements*, Minneapolis: University of Minnesota Press.

20 L. Gatch (2006) 'Local scrip in the USA during the 1930s: Lessons for today?', paper presented at the Conference on Monetary Regionalisation: Local Currencies as Catalysts for Endogenous Regional Development, Bauhaus-University Weimar, Germany, 28–29 September; for examples of these notes see the presentation by Gatch available at: monetary-regionalisation.overip.net/download/slides/02_Gatch.pdf.

21 S. DeMeulenaere, L. Lopezllera-Mendez and T. Greco (1999) 'Towards an economy in the hands of the people: Parallel currencies in the majority world: Study of the Tianguis Tlaloc local currency system in Mexico City', available online at the Appropriate Economics website.

22 North, *Money and Liberation*.

23 G. Seyfang (2007) 'Bartering for a better future? Community currencies and sustainable consumption', CSERGE Working Paper, EDM 04–10, University of East Anglia, p. 17.

24 H. Primavera (2002) 'Wealth, money and power: the ephemeral "Argentinean miracle" of the exchange networks', presentation made at the 2nd panel of the National Journey on Exchange and the Economy of Solidarity, Buenos Aires, 6 September; available at: www.complementarycurrency.org/ccLibrary/543_ENG.rtf; M. S. Cato (2006) 'Argentina in the red: What can the UK's regional economies learn from the Argentinian banking crisis?', *International Journal of Community Currency Research*, 10: 43–55.

25 Lietaer, *Future of Money*, p. 278.

26 Hutchinson et al, *Politics of Money*, p. 187.

6

Green Business: From Maximizing Profits to a Vision of Conviviality

The Sufficiency Economy offers an effective approach to promoting sustainability and managing risks; a survival strategy for travelling down the fast-moving and sometimes treacherous road of globalization, with its illusions and pitfalls. In such a world, what could be more important than a good strategy?

Surayud Chulanont, Prime Minister of Thailand

Green economists have had a fairly turbulent relationship with 'business', which is often blamed in a general way for the environmental crisis. For more radical critics, and especially in the early days of the environmental movement during the 1970s, the response must be one of outright rejection, retreat into smaller communities or even self-sufficient families, providing for themselves on the land without specialization and with only the slenderest interaction with 'business'. More recently, greens have assumed two different but complementary approaches to business. The first is to take a pragmatic view that 'business' is not a monolith and includes many people who are as concerned about preserving the planet as we are. The most positive approach is therefore to work with those engaged in industry and commerce to make their operations as sustainable as possible without challenging significantly the nature of capitalism or its ownership and governance model. The second approach has been to extract one's own life as much as possible from the tainted model of business that dominates in the contemporary economy and to seek to build or support alternative models of economic organization. Both approaches will be covered in this chapter although, as I think is right for a book about green economics rather than environmental economics, the emphasis will be more on the latter approach.

The next section discusses the successes and limitations of attempts to green business, including consideration of how likely it is that technological solutions to be bought and sold within the market will provide an answer to our environmental problems. It covers the agenda of the movement for sustainable production and consumption, a more thoroughgoing attempt to change the direction of business. Then we arrive at a radical critique of the structure of contemporary business and raise questions about ownership and control, resulting in proposed alternatives of smaller-scale, responsible and cooperatively owned business. The final section offers a vision of sustainable business and proposes the growth of the convivial economy.

Limitations of market and technological solutions

For many closely tied to the lifestyle of an industrialized society and the identity it brings with it, a deep green approach to reorganizing the economy is just too challenging. They rely instead on the hope that they can keep their model in place, only substituting low-energy, greener components. This approach is often referred to as 'business-as-usual' or even BAU, which seems a fair label since, although the products and processes may be different, the business model is anticipated to remain unchanged. For many green entrepreneurs, the movement of the ecological crisis from marginal concern to centre stage offers great opportunities for making profits. Hence the central questions greens need to address when approaching business is whether the model itself is faulty or whether it is just producing the wrong products; we summarize this in the simple question, 'Is capitalism sustainable?'

Greens differ in their answer to this question. For those who would answer in the affirmative, the critical next step to 'stop the planet burning' is to find the most efficient technologies. As Monbiot[1] admits, placing hope in 'omnipotent scientists' and 'unproven technologies' is a form of denial that we can all fall prey to, but for greens there is no alternative to significant social and economic change. Monbiot will go as far as agreeing not to fly; other greens go so far as to call for the end of the business model that capitalism relies on. Perhaps the most important reason for this is the increasing pressure for profits at any cost; indeed the limited liability corporation is a legal model that can require the prosecution of board members if they prioritize social and environmental well-being at the expense of profit for shareholders, which it is their sole legal duty to maximize.

Jonathon Porritt's approach to the issue of the sustainability of capitalism is somewhat more wary:

> For fear, perhaps, of arriving at a different conclusion, there is an unspoken (and largely untested) assumption that there need be no fundamental contradiction between sustainable development and capitalism. That assumption stands in stark contrast to the prevailing view of many radical academics and non-governmental organizations (NGOs) that there are profound (and possibly unmanageable) contradictions which demand a completely different world order.[2]

He has none the less invested considerable energy in working with businesses via his Forum for the Future organization in order to encourage the most sustainable practices that do not threaten profitability. The UK household company Marks & Spencer is lauded on the website by green business gurus. It made much of its decision to become carbon-neutral within five years from 2007, but this claim was undermined by the small print indicating that this only applied to the company's UK operations. In other words, by outsourcing production it was able to appear more green while actually being less so because of the increased distance its products needed to be transported.

It is this kind of cynical response that has left greens suspicious of business intentions. For most green economists, business-as-usual cannot be compatible with a sustainable future:

> There are two compelling reasons why a business as usual approach is impossible. One is that the damage being done by a changing climate is already becoming apparent and is costing the insurance industry many millions... The second and even more immediate threat to business as usual is that presented by the arrival of the peak in global oil production... Business will therefore not be able to continue on its present basis.[3]

The business model must change radically not only because its current modus operandi is so damaging but, more importantly, because it relies on fossil fuels which will quite simply not be available beyond the next 20 years or so. In the meantime, most green economists would be pragmatic enough to laud attempts to support the move towards more sustainable systems of production and distribution, if only as preparation for the change in economic structures which more expensive oil makes inevitable.

For more pragmatic theorists with an environmental concern the obvious route to take is one of greater efficiency and lower impact within the same basic structure, an approach often referred to as 'natural capitalism'.[4] Far from questioning the ecological impact of capitalism as a system, it lauds the 'lucrative opportunities' available to green entrepreneurs: 'clever new technologies' and 'living systems', according to this line of reasoning, 'need not be in conflict – in fact, there are fortunes to be made in reconciling them'. The 'natural capitalism' school builds on earlier work by the Rocky Mountain Institute which suggested that, with more efficient energy use, twice as much value could be produced for half as much energy.[5] Lovins and Lovins gave the example of improving a pipe system by straightening the pipe and enlarging its diameter, thus reducing the energy needed to pump fluid through it. Few green economists would argue with the idea of maximizing the efficient use of energy, but there is unlikely to be agreement about whether profit-maximization is compatible with a sustainable future.

Issues of scale and ownership

The issue of the increasing power of the larger multinational corporations in the globalized economy will be discussed elsewhere (see Chapter 8). Combined with the removal of political restraints on the movement of capital this has allowed owners of production facilities to dictate environmental standards as well as rates of pay.[6] The decentralized nature of production allows them to operate with much less concern for social responsibility. Large businesses have huge levels of power to determine the policies of governments and international organizations, and yet their contribution to the creation of employment and the sharing of wealth is minimal:

> In this respect, there remains an extraordinary mismatch between the power of multinationals and their contribution to global employment. The top 300 corporations own an estimated 25 per cent of the world's productive assets; the top 500 account for 75 per cent of all commodities traded. Despite that, the world's top 200 corporations (accounting for 38 per cent of global economic activity) employ less than 0.25 per cent of the global workforce. Estimates vary; but the whole lot of them employ less than 1 per cent of the global workforce – a figure which has not increased for more than two decades.[7]

Most green economists share with Porritt a highly sceptical approach to corporate social responsibility or CSR, which he referred to as a 'seductive illusion'. As discussed in Box 6.1, for many corporations claims to be green are a hollow

Box 6.1 Shell and CSR: A cynical view

Shell is one of the largest global corporations, a key player in the global oil industry and its third largest company behind Exxon-Mobil and BP. In 2001 its revenues were almost US$135 billion and it had 90,000 employees in 140 countries. Shell was one of the first corporations to take up the idea of CSR enthusiastically. This was seen by many as a response to two negative publicity events in the mid-1990s: its disastrous battle with Greenpeace over the disposal of the Brent Spar rig and the even more sinister events in Nigeria, where Ken Saro-Wiwa and other leaders of the indigenous Ogoni people were executed for their activity opposing Shell's oil drilling. Shell gives about £200,000 to environmental organizations annually and the Shell Foundation distributes £7.5 million to development projects around the world. However, Shell has had a far from comfortable relationship with some of the most prominent environmental lobbying groups:

> In May 1996 Shell International Petroleum successfully complained about a joint advertisement by the Body Shop, Friends of the Earth and Greenpeace which criticized Shell's activities in Ogoniland, Nigeria. The advertisement was ruled to be misleading as it implied that Shell was currently operating in Ogoniland. A later complaint (July 1996) by Friends of the Earth about a Shell International advertisement, which also referred to Shell's activities in Ogoniland, was partially successful. The ASA agreed that Shell's claims that sixty per cent of oil spills were caused by sabotage could not be adequately supported.[8]

Shell was a founding member of the Global Climate Coalition, which opposed the scientific findings of the Intergovernmental Panel on Climate Change and has been blamed for slowing policy progress on climate change, although it left the organization in 1997. It has also been criticized by Christian Aid, who challenged the development projects Shell supports in the Niger Delta which have all 'failed or remain unfinished'. In January 2004 Shell was forced to admit it had overestimated its reserves by 3.9 billion barrels, 20 per cent of the total. Worse, this was not the result of errors but failings on the part of Shell's senior executives to revise the reserves figures as they found they were inaccurate. The company's chief executive, Sir Philip Watts, was in essence guilty of misrepresenting the size of the company's reserves, which led to an artificially high stock-market valuation. Nothing could be further from the ideal of CSR: deceiving not only stakeholders, but shareholders themselves.

Source: M. S. Cato, L. Arthur, R. Smith and T. Keenoy (2007) 'CSR in your own backyard', *Corporate Responsibility Journal*, 3/2: 32–8.

attempt to gain PR advantage over their rivals. This is a double-edged sword, since consumers are impressed by the ethical credentials of those they buy from, as demonstrated by a study commissioned by the Co-operative Insurance Society in 2002. The report, called *Sustainability Pays* and conducted by Forum for the Future, found that there was a positive correlation between environmentally and socially responsible business practices and financial performance. In contrast, 'greenwash' rapidly discredits not only the company that is attempting to fake its green credentials, but also the green movement.[9]

A response may be to question both the scale and the ownership of the businesses that will play a part in the sustainable economy of the future: there is a connection between the size and scope of business and its ability to take responsibility for the consequences of its actions. Locally rooted businesses will lose customers if they are known to operate in socially or environmentally threatening ways. When it comes to multinational corporations, or groups of corporations, we cannot be sure what their practices are and are more liable to being manipulated by the PR machine. The film *The Corporation* (2003; www.thecorporation.com) made a similar point about the distance between people's work lives and their lives within their community, allowing them to follow pathological behaviour patterns at work that actually damaged them and their communities in their home setting.

Arguments have also been made linking the ownership of business and its ability to operate in a way that does not threaten the environment.[10] It is easier for employees to act irresponsibly if they think that it is just a job that they can leave when they go home in the evening. Cooperatives, owned by their workers, or even social enterprises where stakeholders are involved in decision making, are less likely to act in an ecologically destructive manner and are more likely to report their environmental performance using systems such as triple-bottom-line accounting. There is also evidence of a close coincidence of interests between social enterprise and environmentally focused businesses, although, according to the UK Social Enterprise Coalition, 'Of all the sectors to which social enterprises are currently contributing, the environment is possibly one of the most difficult to pin down, given the breathless range and diversity of environmental causes and issues, and a lack of analysis into just who's doing what and where'.[11]

We might even go so far as to suggest that the cooperative form of business organization ensures a commitment to more sustainable and accountable business practices:

> *The social economy is a sphere of socioeconomic activities, organizational principles and motivations that is attuned to principles of sustainable development: to considerations such as environmental protection, socioeconomic equality, poverty reduction and encouraging democratic citizenship. This is clearly a bold statement, but it is our contention that the very ethos and structure of social economy organizations promotes sustainable forms of development. Ecological modernization and the broader discourse of environmental economics recognize that profit-maximizing corporations are not inclined to internalize social and environmental considerations and that their activities need to be directed through detailed regulatory and fiscal policy if sustainable development is to be achieved. Our argument is that the organizations within the social economy – cooperatives, mutuals and associations – have an advantage over other institutional forms in that their ethos and structure already reflect principles implicit within sustainable development.*[12]

Box 6.2 Cooperation for sustainability: The alternative food economy in the UK

The alternative food economy in the UK provides a template for how a green economy might develop. It operates on a number of different levels and demonstrates diversity in terms of structure and ownership, while requiring commitment on the part of the consumer as well as the producer. Over the past 30 years or so, largely as a result of dissatisfaction with the quality of food available in the capitalist marketplace, greens have developed their own food economy which now includes production of meat and vegetables, manufacture of food products, wholesale and retail distribution networks, and alternative systems of distribution including box schemes, farmers' markets and small-scale wholefood cooperatives.

The UK has a number of examples of wholefood cooperatives, which have grown from small wholefood shops to become multimillion-pound distributors of huge ranges, while maintaining their commitment to the same suppliers and often their cooperative structure. The foremost example is Suma Wholefoods, set up in 1975 as a wholesaling operation to service wholefood shops in the north of England. It now employs around 150 people and delivers UK-wide. It is still owned by its members, who rotate work tasks including management roles and specialist jobs such as accounting and van driving.

In terms of fresh food there are a variety of options requiring a differing amount of effort on the part of the consumer. Perhaps the simplest is the box scheme, often organized by small and local organic farms, with a minimum of imported food. Farmers' markets have rules about how far produce may travel (usually 50 miles maximum) and so ensure seasonality and support for the local economy. Some provide a livelihood for an organizer who is not also a producer but others, such as Fishguard farmers' market in Wales, are run as cooperative consortia, organized and owned jointly by the food producers. The next stage of involvement is to become a member of a CSA scheme or community-supported farm such as Stroud Community Agriculture in Gloucestershire (see Box 12.5). Members of such cooperatives share the risks of farming with producers, underwriting for them a higher level of income than would be possible for a similar farmer operating in the private market. The return for their investment is a share of what was produced on the farm that week, ensuring seasonality, and in most cases they are also required to commit some work in terms of shared farmdays.

For food that cannot be produced locally, the alternative food economy pioneered fair-trade food. A cooperative form of organization in the producer countries makes fair trade fair; farmers work together to sell their produce direct to the companies who sell it to consumers, thus increasing their market power and ensuring a fair price. At the local level, Country Markets offers opportunities for very small-scale producers in the UK to sell a range of home-produced goods without the need to invest in shop facilities. The combination of all these creative structures operating at different levels of food production, distribution and consumption allows British consumers to choose a range of alternatives to the monoculture of the supermarket.

Sources: B. Cannell (2006) 'Employment law vs. democracy: How Suma is governed and how this may be threatened by statutory employee rights', *Journal of Co-operative Studies*, 39/3: 66–70(5); www.country-markets.co.uk; www.stroudcommunityagriculture.org.

Learning to switch the lights off

The title of this section is taken from a Green Party response to the UK government's energy review undertaken in 2006 which was entitled *Keeping the Lights On*. For many in the green movement such a wasteful attitude towards energy use is precisely the problem; before we even think of questioning our style of living, if we only remove unnecessary waste from our systems of production and consumption we could vastly reduce our impact on the environment. The phrase 'sustainable production and consumption' first emerged at the Earth Summit in Rio in June 1992. Chapter 4 of Agenda 21 issuing from that meeting stated that: 'The major cause of the continued deterioration of the global environment is the unsustainable pattern of consumption and production, particularly in industrialized countries, which is a matter of grave concern, aggravating poverty and imbalances.' As part of a UN process, considerable work was invested in developing this concept.

While energy-efficient production and distribution are important, the consumption side of the economy was also the subject of scrutiny. From a growth perspective, consumption is always beneficial, since it will generate higher levels of sales and greater profits. However, from the perspective of the environment, the overconsumption of Western societies is part of the problem. In February 1994, the Soria Moria Conference proposed a working definition for sustainable consumption: 'the use of goods and services that respond to basic needs and bring a better quality of life while minimizing the use of natural resources, toxic materials and emissions of waste and pollutants over the life cycle, so as not to jeopardize the needs of future generations.'

One aspect of sustainable production is ensuring that businesses are as sustainable as possible in terms of their use of resources and energy. When we think of individual activity, the ecological footprint has become a popular concept to use in seeking to reduce climate change impacts. The parallel concept when considering businesses is known as the 'ecological rucksack':

> *Ecological rucksack is the total weight of material flow 'carried by' an item of consumption in the course of its life cycle. Like the ecological footprint, the ecological rucksack concept deals with displaced environmental impacts but has a more technical focus. It is concerned with reducing material intensity and resource inefficiency* (definition from the International Institute for Sustainable Development: www.iisd.org/).

This concept can be measured by a life-cycle analysis of the production of goods, a useful way of determining, and then reducing, their environmental impact.

Thinking more deeply we can begin to ask questions about how businesses might work in a way that mirrors the way of nature. For some writers, such as Forum for the Future's Jonathon Porritt, defining capital more widely than money alone may help us to value it. This thinking has led to the development of the Five Capitals Framework:[13] natural capital, human capital (education and skills), social capital (a supportive social structure and culture), manufactured capital (infrastructure) and financial capital. Although 'the Five Capitals Framework unhesitatingly asserts the primacy of natural capital', for some the comparison of money with nature is anathema. The framework can also leave those defending nature's interest open to arguments about the possibility of substituting one type of capital for another, when in fact it makes no sense to produce vast quantities of financial capital if you have destroyed the planet.

Industrial ecology takes a different slant on the idea of business compatibility with nature, using intelligent design to create systems that prevent negative environmental and other effects of economic production and government policy:

> *Industrial ecology provides a powerful prism through which to examine the impact of industry and technology and associated changes in society and the economy on the biophysical environment. It examines local, regional and global uses and flows of materials and energy in products, processes, industrial sectors and economies and focuses on the potential role of industry in reducing environmental burdens throughout the product life cycle* (International Society for Industrial Ecology website: www.is4ie.org/).

By taking ecology into account when we create production systems we can gear them to nature's metabolism (see Box 6.3). Jonathon Porritt argues the importance of encouraging businesses to 'match the metabolism of the natural world'.[14] He cites the example of the popularity of biomimicry in design (using designs derived from nature to inspire technology – the most famous example being Velcro™ – as evidence that this process is underway.

Much can certainly be achieved by the strategy of working with businesses to encourage them to fit more closely into the environment, but more radical critics question the appropriateness of the scale and complexity of modern industrial systems. This is a reaction against the logic inherent within capitalism towards larger and more technologically complex systems. In response, in

---

BOX 6.3 PRINCIPLES OF PRODUCTION TO MATCH THE METABOLISM OF THE NATURAL WORLD

- Buildings that, like trees, produce more energy than they consume and purify their own waste water;
- factories that produce effluents that can be used as drinking water;
- products that, when their useful life is over, do not become useless waste but can be tossed on to the ground to decompose and become food for plants and animals and nutrients for soil; or, alternatively, that can be returned to industrial cycles to supply high-quality raw materials for new products;
- billions, even trillions, of dollars' worth of materials that accrue for human and natural purposes each year;
- transportation that improves the quality of life while delivering goods and services;
- a world of abundance, not one of limits, pollution and waste.

Source: J. Porritt (2006) *Capitalism as if the World Matters*, London: Earthscan.

1970 Schumacher established the Intermediate Technology Development Group, initially to transfer technology to developing countries at a scale appropriate to their needs, but the phrase 'intermediate technology' has since been used by greens generally as a way of defining a limit to the expansionist process of economic development under capitalism. Schumacher encouraged many to: 'Question the future and values of the marketeering, consumer society, and to make radical changes in their own lifestyles... He exhorted all to rely on people power and their own mental and physical inventiveness, rather than basing their futures on capital and energy-intensive technologies.'[15]

Low-carbon growth as the flourishing of the convivial economy

Climate change will have a major impact on the future path of our economy and the businesses which form part of it. We are no longer arguing about theories of climate change; we are living with the reality. Yet links are not being made between the need to reduce CO_2 emissions and the way we manage and direct our economic activity. Figure 6.1 illustrates the carbon cycle, the natural process of the fixing of carbon from the atmosphere and its release after a certain length of time – short in the case of cattle eating grass, very long in the case of fossil fuels. Climate change is the result of the burning of fossil fuels that have stored carbon for thousands of years, thus disrupting this natural cycle. From an economic development perspective the key basis for building a sustainable economy is the understanding that there are three main systems producing greenhouse gases that are part of our broad economic activities: the growth and decay cycle of living organisms, our interaction with the land via agriculture, and our use of fossil fuels. Of these it is the third that is mainly causing the breakdown in the natural system. Any economic activity that adds to the downwards arrows by absorbing CO_2 (such as planting trees) or reduces the size of the upwards arrows by reducing the emissions of CO_2 (such as switching from fossil-fuel-intensive agriculture to organic agriculture) in this figure is in a sector that is bound to grow in the future.

As the figure shows, some human activities – agriculture and transport, but especially activities which depend on the burning of fossil fuels – put CO_2 into the environment. However, other economic activities actually remove CO_2, especially activities that fix carbon over the medium term, such as forestry and building with wood. Within such a scenario we can make two firm predictions about the future course of industry: economic sectors which have a positive impact on CO_2 emissions are likely to contract, while those which have a neutral or negative impact on them are likely to increase. So in the construction sector we will see a shift from building using concrete and other energy-intensive materials to building in wood; in agriculture we will see a shift from fossil-fuel-intensive agriculture towards organic agriculture; recycling and reuse businesses will thrive, while those concerned with extraction of raw materials and waste disposal will diminish in size. Table 6.1 offers a compari-

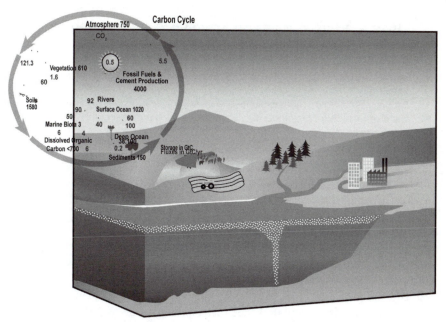

Figure 6.1 *The carbon cycle*

Note: The figure shows the natural transfer of oxygen and carbon dioxide between plants and animals and other systems of CO_2 circulation. It is the burning of fossil fuels that has disrupted this cycle.

Source: Image provided free of charge by Wikimedia commons.

son of those sectors likely to increase and decrease in size as we make the transition to a low-carbon economy.

This is the most basic cycle that we must rebalance to achieve sustainability – the carbon cycle – but beyond that we must also learn to use resources in a way that does not exceed nature's ability to replenish them. This leads us to the principles shown in Box 6.4, taken from the research and pressure group, Natural Step. Other green economists call for a tool for rebalancing the demands of capital and the need for a period of respite for the Earth that is the source of all our resources. Charles Hall has called for a new way of measuring

Table 6.1 *Success of various sectors within a low-carbon economy*

Sectors likely to expand	Sectors likely to contract
Organic farming	Intensive farming
Community renewable energy schemes	Large fossil-fuel power stations and the National Grid
Recycling	Waste disposal
Sustainable construction using local materials that fix CO_2, e.g. wood, straw, hemp, etc.	Construction based on concrete and materials with high levels of embodied energy
Biofuels based on recycled oil	Crop-based biofuels
Mend and repair	Extractive industries

Box 6.4 Principles for achieving sustainability according to the Natural Step

- Substances produced from the Earth's crust cannot systematically increase in the biosphere.
- Substances produced by society cannot systematically increase in the biosphere.
- The physical basis for the productivity and diversity of nature must not be systematically deteriorated.
- There must be fair and efficient use of resources to meet human needs.

Source: R. Douthwaite (2007) 'The economics of responding to climate change', paper for the Institute of European Affairs, Dublin.

---

investment productivity to replace that of ROCE (Return on Capital Expended), which is a purely capital-based measure. He proposes instead the EROI (energy return on energy invested).[16] He has calculated that each unit of energy invested in oil exploration and production in the US in the 1930s generated 100 units of energy in return; by the 1990s this had been reduced to 11–18 units. He also calculated that for each megajoule worth of oil the US imported in 1970 it gained 30MJ, but by 1980 the ratio had dropped to 3 : 1. This sort of measurement indicates how inefficient our economy really is: being more careful of the energy invested in production could move us towards a lower-carbon production curve.

Photo 6.1 *Conviviality: Building the bread oven at Springhill co-housing, June 2008*

As discussed in Chapter 4, we are also likely to see a reduction in working hours and less concentration on formal employment, with more focus on relationships, solving problems together within our communities. As items and pastimes that have a heavy carbon impact become more expensive we will find ways of making-do-and-mending and entertaining ourselves. Thus the businesses of the future will be those that can facilitate this sort of lifestyle, rather than those using fossil fuels to provide exotic products with high embodied energy content. We cannot say at present exactly what such an economy will look like or feel like, or what novel ways we will come up with to meet our needs and provide us with joy and satisfaction in life. However, those of us working towards developing this sort of economy have a vision of how it will be, summed up in the term 'the convivial economy'. Here is how Illich describes conviviality:

> *I choose the term 'conviviality' to designate the opposite of industrial productivity. I intend it to mean autonomous and creative intercourse among persons, and the intercourse of persons with their environment; and this in contrast with the conditioned response of persons to the demands made upon them by others, and by a man-made environment. I consider convivality to be individual freedom realized in personal interdependence and, as such, an intrinsic ethical value. I believe that, in any society, as conviviality is reduced below a certain level, no amount of industrial productivity can effectively satisfy the needs it creates among society's members.[17]*

This provides an inspiring vision to strive for in our working and personal lives and in our roles as business managers and employees and as their customers.

Notes

1　G. Monbiot (2006) *Heat: How to Stop the Planet Burning*, Harmondsworth, Penguin.

2　J. Porritt (2006) *Capitalism as if the World Matters*, London: Earthscan, p. xiv.

3　R. Douthwaite (2007) 'The economics of responding to climate change', paper for the Institute of European Affairs, Dublin.

4　P. Hawken, A. Lovins and L. H. Lovins (1999) *Natural Capitalism: Creating the Next Industrial Revolution*, Snowmass, CO: Rocky Mountain Institute.

5　A. B. Lovins and L. H. Lovins (1997) 'Climate: Making sense and making money', paper published by the Rocky Mountain Institute, Snowmass, CO. Extensions of this work can be found in E. U. von Weizsäcker, A. Lovins and L. H. Lovins (1997) *Factor Four: Doubling Wealth – Halving Resource Use: The New Report to the Club of Rome*, London: Earthscan; W. McDonough and M. Braungart (2002) *Cradle to Cradle*, New York: North Point Press.

6　M. S. Cato, L. Arthur, R. Smith and T. Keenoy (2007) 'CSR in your own backyard', *Corporate Responsibility Journal*, 3/2: 32–8.

7　Porritt, *Capitalism*, p. 251.

8   Beder, *Global Spin*, p. 178.
9   S. Beder (1997) *Global Spin: The Corporate Assault on Environmentalism*, Totnes: Green Books.
10 Cato et al, 'CSR'.
11 Quoted in G. Smith and S. Young (2007) 'Social economy and the environment', paper prepared for the conference Social Economy: Towards a Worldwide Perspective, Leuven, 4–5 June.
12 J. Barry and G. Smith (2005) 'Green political economy and the promise of the social economy', in P. Dauvergne (ed) *International Handbook of Environmental Politics*, Cheltenham: Edward Elgar, p. 256; see also N. Carter (1996) 'Worker cooperatives and green political theory', in B. Doherty and M. de Geus (eds) *Democracy and Green Political Thought: Sustainability, Rights and Citizenship*, London: Routledge.
13 Porritt, *Capitalism*, p. 137.
14 Porritt, *Capitalism*, p. 174.
15 D. Schumacher (1998) 'Introduction', in *This I Believe*, Totnes: Green Books.
16 See details in Douthwaite, 'Economics of Responding'.
17 I. Illich (1974) *Tools for Conviviality*, London: Marion Boyars.

PART 3

Policies for a Green Economy

7
The Policy Context

*We cannot solve our problems with the same thinking we used
when we created them.*

Albert Einstein

As the ecological crisis has moved towards the centre of political debate, the
pioneers of policy responses have found their consensus over solutions
challenged by newcomers with a range of prescriptions based in a whole
variety of ideological outlooks. As a colleague recently pointed out to me,
before very long the only issue in the social sciences will be the environmental
crisis. Soon the ecological issue may occupy the hegemonic position that the
relationship between capital and labour did in the late 19th and early 20th
centuries. Just as Karl Kautsky, leader of the German Social Democrats,
proclaimed that 'We are all socialists now,' it is not too difficult to see the
plausibility of saying that the motto for politics in the 21st century might be
'We are all environmentalists now.' This may be a rather extreme position, but
all the academic disciplines, beginning with the natural and technological
sciences and now moving on through the social sciences to philosophy, art and
literature, are responding to the most pressing issue of our time.

On the one hand, this is gratifying and a relief to those of us who have been
feeling like political Cassandras or lone voices in the wilderness for many
years. On the other, we are required to adjust to a situation where we no longer
have a monopoly on solutions to issues such as climate change. Green critics of
the status quo have never had a monolithic approach; there have always been
debates within the movement, but there have been some basic assumptions that
were shared. Many of these have already been presented in Chapters 2 and 3,
and by far the most fundamental is a commitment to egalitarianism, not only
between living human beings across the globe, but also across generations and
species. As others rush into our political space we are having to negotiate this
basic tenet of our philosophy. To take the issue of climate change again, the
basic green position (that the right to pollute the global atmosphere should be
equally shared) now has to negotiate with those who attack China for increas-

ing its pollution when it is still producing much less CO_2 per capita than the US, or those who propose market trading solutions.

This chapter describes the policy context facing green economics. As a system of thought and policy prescriptions that have been developed outside the political mainstream, and very largely outside the academic mainstream too, the policy arena represents hostile territory. For a philosophy which has 'small is beautiful' as its most memorable adage and displays many anarchistic features, dealing with the centralized and bureaucratic policy-making structure was always going to be problematic. The first section of this chapter presents the explicit clash between these cultures through what is known in academic and policy circles as ecological modernization, focusing the discussion around the issue of sustainable construction. I then move on to present the clash in the most urgent policy arena: that of climate change. The final two sections address the issue of measurement: for conventional policy makers measurement is central to policy making, but green economists have long argued that the way the economy is measured is fundamentally flawed. This critique is presented and in the following section alternative ways of measuring economic activity that more accurately represent what we really value are discussed.

The ecological modernization discourse

The originator of the concept, Maarten Hajer, defines ecological moderniza- tion as 'the discourse that recognizes the structural character of the environmental problematique but none the less assumes that existing political, economic, and social institutions can internalize the care for the environment'.[1] John Barry's summary is neater: 'The basic tenet of ecological modernization is that the zero-sum character of environment–economic trade-offs is more apparent than real.'[2] For the ecological modernizers the solution to the environmental crisis relies on 'eco-efficiency', on the same corporations who (for many greens) created the problem now simply shifting their focus and using the same drive for efficiency (producing maximum value from minimum inputs) to achieve maximum environmental quality.[3] For greens this is a nonsense: it is this system of thought and way of designing systems itself that is the problem; to solve the problem we need a whole shift in paradigm. However, green parties which have moved into government – especially Die Grünen in Germany – have tended to make exactly this adjustment to the exist- ing policy culture, which initially they were diametrically opposed to. While for some within the green movement this marks the 'de-radicalization' and 'domestication' of green parties (the triumph of the 'realos' over the 'fundis'), for others both within and outside the movement, this is seen as a welcome sign of political maturity and evolution of the greens from a party of protest to one of power.

For the majority of green economists, a sustainable economy will not be a capitalist economy (which of course is not the same as saying it is a 'post- market' or centralized economy), it will not be dominated by a small group of transnational corporations, it will not focus solely on formal, monetary exchange, work and production, and it will not be a globalized economy (which is not to say that trade is completely ruled out). In other words, green economics proposes massive, significant and radical changes to the way our economic lives are organized, central to which is the need for new models and ways of thinking about economics itself. These are the conclusions of the people who first alerted the policy community to the environmental crisis and who have spent longest considering the problem and its solution. This is a threatening reality for all those with investment in the existing power structures, and their response has been to attempt to strip out the technological aspects of the proposed solutions while leaving the basic structures untouched. This explains the dominance of technology in suggested solutions to climate change, for example, and also why production rather than consumption of energy and goods and services is the focus of state policies. The inertia within the current economically and politically sustained system is such that policies which suggest reducing consumption as part of dealing with the environmental crisis are edited out, since these threaten business-as-usual.

Clearly greens are not content to see their vision of an egalitarian future translated into a model of business-as-usual with only a slight shift in emphasis and range of products available. A world where B&Q sell hemp insulation rather than fibreglass insulation and where we continue to fly long haul for our holidays but now spend the time photographing zebras rather than lying on a beach, fly in aircraft that use biodiesel rather than kerosene, and then pay money to offset our carbon emissions on our return, will not meet the aspirations of those who have carried the sustainability torch for so long. From a practical perspective, however, the more important question is whether such a strategy – which was unquestionably designed to remove the radical political potential from the green agenda – can actually work.

Heather Lovell has studied this question in connection with the sustainable construction sector and her conclusion is that it will not. Lovell frames this discussion about the centrality of social aspects to the process of sustainable construction in terms of a conflict between a 'deep green' approach, relying on bottom-up individual or community responses to the need for energy-efficient housing, and the 'ecological modernization' discourse. In the context of sustainable housing, this discourse begins with an attempt to manipulate the discussion away from sustainability and towards 'low-carbon' and then moves to separate the technological aspects of sustainable building from the social:

> *The low-carbon discourse coalition has actively tried to de-link environmental and social values from technologies pioneered by sustainable housing advocates... Sustainable houses are, perhaps, more realistically viewed as the end products of social processes, rather than technical demonstrations.*[4]

Lovell's central concern is that those without the motivating deep-green values that created such solutions may lack the commitment to ensuring sufficient low-energy housing is built: 'Early experience suggests deep green values may continue to be critical in sustaining the degree of commitment required to actually build sustainable housing.'[5] Green economics might ask more searching questions about the sharing of value: if the expertise, technological and social, that ensured the development of sustainable housing was developed largely by those with a commitment to common ownership and community control, how can the value this represents be extracted to increase the profits of private companies and perhaps even be constrained by the use of 'intellectual property' laws? Such concerns lead us to raise questions about the potential for commodification of such knowledge and the means we can use to prevent this and allow its maximum dissemination.

The latest move in the ecological modernization discourse with regard to housing in the UK is the call for 'zero-carbon housing' for new-build by 2016. The definition of zero-carbon is unclear; in fact it will rely on the ability of each house to generate electricity that it feeds back into the grid with each house operating as a miniature power station.[6] This policy proposal is appealing at the level of media interest but it has two central flaws. First, most people in the UK do not live in new homes (for example, 97 per cent of London's housing was built before 1995);[7] second, because of the progressive tightening-up of energy efficiency requirements in the building regulations over the years, new homes are already massively more energy efficient than older homes.[8]

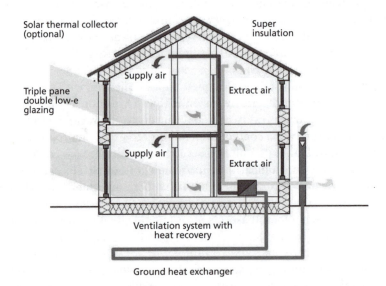

Figure 7.1 *The* Passivhaus

Source: The *Passivhaus* has the highest levels of insulation; uses natural air flows for ventilation; windows face south to maximize solar gain.
Source: Image provided free of charge by Wikimedia commons.

Box 7.1 The European Union Packaging Directive

Following the introducing of a 'packaging ordinance' by Germany in 1991 the EU adopted a Packaging Directive in 1994 to prevent obstacles to EU trade. It included targets of 50–65 per cent for recovery of packaging waste and recycling rates of 15–45 per cent of such waste. As with all EU Directives, national governments were responsible for determining how it should be implemented within their states. In the UK, the objective was to create the least burden for industry; Germany, by contrast, placed the burden entirely on industry, making it responsible for reusing and recycling the packaging it created. The table indicates that the German policy was considerably more effective at achieving reduction in packaging with nearly 60 per cent of businesses reducing their consumption and recycling rates, more than double those in the UK.

Table 7.1 *Percentage of firms engaged in various waste-management activities in UK and Germany, 2001*

Action	UK	Germany
Reduction in consumption	12.7	57.1
Reuse	23.8	52.4
Collection from business premises	64.5	85.4
Collection from customers	13.4	18.4
Purchase of recycled packaging	24.5	53.2

Source: I. G. Bailey (2002) 'European environmental taxes and charges: Economic theory and policy practice', *Applied Geography*, 22/3: 235–51.

We can also contrast the UK policy approach – which relies on the existing corporate construction industry and a uniform design model – with that in Germany, where emphasis is rather on the *Passivhaus*. The *Passivhaus* is energy neutral because of the way its design is uniquely suited to its local environment – it is thus the perfect green economics exemplar for construction. As the profit-driven construction industry has focused on cheapest and fastest construction methods, the old adage for building in cold, damp climates: 'wrap up warm and face south', has been forgotten. But this is exactly the principle used by designers of the *Passivhaus* model, allowing maximum solar energy gain, installing the highest possible amount of insulation, and installing a natural ventilation system based on wind and heat flows. This can only ever be a model, because every *Passivhaus* will be different, responding to its location's microclimate. Such bespoke construction is clearly impossible for the construction corporations to replicate, hence the choice by the UK government of the zero-carbon route. Box 7.1 details the results of a parallel policy difference between the UK and Germany in the case of industrial packaging.

Policy responses to climate change

In a book such as this the space available to compare different attempts to affect green policy outcomes is clearly limited, so a detailed discussion is restricted to the most import environmental issue facing the world's politicians:

climate change. This is used as a case study to illustrate the advantages and disadvantages of different approaches that governments can take. We will look at four main policy approaches: international negotiations for agreements between countries to limit their emissions; carbon trading; systems that treat the atmosphere as a global commons; and carbon rationing.

Since climate change is a global problem, the international level of agreement over policy responses is crucial. In other areas of relevance to the environment governments have achieved some success: for example, the limited 'club' of nations that makes up the EU has introduced limits on packaging which national governments have then implemented in different ways (see Box 7.1). However, emissions reductions are far more painful and their effects more far reaching – and to make a serious impact on the problem the largest countries, with their conflicting economic systems and cultural values, need to agree. The danger with attempts to reach global agreements on such issues is that we arrive at a lowest-common-denominator treaty such as the Kyoto Protocol, whose CO_2 limits were grossly inadequate. Not only is this serious in itself, but it also creates the illusion that something is being done about the problem and thus reduces any sense of urgency about the need to do more.

Within the conventional economic paradigm, the proposed solution to any problem is based around the market – in the case of climate change the resulting structure is an arrangement for CO_2 exchange such as the EU's Emissions Trading Scheme (ETS). Such a scheme decides on the limited amount of CO_2 that will be permitted, and then issues the right to produce it in terms of tradable permits. In the case of the ETS these permits were allocated by national governments to their most energy-intensive industries. The major problem facing any policy that emerges from the culture of business is that the interests of corporations have probably played a large part in designing it and that it therefore only mildly constrains their activity, however environmentally damaging it may be. In the case of ETS, industry lobbied for some of the most polluting sectors (including aviation) to be excluded altogether, so that only 45 per cent of total emissions were included.[9] In the European context, the UK government is most beholden to the 'ever-moaning CBI' (Confederation of British Industry), which lobbied for such a meaningless cap on emissions that the ETS was farcically ineffective:

> *The short-sightedness of this position became all too apparent in 2006, when the ETS all but collapsed. Governments had given away so many credits to industry through their respective National Allocation Plans that not a single company was forced to do anything more than it would have done anyway! With nobody needing to buy anybody else's credits, the price of a tonne of CO_2 plummeted, hitting a low of less than €0.30 in 2007.*[10]

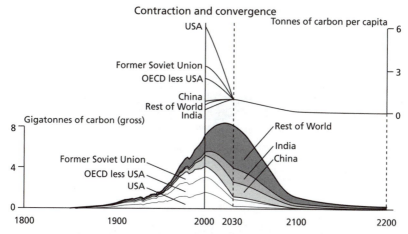

This example shows regionally negotiated rates of C&C.
This example is for a 450ppmv Contraction Budget, converging by 2030

Figure 7.2 *Illustration of the contraction and convergence model for global CO_2 emissions reductions*

Source: Thanks to Aubrey Meyer and Tim Helweg-Larsen of the Global Commons Institute.

A more radical green critique of the scheme would question the justice of allocating the right to pollute to a tiny sector of the global population – the shareholders of corporations. Since enforcing a carbon cap via tradeable permits effectively creates a huge economic value, it should belong to all citizens rather than a small minority.

Such a commitment to equity leads to a plan for the sharing of the global commons, such as the Global Commons Institute's Contraction and Convergence – the first approach to tackling climate change that began from the simple notion that each person on the planet had an equal right to produce CO_2. The 'convergence' was the name given to the commitment to share these emissions fairly within a meaningful cap on total output of CO_2. Overproducing countries would then be required to compensate underproducing countries. The 'contraction' is the process of all countries, in step, reducing their emissions gradually over the next 50 years. The scheme is illustrated in Figure 7.2. The rising curve is the historical increase in CO_2 emissions; these are portrayed following a sharp descent over the next century (the contraction) during which time countries also converge towards a share of the global total that represents the size of their population.

The cap-and-share proposal takes this thinking further: proposing a policy for effecting the necessary reduction. Each citizen would receive a 'fossil-fuel pollution authorization permit' representing their right to a share of each year's global emissions. These would not operate as a ration but rather as a permit to allow fossil-fuel production. Governments could sell these permits in an international auction – without buying them fossil-fuel companies could not operate. The proceeds from the sale, which is after all a 'universal dividend'

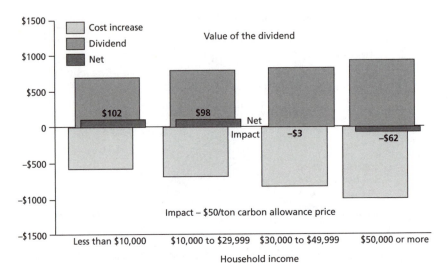

Figure 7.3 *Sharing of 'universal dividend' from sale of carbon permits and its impact on incomes in different groups of the US population*

Source: Thanks to John Bailey of the Institute for Local Self-Reliance for permission to reproduce this graphic.

derived from an international commons, could provide cash to fund a Citizens' Income scheme (see Chapter 11). This additional income would provide some relief for the poorer members of society from the increasing costs of energy resulting from such a system. The impact of a similar policy on different income groups has been calculated for the US and is illustrated in Figure 7.3. For each income band (as represented on the x-axis) the graphic illustrates the size of the dividend as well as the extra cost associated with the carbon quota that will result from a system of charging for the production of carbon. As the graph shows, those in the lower income groups will see a net gain, whereas the better off will experience a small net loss. Under the original scheme, people could also choose to forgo this income and destroy their own permits. Whichever way it worked it would reward climate-friendly consumers and encourage individual behaviour that would move the economy in a more carbon-efficient direction.

In the Irish context, it has been argued that the best strategy for the Irish economy in the long term would be for the government to engineer the price of fossil fuels on a smooth trajectory towards where it will be as scarcity drives it relentlessly upwards. This would encourage investment in the technologies, including renewable energy technologies, that will be needed in the post-fossil-fuel economy of the future. Dowthwaite suggests the use of a judicious combination of carbon tax (see the discussion in Chapter 10) and cap-and-share.

The final type of policy that might be considered to reduce our emissions of CO_2 is some form of rationing. The most popular version in the UK context is Tradable Emissions Quotas or TEQs.[11] This is a scheme proposed by David

Fleming of the Lean Economy Connection and a former economics speaker for the UK Green Party, who first published the idea in 1996. The right to produce CO_2 ('carbon units') is limited by global agreement and then allocated whenever people buy any form of energy. The scheme is also based in a global per-capita equity framework, with carbon units being allocated free to adults, while organizations have to purchase the units they need in a national market. The main advantage of the scheme is that it makes clear to consumers the energy impact of their choices. The main criticisms of the scheme are that it would require people to carry a TEQ card as well as money (it is suggested that an electronic card might serve) and that it also only covers fuel, not other energy-related sectors; these are covered indirectly through one's need to buy TEQs to cover one's own energy use. It would not tackle the problem that energy used to produce our consumer goods in China would need to be paid for by Chinese citizens out of their quota. It would encourage energy frugality and an awareness of energy use, but would do nothing to share the proceeds of the market in emissions to subsidize fuel poverty, which can be achieved through cap-and-share.

This is still a relatively new discussion and the green movement is fully engaged in debate about the possible options. It seems fair to conclude that green economists would argue for a scheme which:

- included a serious and declining cap on CO_2 emissions;
- was based on an equal, per-capita global share;
- did not allow countries to export their emissions by consuming goods produced overseas without being responsible for the CO_2 emitted during their manufacture.

What's wrong with GDP?

Policy makers are convinced that they cannot operate without some means of assessing what our economy is achieving, and for most developed economies today the basic measure of 'economic activity' is GDP (formerly GNP). This has been the target of sustained attack by environmentalists and green economists in terms of being a measure of what our economies achieve:

> *Our standard of living is calculated in terms of the market prices of the goods that it includes. These do not distinguish between, on the one hand, the gadgets that we do not really need and such essentials as unpolluted water, air and food on which our health must depend ... It is in terms of these market prices that the GNP is calculated and, as we have seen, this provides the most misleading indication of our well-being.*[12]

National income accounting is a means of measuring all the economic activity that takes place in a country. So any action by any one of us that has economic value should be included. Measurement is obviously influenced by subjective judgements of what is valuable or deleterious. The assumptions of standard economics tend to go largely unchallenged. Its main assumption is that doing anything is better than doing nothing, which explains Keynes' well-known remark about being able to make a highly successful economy merely by digging holes and filling them in. The two most important conventional indicators are GDP (gross domestic product) and GNP (gross national product); the distinction between these two depends on whether production by citizens of a country earned overseas is included or not, and since rapid globalization began GDP has become the favoured measure among economists and policy makers.

In the prologue to her book *If Women Counted*, Marilyn Waring, a New Zealand feminist economist, writes of her realization of the importance of national accounts during her experience as a member of the NZ Public Accounts Committee:

> *I learned that in the UNSNA [United Nations System of National Accounts], the things that I valued about life in my country – its pollution-free environment; its mountain streams with safe drinking water; the accessibility of national parks, walkways, beaches, lakes, kauri and beech forests; the absence of nuclear power and nuclear energy – all counted for nothing. They were not accounted for in private consumption expenditure, general government expenditure, or gross domestic capital formation. Yet these accounting systems were used to determine all public policy. Since the environment effectively counted for nothing, there could be no 'value' on policy measures that would ensure its preservation.*[13]

During her consequent thorough research into how the UN established the system she found that the influence of the UK in establishing its war economy in 1939 was of key importance. That is, the main purpose of the origins of GDP was to measure the war-fighting capacity of a nation. Her conclusion was that we are still organizing our economies on a warlike footing, which explains our failure to achieve settled peaceful lives for our citizens.

The critics of GDP as a measure have identified four main problems with it:

1   *The exclusion of unpaid, domestic and primarily women's work.* The subsistence-based economies of the world, and the core economies in more developed countries on which the wider economy depends, are not considered economically valuable. Feminist economists point to the undervaluing of mothers: the complex range of skills that they need – including healing, caring, nutrition, psychology, diplomacy, education and so on – are ignored. The inadequacy of the present method of measuring economic activity is shown by the fact that if a woman goes out to work and sends

her children to a nursery, the work of the care assistants is measured in the national accounts, so this will show up as an increase in growth. Similarly, if she buys more convenience foods she will be stimulating the food-production sector, again causing an increase in GDP.

2   *Environmental and social catastrophes add to GDP.* An example often used in green circles to indicate the inappropriateness of GDP as a measure of national well-being is that of a tanker disaster. When the tanker runs aground it is universally seen as a 'bad thing', but in fact this environmental catastrophe adds to GDP in many ways: extra activity cleaning the beaches; the jobs created in the refitting work; the extra medical work for the children who suffer respiratory and probably long-term health damage. And, conversely, because pollution and wildlife are not measured in the national accounts there will be no negative entry to balance these positive entries. A similar point can be made about social disasters, such as an epidemic of relationship breakdown. During the period of separation economic activity is boosted by the interventions of solicitors and counsellors, as well as the additional spending on alcohol and/or antidepressants. After the separation both partners need to provide themselves with homes, sofas, electrical goods and so on, greatly adding to GDP. Again it becomes clear that a measure that does not take the worth of the activity into account is going to guide our economy in perverse directions. For this reason, many green economists support the creation of 'materials flow' accounting systems to measure and track the increase or decrease of energy and materials flowing through an economy. GDP only measures monetary values and flows, whereas from a sustainability point of view we need both to measure the actual ecological and carbon footprint of our economic activity and to keep a measure of actual physical assets and resources, not just their monetary value.

3   *Inequality.* Even if national income accounts measured the right things, they would still be inadequate in terms of measuring human welfare, since they give no idea of how the goods produced are shared out. Standard national accounting ignores inequality of distribution, and so gives little indication of the quality of life of any given individual in the country.

4   *National accounts measure movement, not stores of wealth.* National accounting is about the movement of money and resources, but as individuals and as nations we would be foolish not to measure the stocks of value that we have as well as the incomings and outgoings:

> *The inadequacy of GDP stems, in part, from the failure of accounting systems to fully account for 'natural capital'... Evidence of this incomplete accounting is abundant. For example, while governments may account for the timber which is extracted from forests, they do not account for the ecosystem services provided by that forest. These include water storage, soil stability, habitat maintenance, and the regulation of the atmos-*

Table 7.2 *Comparison of costs to society of various psychological 'escape routes' compared with spending in various areas, UK c. 2001*

Category	Cost (£ billion)	Category	Spend (£ billion)
Alcohol	20	Law and order	20.5
Illegal drugs	20	Defence	23.5
Depression	9	Transport	9.1
Gambling	3	Housing	3.5
Smoking	1.5	Rail services	1.3
Total	52	All spending	368.3

Source: 'Counting the costs: Introductory report', Centre for Holistic Studies. J. Seabrook, M. Tully and M. S. Cato (2005).

phere and climate. Unfortunately, the costs of losing those essential ecosystems services only become apparent when they start to break down.[14]

Herman Daly summed up his criticism by pointing out that if the whole of US virgin forest were cut down and turned into gambling chips, according to GDP measurement this would be an economic improvement. Environmentalists consider this criticism to be particularly important in terms of the planet's resources, since the amount of these that remains is an important indicator for the future.

The fast-pace, rapid-growth economy of advanced capitalism may produce impressive GDP measurements but it is destructive of human well-being. Table 7.2 gives an example of activities relating to the need to 'escape' that are counted in the UK GDP but which impose huge costs on society and require government spending to rectify the problems they cause; this spending also figures in the UK's national accounts.

Measuring what we value

I began the previous section by stating the conventional economists' certainty that a clear measurement was essential before policy making could begin. A green economist is likely to be considerably less sanguine about the ability of statistics to teach us much about what we really value. As Joan Robinson so wisely pointed out, this is a challenging task:

> *One of the great metaphysical ideas in economics is expressed by the word 'value'. ... It does not mean market prices, which vary from time to time under the influence of causal accidents; nor is it just an historical average of actual prices. Indeed, it is not simply a price; it is something which will explain how prices come to be what they are. What is it? Where shall we find it? Like all metaphysical concepts, when you try to pin it down it turns out to be just a word.*[15]

A recent report from the Centre for Holistic Studies agrees, finding that much of the policy aimlessness of recent years is the result of relying on measurement rather than judgement.[16] As Funtowicz and Ravetz pointed out in a seminal paper in the related field of ecological economics, in which they ask, 'What is the value of a songbird?', the most valuable things in life are, quite literally, priceless. Unfortunately, this can mean that they are therefore accorded no economic value and not protected.[17]

The call for alternative indicators comes down to a question of how we, as citizens concerned for the well-being of others and of the planet we share, would choose to measure the well-being of a nation. To begin this process we should follow the scheme outlined in the figure below, beginning with defining what we think we should aim to be measuring, then deciding what we should consider as positives and negatives, including some consideration of aspects of life that are difficult to measure, for example the existence of whales as a species.

What item do we want to measure: economic activity? socially beneficial activity? happiness? health?

What goods are we going to add in?

What bads are we going to deduct?

How can we handle things we can't measure easily?

There is no shortage of alternative measures of economic progress: this section covers a few of the most prominent. In his 1991 book Victor Anderson began by identifying the criteria for choosing a good economic indicator,[18] which should:

- be based on data that are readily available, especially for less-developed countries;
- be easy to understand – not based on abstruse maths – e.g. infant mortality;
- relate to something measurable, e.g. not 'loss of community';
- measure something believed to be important in its own right, e.g. infant mortality is an indicator of general standard of health and living;
- be rapidly available, as an early warning signal;
- be based on information that is geographically comparable;
- be internationally comparable, e.g. access to clean water.

The measurement criterion is problematic, since some of the things we value most are not conducive to numerical measurement, hence the philosophical

Table 7.3 *Additions and subtractions from GDP to arrive at the ISEW*

	Total consumer expenditure
minus	*plus*
inequality	housework and homework
commuting	services from consumer durables
traffic accidents	state education
pollution	health expenditure
depletion of resources	
long-term environmental damage	

discussion in the environmental economics literature about the value of a songbird or a sunset. This requires us to be aware that even when we have a well-grounded measure of economic activity it still cannot assess the success of our society.

Tim Jackson and Nick Marks, working for the New Economics Foundation, devised an index for the UK called the Index of Sustainable Economic Welfare (ISEW). They attempted to take into account many of the problems outlined above, as shown in Table 7.3. They compared these two alternative ways of measuring economic well-being in the UK and found that from 1974, although GDP in the UK continued to increase, the ISEW fell, and that by 1990 it was only 3 per cent higher than it had been in 1950, having dropped by more than 50 per cent since they had started their analysis (see the graph in Figure 7.4). The ISEW provides a more balanced measure of well-being than narrow economistic values such as GDP. A similar graph was also produced in a recent report by the UK Cabinet Office's Strategy Unit, which

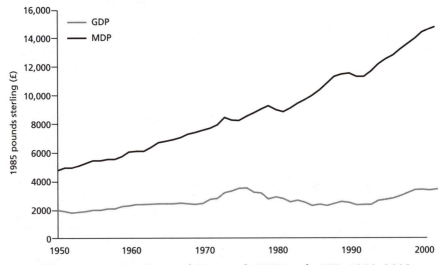

Figure 7.4 *A comparison of GDP and ISEW in the UK, 1950–2002*

Note: ISEW has been relabelled as MDP (measure of domestic progress).
Source: The figure is reproduced with kind permission of the New Economics Foundation from T. Jackson (2002) *Chasing Progress: Beyond Measuring Economic Growth*, London: New Economics Foundation.

BOX 7.2 NORWAY'S EXPERIENCE WITH NATIONAL RESOURCE ACCOUNTING

Norway's Ministry of the Environment began the process of compiling National Resource Accounts (NRA) in 1974. Because of Norway's reliance on the oil industry the future depletion of oil reserves was of primary economic importance and this was the basis of the first accounts. Accounts were also produced for minerals, hydropower, land use and a selection of air and water pollutants. The decision about which resources or pollutants to measure is pragmatic and policy-driven. By the early 1980s Norwegian natural resource accounts were in place for energy, minerals, forestry, fish and land use. In the following years environmental issues have increased in importance relative to the resource-depletion issues and this has been reflected in changes in the accounting procedures. Norway's energy accounts show that between 1976 and 1993 total energy consumption increased by an average of 1.2 per cent annually. Electricity consumption increased by an average of 2.5 per cent during the same period, i.e. by more than the overall energy consumption. Norway's other important strategic resource is its fisheries, and accounts for these have been produced since the 1980s. This has enabled the country to chart the decline in the two most important species: spring-spawning herring and northeast Arctic cod. Norway has also been monitoring emissions of pollutants to the air since the 1970s, which has allowed the country to substantially reduce emissions of sulphur dioxide (SO_2) and lead (Pb): the levels in 1991 were less than half those in the early 1970s.

Source: Statistics Norway (SSB); S. Simon (1999) 'Green national accounting: Conceptual shift, construction and implementation', in M. Scott and M. Kennett (eds) *Green Economics: Beyond Supply and Demand to Meeting People's Needs*, Aberystwyth: Green Audit.

---

concluded that 'above a certain threshold of consumption, there is no clear relationship between economic growth and quality of life.'[19]

There has been some response to this critique on the part of national governments, whose policies rely so heavily on the GDP measure, generally in the form of the construction of satellite accounts. These include measures of natural assets such as usable land, wilderness resources such as forests, and natural systems such as the quality of air, water and subsoil. This helps to address the criticism of GDP that it measures flows rather than stocks and helps to track individual resources, but it does not address the way that GDP only values some aspects of economic activity (ignoring domestic, unpaid work, for example) or the way that it counts 'bads' as 'goods' (as in the example of the generation of activity caused by environmental disasters). Norway was the first country to begin preparing natural resource accounts including categories of 'mineral resources', 'biological resources', 'inflowing resources' (solar radiation, wind, ocean currents), and 'environmental resources' (air, water, soil, space) (see Box 7.2).

Bhutan has recently attracted attention because of its king's decision to substitute GDH (gross domestic happiness) for GDP. By conventional economic measures Bhutan is struggling, being ranked as one of the ten least-developed countries in the world by the United Nations. Yet visitors report little sign of malnutrition, bad clothing or poor housing. All economic planning decisions are tested against their environmental and social consequences. Bhutan once earned valuable foreign exchange by exporting timber but this was stopped because of the environmental impact of deforestation. For social reasons, individual ownership of any business was limited to 10 per cent, while plastic bags have been banned because of problems with litter and dioxin releases. The London-based think tank, the New Economics Foundation, has come up with a measure of happiness across societies which it calls the 'happy planet index' (HPI). It is a measure of the ecological efficiency with which well-being is derived: a ratio of well-being to resource consumption in a given society. Well-being is measured by a combination of survey-based data of perceived satisfaction and the more objective data on life expectancy at birth. This is then compared with the ecological footprint of society as an indicator of the resources needed to achieve that level of well-being. The index shows that Europe is actually less carbon-efficient than it was 40 years ago and that some European countries produce well-being much more efficiently than others. The punchline of the research is that: 'People are just as likely to lead satisfied lives whether their levels of consumption are very low or high. This means there is huge potential to reduce environmentally damaging consumption, and that good lives don't have to cost the earth.' The International Labour Organization reached a similar conclusion, finding that:

> People in countries that provide citizens with a high level of economic security have a higher level of happiness on average, as measured by surveys of national levels of life-satisfaction and happiness... The most important determinant of national happiness is not income level – there is a positive association, but rising income seems to have little effect as wealthy countries grow wealthier. Rather the key factor is the extent of income security, measured in terms of income protection and a low degree of income inequality.[20]

Table 7.4 *HDI and HPI rankings for the G8 countries and other nations with high gross GDP, 2007*

Country	Ranked by GDP	GDP per capita	HDI	HPI
US	1	4	10	150
China	2	97	84	31
Japan	3	13	11	95
India	4	119	125	62
Germany	5	14	20	81
UK	6	18	15	108
France	7	15	16	129
Italy	8	19	18	66
Brazil	9	66	62	63
Russia	10	61	61	172
Canada	11	7	4	111

Note: More details on how the index is compiled are available here:
www.neweconomics.org/gen/uploads/zeyhlcuhtfw0ge55lwnloi4520082007141551.pdf.
Source: S. Thompson, S. Abdallah, N. Marks, A. Simms and V. Johnson (2007) *The European Happy Planet Index: An Index of Carbon Efficiency and Well-Being in the EU*, London: New Economics Foundation.

This has led one prominent green economist to argue that governments should shift their focus from economic growth towards economic security, reducing socioeconomic inequality and focusing on sufficiency and the concept of 'enough'.[21]

Table 7.4 provides comparative data for a range of economies in terms of the conventional GDP measure, GDP per capita as a measure of equality, the UN's Human Development Index and NEF's happy planet index.

Notes

1   M. Hajer (1995) *The Politics of Environmental Discourse*, Oxford: Oxford University Press, p. 25.
2   J. Barry (2003) 'Ecological modernisation', in J. Proops and E. Page (eds) *Environmental Thought*, Cheltenham: Edward Elgar, pp. 191–214.
3   S. Young (2000) *The Emergence of Ecological Modernisation*, London: Routledge.
4   H. Lovell (2004) 'Framing sustainable housing as a solution to climate change', *Journal of Environmental Policy & Planning*, 6/1: 35–55: 51–2.
5   Lovell, 'Framing sustainable housing', p. 37.
6   DTI (2006) *Energy Review: The Energy Challenge*, London: TSO.
7   DCLG (2006) *Building a Greener Future: Towards Zero Carbon Development*, London: TSO.
8   J. Lambert (2007) *Hot Houses: Climate Change and London's Housing*, London: Green Party.
9   Feasta (2007) 'Controlling the environmental impact of the transport sector', www.feasta.org/documents/energy/Aviation_background_briefing.pdf.
10 J. Porritt (2007) *Capitalism as if the World Matters*, London: Earthscan, pp. 152–3.
11 R. Starkey and K. Anderson (2005) *Domestic Tradable Quotas: A Policy Instrument for Reducing Greenhouse Gas Emissions from Energy Use*, Norwich: Tyndall Centre for Climate Change Research.
12 E. Goldsmith, R. Allen, M. Allaby, J. Davoli and S. Lawrence (1972) *A Blueprint for Survival*, Harmondsworth: Penguin, pp. 65–6.
13 M. Waring (1988) *If Women Counted: A New Feminist Economics*, New York: Harper and Row.
14 Porritt, *Capitalism*, p. 224.
15 J. Robinson (1962) *Economic Philosophy*, Chicago: Aldine, p. 26.
16 J. Seabrook, M. Tully and M. S. Cato (2005) 'Counting the costs: Introductory report', paper for the UK Network of the Centre for Holistic Studies, India and the New Era Coalition.
17 S. O. Funtowicz and J. R. Ravetz (1994) 'The worth of a songbird: Ecological economics as a post-normal science', *Ecological Economics*, 10: 197–207.
18 V. Anderson (1991) *Alternative Economic Indicators*, London: Routledge.
19 J. Foley, 'Will more consumption choices leave us better off?', reported in *Progress*, 11 February, London: IPPR.
20 International Labour Organization (2004) *Economic Security for a Better World*, Geneva: ILO.
21 J. Barry (2007) 'Towards a model of green political economy: From ecological modernisation to economic security', *International Journal of Green Economics*, 1/3: 446–64.

8
Globalization and Trade

Look at the world, and see it whole.

E. F. Schumacher

The dominant process in our economic lives for the past 60 years, and accelerating since the 1970s, has been that of globalization, 'the ever-increasing integration of national economies into a giant one-size-fits-all global economy through trade and investment rules and privatisation, aided by technological advances, and driven by corporate power'.[1] As the world's economies have become integrated, an increasing proportion of what we produce and consume is traded – and over ever-increasing distances. This chapter considers the consequences of this way of organizing our economic affairs, its environmental problems, and a range of policies and structures proposed by environmental campaigners, green economists and politicians to move us towards a more sustainable path.

The major achievement of the system of 'free trade', the global regime governing the exchange of goods between nations since 1945 (the promotion of free trade is written into the Articles of Agreement of the IMF and World Bank), has been an ideological one: to convince politicians and economists the world over that it is the best system. World Bank President Barber Conable stated in a press conference in 2000 that, 'If I were to characterize the past decade, the most remarkable thing was the generation of a global consensus that market forces and economic efficiency were the best way to achieve the kind of growth which is the best antidote to poverty.'[2] His identification of a 'consensus' is evidence of the narrow range of views attended to by the denizens of such global institutions. For, as reported in this chapter, from the ranks of green economists, and from the producers in poorer nations, dissenting voices are questioning the disastrous consequences of the globalized trade system for the planet and its people.

In this section we will first explore the economic theories that have been used to justify global free trade, particularly the theory of comparative advantage. The following section explores who are the winners and losers in the global trade game. We then come to the heart of the matter from the perspective of a green economist: the impossibility of persisting with the present volume of movement of goods during this era of climate change and movement towards lower use of fossil fuels. Finally we explore policies and practices for greening trade at the local and global levels.

Whose comparative advantage?

The earliest attempt to formalize a discussion of the benefits of trade within economic theory was made by David Ricardo, whose 'theory of comparative advantage', first published in 1817, is still relied on by mainstream economists. It was made in contrast to the theory of absolute advantage, which suggests that if a country can produce one good more efficiently than another country it would gain economically if it concentrated its efforts on its best good and traded this with other countries for goods that they produced more efficiently. This is intuitively reasonable. The next step is to argue that, even if one country produces everything less efficiently than its neighbour, it is still better placed to concentrate on the good it produces most efficiently itself and trade for other goods with its neighbours.

This theory of comparative advantage is counter-intuitive, because it contains crucial theoretical flaws, although it can be made to appear convincing when demonstrated using a specific numerical example, as was done by Ricardo and repeated in countless economic textbooks since his day. Ricardo based his argument on two goods where the UK and Portugal obviously have absolute advantages: woollen cloth and wine. During a recent trip to Lisbon I realized why he used these examples and thereby began to understand the true meaning of the theory. My helpful guidebook informed me that the reason there was free trade between these two countries is that it was bought some 50 years earlier at the barrel of a gun, or rather to allow Portugal to avoid the barrels of Spain's guns. Britain offered military protection under the Methuen Treaty and in exchange Portugal had to agree to the import of subsidized UK cloth, undercutting domestic production and putting thousands of textile workers out of jobs. So Ricardo's example in fact makes clear that trade is always about politics rather than free markets – as true today as in Ricardo's time.

The textbook examples always rely on fixed numerical terms of trade, say 10 barrels of oil for 1 tonne of grain, whereas in reality it is precisely these terms which are not fixed; rather they are negotiated in a political arena within which the two countries negotiating are not equally powerful. The theory is also based on a number of assumptions which did not hold true in Ricardo's day, much less today; for example that labour can move freely from country to country without immigration restrictions, that workers are identical, and that labour productivity is fixed. More importantly from the standpoint of green economics, the theory is set in a world without concern for environmental limits, and where the pollution associated with transport is considered an 'externality' which can be absorbed by nature without cost to the trading nations.

Even accepting the basic conclusion of the theory – that countries should specialize in producing the good they are most efficient at producing and trade for others – trade is still likely to lead to growing inequality for the less productive economies:

> *This widening of the gap between the least well paid and all other income earners in their societies is, in fact, exactly what standard economic theory predicts. In the 1930s Eli Heckscher and Bertil Ohlin developed the theorum which is now named after them and which states that each country tends to export goods that use the highest proportion of its most abundant, and hence relatively cheapest resource. For most 'developing' countries this resource is its unskilled labour and, as competition in international markets between such countries will tend to force the prices of their exports down, the earnings of the unskilled will be reduced by more than those of more highly skilled workers less exposed to foreign competition. All workers in sectors exposed to international competition may therefore see their wages fall as markets open up, but those most exposed will fare the worst.*[3]

More fundamentally, trade means the exchange of goods in the medium of money, and that money is not, as economic theory assumes, a neutral medium. Rather, because of the way the countries controlling reserve currencies have a disproportionate amount of power in the world economy (for more on how this works see Chapter 5), they are able to run huge trade deficits, effectively importing goods for next-to-nothing:

> *Allowing the free market to determine the price of surplus goods offered to corporate monopoly buyers based in powerful industrial nations, produced by underdeveloped nations, carrying massive debts, under pressure to export – this is bound to lead to low prices. In economists' jargon, instead of being a process*

involving mutual gain and 'equal exchange', there is 'unequal exchange' with the benefits accruing principally to commerce based in the wealthy nations.[4]

Rowbotham assigns this criticism to Ricardo himself, who identified the limitations of the free-market system even in the era of mercantilist capitalism. For most green economists the argument that trade is always an unquestionably beneficial process needs to be rigorously explored, rather than relying on the theories of a defunct economist from two centuries ago.

How free is free trade?

Green economists identify a range of problems with trade. Colin Hines identified the three 'c's which undermine arguments suggesting that trade can solve problems of poverty in the poorer countries: competition, control and climate change.[5] We will deal with the third in the next section, but what of his second 'c', control? Green economists are keen to ask searching questions about the power games that take place at international trade negotiations. According to an UNCTAD (United Nations Conference on Trade and Development) report, 'The volume of commodity exports from LDCs [least developed countries] increased by 43 per cent between 1986 and 1999… But the value of LDC commodity exports increased by only 26 per cent over this period, and the purchasing power of commodity exports increased by only 3 per cent between 1986 and 1999.'[6] Together with the fact that real commodity prices were substantially lower in 2004–2006 than they had been in 1977–1979, Hines interprets this as meaning that: 'The poorest countries had to run ever faster in order to stay where they were: an increase of more than 40 per cent in the quantities they exported brought virtually no increase in what they could buy with the proceeds.' This is the result of the international trade game, where countries that control reserve currencies and have the power in trade negotiations benefit increasingly from the growing volume of trade, while those who export commodities come under ever more pressure. This results not only in growing poverty in the poorer, weaker countries but also more pressure on the environment, which they are forced to exploit to provide commodities to sell on international markets (see further details in Table 8.1).

Studies from the World Bank itself indicate that 'Globalization generally widens the income gap between the world's poorest people and the richest.'[7] A study reviewing household income data for 88 developing countries between 1985–1991 and 1992–1997 concluded that the main impact of the regime of trade and investment liberalization had been to increase inequality within poor countries. The average income of the poorest 10 per cent of people in the countries studied fell from 30.7 per cent of the average income to 24.8 per cent. By contrast the income of the richest 10 per cent increased from 273.5 to 293.4 per cent of the average (further details from the report are presented in Box 8.1).

Table 8.1 *Changes in the terms of trade of some country groups, 1980–1982 to 2001–2003*

Group	Annual average 1980–1982	Annual average 2001–2003	% change
Developed economies	95.7	103.3	+7.9
Developing economies	117.3	97.7	-16.7
Developing economies: Africa	131.7	100.0	-24.1
Least developed countries	144.0	93.3	-35.2
Landlocked countries	114.7	96.3	-16.0
Sub-Saharan Africa	124.0	98.3	-20.7

Source: Data from UNCTAD; calculations in T. Lines (2008) *Making Poverty: A History*, London: Zed.

Hines' first 'c' – competition – is illustrated in the markets for such commodities as coffee, sugar and tea, as well as in manufactures such as textiles, although the situation has changed somewhat since the publication of the UNCTAD report, with competition for resources from China leading to increasing prices and some gains for countries which rely heavily on the export of raw materials. The southeast Asian tsunami brought into relief the vulnerability that results from relying on one sector, since overdevelopment of the coasts of countries such as Sri Lanka is a direct result of competition for foreign cash through the development of the global tourist industry. The change to the ecosystems of coastal areas of the Indian Ocean, especially the removal of native mangrove to open up leisure beaches, greatly exacerbated the effects of the tsunami – another example of how environmental destruction

---

BOX 8.1 TRADE AND INEQUALITY

This process [of globalization and increased trade] has been one of the factors widening the gap between the rich and the poor, both within countries and between them. An UNCTAD report shows that in nine out of a sample of ten Latin American countries the differential between the earnings of more highly skilled workers and their less skilled colleagues increased markedly between 1984 and 1995 as a result of freer trade. Indeed, in most cases, the real purchasing power of the least skilled workers actually declined, in several cases by over 20 per cent. Similarly, an International Labour Office (ILO) study of 30 countries in Africa, Asia and Latin America found that in two thirds of the countries the real wages of all workers fell between the late 1970s and the late 1980s, with the least skilled falling by the greatest percentage. And a 1999 World Bank paper reported that data from a sample of 38 countries between 1965 and 1992 had shown that greater openness to trade had reduced the incomes of the poorest 40 per cent of the population but strongly increased those of the remaining groups. 'The costs of adjusting to great openness are borne exclusively by the poor', the Bank said in a commentary [emphasis in original].

Source: Douthwaite (personal communication, 2004); UNCTAD data from *Trade and Development Report* (1997) pt 2, ch. 4, § B.1; ILO data from *World Employment Report 1996/97*, Table 5.9; World Bank data from M. Lundberg and L. Squire (2003) 'The simultaneous evolution of growth and inequality', *Economic Journal*, 113/487: 326–44

results from a focus on trade as the means of solving poverty in the South. In the global trade regime there are winners and losers among the poorer nations and the gains are highly concentrated. In the horticulture sector, for example, two-thirds of exports from developing countries are accounted for by just eight countries, none of which is an LDC. All the increase in the value of vegetables exported from sub-Saharan Africa has accrued to Kenya, and within Kenya to the larger farmers, who are actually depriving their neighbours of the water they need for subsistence farming (Lines 2008). The rise of China as a trading power has been a mixed blessing; its hunger for raw materials has benefited some countries, while competition in manufacturing markets has been disastrous for many poorer nations who formerly gained export earnings from manufactures, for example textiles.

The nature of the international trading regime has become increasingly politicized over recent years, with cultural icons entering the fray and calling for 'trade justice'. However, expecting the countries that dominate the existing system to change to a regime that means consumers in their countries pay more was always going to be hard work, and the successes of the trade justice coalition have been very limited. What we have seen is increasing pressure for 'free trade', which means pressure exerted by powerful nations in the international organizations on poorer nations to open up their markets to Western goods. In spite of the rhetoric about trade offering an end to global poverty, it is not poorer countries that gain from the opening up of markets. Taking the example of vegetable exports from Africa, Lines shows that, while total exports from sub-Saharan countries increased by in value by US$92 million between 1990 and 2005, their imports increased by US$295 million; the actual volume of exports fell during this period.

Partly as a result of the continuing trade injustice at the global level, consumers have begun to buck market predictions and choose higher prices for goods themselves, buying the fair trade products that are increasingly available. Fair trade began as a marginal movement among Christian consumers in Europe and the US, but has spread into the mainstream. While what the consumer is most conscious of when buying fair trade products is the price premium, for producers the long-term trading relationship with a guaranteed price can ensure a security not possible given the huge fluctuations in the prices of commodities on world markets. This allows producers in poorer countries to provide basic necessities such as education for their children and also to invest in improving their business. As Figure 8.1 indicates, fair trade has expanded rapidly in some of the richer countries. Figures from the Fairtrade Labelling Organizations International indicate that consumers worldwide spent £1.1 billion on certified products in 2006 – an increase of 42 per cent on the previous year. Particularly large increases were found for cocoa (93 per cent), coffee (53 per cent), tea (41 per cent) and bananas (31 per cent).

Fair trade has three main objectives in terms of social justice: first, drawing attention to the unfairness of the low prices we pay for basic commodities;

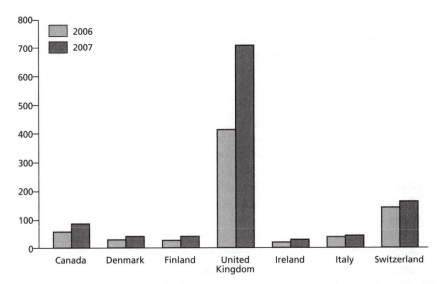

Figure 8.1 *Fair trade sales in the leading consumer countries in 2006 and 2007 (estimated retail value in £ million)*

Source: Data from the Fairtrade Foundation.

second, improving the human connection between producer and consumer; and third, ensuring that a larger share of the value of the product stays with the producer.[8] It has been successful in the first, largely as a result of the support of iconic figures from the worlds of music and fashion. When organized along cooperative lines, producers of commodities can also increase their market power and negotiate a better price for their product, thus achieving the third aim.[9] The second aim is harder to achieve (in spite of the imaginative use of images of producers themselves on some fair trade packaging), although it may have opened up the way to more creative solutions, such as the solidarity economy idea discussed later.

Trade in the era of climate change and peak oil

As explained in the first section of this chapter, conventional economic support for trade has been based on arguments about productive efficiency – closely related to profitability – and has been set in an unreal world of impossible assumptions and limitless resources. It is important to put this understanding of trade as a natural way to exchange virtually identical goods across the globe in its historical context, which is contemporaneous with a particular economic system and the massive abundance of fossil fuels over the past 200 years:

> *A fashionable defence of economic globalisation is to point out that markets, the profit motive and international trade are as old as human civilisation. The claim could not be more misleading.*

> *For much of human history, the long distance exchange of fancy goods and luxuries was a relatively marginal activity compared to the routine, and more local, day-to-day meeting of human needs. It was something that is quite different from organising the entire global economy as a market system.*[10]

A common joke in green circles is that we used to make the cake and import the icing, whereas now we make the icing and import the cake! The reality of globalization and trade for necessities rather than luxuries is that this era is rapidly coming to an end, undermined by the depletion of oil supplies and the need to massively reduce emissions of CO_2 to prevent runaway climate change.

Figure 8.2 indicates the close relationship between CO_2 emissions and world trade. Amid the growing consensus that climate change is caused by the burning of fossil fuels it is becoming inevitable that each gram of CO_2 emitted must achieve the maximum in terms of human well-being. This is not the case for emissions used to ferry apples backwards and forwards across the globe when the people who eat those apples could happily eat the ones grown in their own countries. Such a system is efficient at generating profits – by concentrating production in countries with low wages and low standards of environmental protection, and concentrating consumption in the wealthier countries – but inefficient at using the capacity of the planet to absorb pollution.

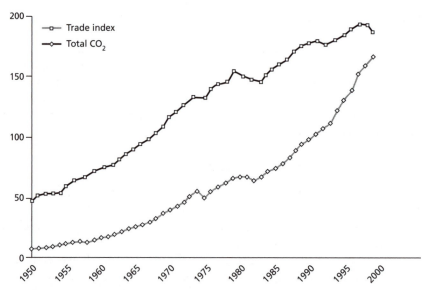

Figure 8.2 *Relationship between growth in trade and growth in CO_2 emissions*

Note: The trade figures are calculated as an index based on 1990 = 100 and include agricultural and mining products and manufactures. The CO_2 emissions are for solid, liquid and gas fossil fuels divided by 33 to achieve proper scaling.

Source: Carbon dioxide data from Oakridge Research Laboratory, California; trade data are from the WTO.

The corporate supporters of free trade have been quicker than the environmentalists to see that this is where the discussion is moving and have begun a debate about the relative advantage of food produced locally in an energy-intensive way versus that produced in sunnier climes and then transported to our markets. This is often a false debate – for example comparison between pineapples grown in Malaysia and those grown in European greenhouses, whereas the real solution might be for consumers in Europe to eat more apples. In the UK Tesco has donated £25 million to Manchester University to create a Sustainable Consumption Institute. It seems unlikely that the academics funded by Tesco will discover that a local, self-sufficient economy is the most sustainable way forward.

Greening trade locally

From free trade to trade subsidiarity

The priority for green economics is to meet our needs as close to home as possible, but how local is local, and how far should goods travel? One concept for helping this discussion is that of 'trade subsidiarity': 'the extension of the concept of "subsidiarity" into the realm of production and consumption, so that we naturally tend to look to purchase goods produced as close to where we live as possible':

> *The principle of trade subsidiarity states that distance between production and consumption should be as short as reasonably possible... Thus, market areas for goods and services that are relatively easy to produce, such as staple food crops, should be the most localised. Goods that depend on highly capital-intensive production, such as cars and computer chips, could in principle also be manufactured on a highly localised basis, but in practice this would be highly inefficient and their domestic market area would therefore need to be larger, perhaps even the size of the EU.*[11]

In determining where goods should be produced there are two important variables to consider: the physical inputs that are required to make the goods; and the amount and type of work required. If we simplify these into local versus global, and labour-intensive versus non-labour-intensive, we generate four types of good:

1　local, non-intensive goods such as seasonal fruit and vegetables and other raw materials which can be grown without much complex labour input;
2　global, non-intensive goods, which do not need much labour but require a different climate from our own;
3　local, complex goods that require skill and time to produce but not the import of raw materials;

Labour		Raw materials	
		Local	Global
	Non-intensive	Farmers' markets; self-build; domestic textiles	Fair trade; replace WTO with GAST
	Intensive	Support of local craft workers	Mending to replace obsolescence; end to intellectual property laws

Figure 8.3 *Production grid illustrating trade subsidiarity*

Source: Author's graphic.

4   global, complex goods that need technical expertise and considerable time to produce and for which raw materials or the size of market suggests a problem with local production.

As we move up this hierarchy the environmental problems generated by the consumption of the goods increases. The hierarchy also represents a movement away from control over the goods by local people, so that those in category 4 are completely dominated by corporate, globalized trade. Figure 8.3 illustrates the way we might meet our needs for goods in the different sorts of categories.

From fair trade to the sufficiency economy

> *A watchword of sustainable economics is self-reliance – not self-sufficiency, which I believe holds very few attractions. Self-reliance entails combining judicious and necessary trade with other countries with an unapologetic emphasis on each country maintaining security of supply in terms of energy, food and even manufacturing.*[12]

Many who are concerned about the injustice surrounding global trade and the massive carbon emissions associated with it have concluded that local, self-reliant economies are the most positive way forward. Here we are in a process that is sometimes referred to as 'learning from the South', in particular from the work of Gandhi, whose political action was directed at liberation from colonialism but also from the version of neocolonialism that he identified in the global trade system. Gandhi's most relevant contribution is his concept of *Swadeshi*, or self-reliance, which offers a prototype for the localization of the economy (as discussed in the next chapter). Gandhi called for a self-reliant economy based on a system of production and consumption of goods that was locally based and human-focused rather than dominated by the market. His salt marches and campaign for homespun cloth or khadi (the origin of the spinning wheel on India's national flag) were designed to achieve not just national independence but local and personal independence too:

Box 8.2 The fight-back: Trade-related direct action in India

- Shut-down of a Coca-Cola plant in Plachimada, Kerala by local tribal women; the company had been exploiting the valuable local water resource to the extent of 1.5 million litres a day;
- blockades of 87 Coca-Cola and Pepsi plants nationwide inspired by the Plachimada example;
- students at Jawaharlal Nehru University voted to replace their campus Nestlé outlet with a café serving indigenous cuisine from the northeast tribal region of India
- Seed Sovereignty: a nationwide movement encouraging non-cooperation with seed patent laws;
- development of sufficiency agriculture policies around the slogan – Food Sovereignty, Seed Sovereignty, Water Sovereignty;
- creation by communities of 'freedom zones' protected from GM seeds, pesticides, unfair practices by corporations and monopolistic markets.

Source: C. Lucas, V. Shiva and C. Hines (2005) 'Making poverty inevitable: The consequence of the UK government's damaging approach to global trade', download available from Caroline Lucas' website: www.carolinelucasmep.org.uk.

Swadeshi *carries a great and profound meaning. It does not mean merely the use of what is produced in one's own country. That meaning is certainly there in* swadeshi. *But there is another meaning implied in it which is far greater and much more important.* Swadeshi *means 'reliance on our own strength'. 'Our strength' means the strength of our body, our mind and our soul.*[13]

This call for self-reliance was a clear inspiration to the self-sufficiency movement in Europe and the US from the 1960s onwards, with its impetus to move back to the land and provide for one's own needs.[14] As shown by the activities of Indian peasants listed in Box 8.2, Gandhi's message is still inspiring emancipatory activity in the poorer countries of the South. Following its negative experiences on the boom-and-bust roller coaster, Thailand has now stepped aside to follow its own path to human-scale development, as reported in the latest (2007) UNDP Human Development Report for that country. The King of Thailand, who has inspired this philosophy, describes it as a middle way – neither extreme isolation from the outside world, nor leaving oneself vulnerable to the forces of globalization: 'This self-sufficiency does not mean that every family must grow food for themselves, make clothes for themselves; that is too much. But in a village or subdistrict there should be a reasonable amount of sufficiency. If they grow or produce something more than they need they can sell them. But they do not need to sell them very far; they can sell them in nearby places without having to pay high transport costs.'[15]

For many in the West the path being followed by Thailand offers inspiration. The Transition Towns movement calls for greater self-sufficiency within local communities – both to reduce the carbon impact of economic activity and also to increase resilience against increasing oil prices and the harsh climatic conditions climate change will bring. Communities following this model of transition to a low-carbon economy are establishing more local production and distribution, bringing more fun into shopping by developing systems of 'fayre trade', somewhere between a car-boot sale and a medieval market – a far cry from the sterility of the supermarket. For goods that cannot be produced locally there is the 'solidarity economy' – the attempt to go beyond fair trade and build real relationships with producers in the South and link communities across the globe. An example is the work of Birmingham-based Globally Local, focusing on collaborative regional self-sufficiency.

Greening trade globally

The global architecture for the trade regime was created as part of the Bretton Woods framework to ensure international peace and harmony following the disaster of the Second World War. At this time most of the countries that now make up the United Nations did not even exist – they were still the 'possessions' of the Western industrialized countries, which under the colonial system claimed ownership of their resources as well. It is little wonder that this system has failed to protect the interests of the newly emerging states. A managed system for global trading would be based around attempts to ensure balanced budgets, so that countries could run neither large-scale surpluses nor deficits (an idea which UK negotiator J. M. Keynes took to the Bretton Woods negotiations nearly 70 years ago). As part of the reordering of international economic relations that is a central thread running through green economics, a new international trade system is of crucial importance. Several have labelled this GAST – the General Agreement on Sustainable Trade. The key provisions of such a system are listed in Box 8.3; they are analogous to the rules presently governing fair trade, which are adopted voluntarily by many consumers and guarantee decent wages, working conditions, environmental standards and fair prices to producers and consumers.

Colin Hines suggests a regime of 'managed trade', which may also include tariffs (a form of import tax) to prevent the import of goods with an environmentally or socially negative impact or to protect industries whose import role supports a specific community.[16] An example might be the introduction of a tax on US goods to reflect the fact that the country is not engaging in CO_2 reductions, thus increasing the relative value of production in countries that are. In general, the managed regime would be a means of moving trade in a more environmentally and socially benign direction. The 'national treatment' rules of the WTO, which prohibit the promotion of domestic above imported goods, might be changed under GAST to a provision permitting trade controls 'that increase local employment with decent wages, enhance protection of the environment, ensure adequate competition and consumer protection, and otherwise improve the quality of life... States

---

BOX 8.3 KEY PROVISIONS OF THE GENERAL AGREEMENT ON SUSTAINABLE TRADE

Support the local	Provisions preventing governments from giving favourable conditions to domestic producers will be abolished.
Favouring certain partners	States will be allowed to choose to give preferential trade terms to goods and services from other states which respect human rights, treat workers fairly, and protect the environment.
Performance requirements	States may impose requirements on corporations opening production facilities in their territories based on: a minimum level of domestic input to the production process; a minimum level of local equity investment; a minimum level of local staff; minimum environmental standards.
Standstill and rollback	No state party to GAST can pass laws or adopt regulations that diminish local control of industry and services.
Dispute resolution	Citizen groups and community institutions should be able to sue companies for violations of this trade code, under a transparent and public process.

Source: Adapted from C. Hines (2000) *Globalisation: A Local Manifesto*, London: Earthscan.

---

are urged to give favourable treatment to domestic products and services which best further these goals.'

Conventional economics wisdom is that free trade is superior to managed trade, but this is only true if those involved in trade negotiations have equal power – this is not the case in the present system. Measures to manage global trade – such as tariffs and quotas – are frowned on by conventional economists. Yet they represent one way that the richer, more powerful countries, can act more justly in a system where they have a disproportionate amount of power. Following the break-up of empires, countries such as the UK and France felt a paternalistic sense of responsibility for their former colonies, and introduced systems favouring their crops and products; since the creation of the WTO these systems of tariffs (an extra price imposed on goods coming into a country before they are sold there) and quotas (a limit on the amount of a certain product that can be imported) have been progressively dismantled, leading to increasing insecurity and poverty in the South. Meanwhile Western nations have in many cases subsidized their own industries and forced their cheap exports onto world markets, a process known as 'dumping'.

A GAST would allow selective tariffs to be reintroduced by negotiation, preventing the dumping of European food on the markets of poorer countries. Similarly quotas, which play a crucial role in ensuring security of access for exports from poor countries into rich ones, would be permitted as a way of supporting producers in poorer countries. In the market for textiles, for example, there is fierce competition between poorer countries, which produce more than half the world's textile exports and nearly three-quarters of its clothing exports.[17] Producer countries enjoyed some protection through the

Multi-Fibre Arrangement (originally negotiated by developed countries to protect their post-war markets against imports) until this was removed under WTO pressure at the end of 2004. This has led to the collapse of an important sector of production in countries whose workers were paid slightly more – the so-called 'race to the bottom' in production.[18]

From a development economics perspective and in a book with a strong focus on poverty alleviation, Tom Lines argues the case for a fundamental restructuring of commodities markets. He also suggests informal cooperation between poorer countries dependent on commodities to earn foreign exchange to increase their market power:

> *For example, in May 2005 a new government in Ecuador (which exports more bananas than any other country) signed a decree to regulate the volume of bananas leaving the country. Two months later, Malaysia and Indonesia announced a bilateral plan to cooperate on the palm oil, rubber, cocoa, timber and other markets in order to ensure price stability and eliminate the undercutting of their position by others ... On the world tea market, discussions have been reported involving all four leading tea producers, China, India, Kenya and Sri Lanka.*[19]

This may be considered 'unfair trade' as it represents effective cartels in the markets for different commodities but it is a response to the unfairness of the negotiations in those very markets, which have for centuries been dominated by the rich Western nations to the detriment of the South.

Notes

1   M. Woodin and C. Lucas (2004) *Green Alternatives to Globalisation: A Manifesto*, London: Pluto, p. 6.

2   Quoted in M. J. Rowbotham (2000) *Goodbye America! Globalisation, Debt and the Dollar Empire*, Charlbury: Jon Carpenter, p. 52.

3   Richard Douthwaite, quoted in M. S. Cato (2006) *Market, Schmarket: Building the Post-Capitalist Economy*, Gretton: New Clarion Press, p. 64.

4   Rowbotham, *Goodbye America!*, pp. 75–6.

5   C. Hines (2002) 'Oxfam's Jekyll and Hyde approach to trade will worsen the lot of the poor'; www.gaianeconomics.org/colin_hines.htm.

6   Cited by T. Lines (2008) *Making Poverty: A History*, London: Zed Books.

7   B. Milanovic (1999) 'The world income distribution, 1988 and 1993: First calculation based on household surveys alone', World Bank Policy Research Working Paper No. 2244.

8   G. Fridell (2007) 'Fair-trade coffee and commodity fetishism: The limits of market-driven social justice', *Historical Materialism*, 15/4: 79–104.

9   A. Bibby and L. Shaw (2005) *Making A Difference: Co-operative Solutions to Global Poverty*, Manchester: Co-operative College.

10 A. Simms (2000) *Collision Course: Free Trade's Ride on the Global Climate*, London: New Economics Foundation, p. 3.

11   Woodin and Lucas, *Green Alternatives*, p. 74; for a full discussion see Cato, *Market Schmarket*, ch. 4.

12   J. Porritt (2006) *Capitalism as if the World Matters*, London: Earthscan, p. 18.

13   M. K. Gandhi (1909) 'New Year', *Indian Opinion*, 2 January; reprinted in I. Raghavan (ed) *The Essential Writings of Mahatma Gandhi*, Delhi: Oxford University Press, 1991.

14   You can find out more about these movements in both historical and contemporary context from the websites of Diggers and Dreamers (www.diggersanddreamers.org.uk/) and The Land Is Ours (www.tlio.org.uk/).

15   UNDP (2007) *Sufficiency Economy and Human Development: Thailand Human Development Report 2007*, Bangkok: UNDP.

16   C. Hines (2000) *Localisation: A Global Manifesto*, London: Earthscan.

17   EU data for World Textile and Clothing Exports, 1962–2000, cited in C. Lucas, V. Shiva and C. Hines (2005) 'Making poverty inevitable', *Sustainable Economics*, 13/2, www.sustecweb.co.uk.

18   EU (2005) *Draft Report on Prospects for Trade Relations between the EU and China*, Committee on International Trade, Rapporteur: Caroline Lucas.

19   Lines, *Making Poverty*.

9
Relocalizing Economic Relationships

Such a vision offers greater community and personal satisfaction: a world where conviviality replaces consumption, where local identity replaces global trade, and where community spirit replaces brand loyalty.
Lord Beaumont of Whitley, speaking in the House of Lords

For a couple of decades the proponents of globalization have been winning the ideological battle, in spite of strong and growing opposition and proposals for more humane ways of organizing international economic relationships, as outlined in the previous chapter. During this time the few green economists calling for local food and energy security, or protection of local economies and communities, have seemed like voices in the wilderness. Yet, partly as a result of the imminence of climate change and increasing oil prices, putting all our eggs in the globalization basket has begun to seem rather a risky strategy. Put this together with the recognition that globalization means vastly more carbon-intensive transport of people and goods and localization begins to be an increasingly popular strategy.

Localization to replace globalization

In his 'global manifesto' for localization Colin Hines defines globalization as follows:

Globalization n. 1. the process by which governments sign away the rights of their citizens in favour of speculative investors and transnational corporations. 2. The erosion of wages, social welfare standards and environmental regulations for the sake of international trade. 3. The imposition world-wide of a consumer monoculture. Widely but falsely believed to be irreversible – See also financial meltdown, casino economy, Third World debt and race to the bottom (16th century: from colonialism, via development).[1]

This is, as Hines himself concedes, a blunt and indeed a savage critique. He sees globalization not as a positive move but rather as an economic delocalization or dismantling of local economies on a global basis.

Woodin and Lucas refer to globalization as 'the economics of insecurity', making a strong case that it was a politically motivated project justified on the basis of economic efficiency but in reality operating for the benefit of transnational corporations or TNCs:

> *There is plenty of evidence to show that the beneficiaries of this massive expansion in international trade are the transnational corporations (TNCs) that control it. For example, 51 of the top 100 economies in the world are TNCs. Just 500 TNCs control 70 per cent of international trade and a mere 1 per cent of TNCs control half of the world's foreign direct investment. And while the global economy typically grows at 2 to 3 per cent every year, large corporations have an 8–10 per cent growth rate.*[2]

As well as political concerns about the shifting of economic power from governments to corporations, there is the obvious concern that the increasing amount of transport of goods and increasingly people too has severe environmental consequences. In addition there are anxieties about the failure of security of supply of our most basic necessities such as food and energy. These will be discussed further in later sections, but the problem was graphically illustrated in 2006 when Christmas for UK consumers was imported on the world's largest container vessel's maiden voyage from China. If anything had happened to the 'quarter of a mile long, 200ft-high [61m] behemoth', then Christmas might have had to be cancelled.[3]

The situation is particularly serious in the case of economies which are dependent on food imports. Figure 9.1 shows the decline in the UK's self-sufficiency in terms of food, feed and drink since 1960.

> *The UK's dependence on food imports makes us particularly vulnerable to rising energy prices. We currently rely on imports to provide almost one third of the food consumed in the UK, and have one of the lowest self-sufficiency ratios in the EU8. Although the UK has been a net importer of food for a long time, imports are currently growing at a significant rate. Defra figures show that imports in tonnes increased by 38 per cent from 1988 to 2002. For some types of food, the increase has been even more dramatic. Imports of fruit have doubled, for example, while imports of vegetables have tripled. Half of all vegetables and 95*

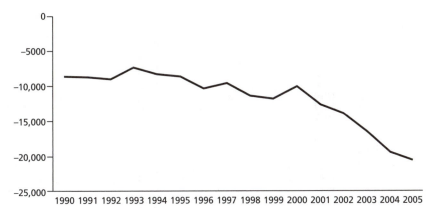

Figure 9.1 *Trade gap in agricultural products in the UK, 1990–2005 (US$ million)*

Note: Total agricultural trade is the sum of all the commodities traded between countries, encompassing food for humans, animal feed, livestock itself and most products derived from animals and vegetables, such as fibres, oils, wood and skins. It excludes fish, fertilizers and items like machinery.

Source: Author's graphic: data from the Food and Agriculture Organization.

per cent of all fruit consumed in the UK now come from overseas.[4]

The problem for the proponents of localization is that the rules of the economic game are stacked against them. Although globalization has resulted in a single economy for sales, there is no global rate for wages, nor internationally agreed standards of employment or environmental protection. In such a world it is inevitable that there will be what critics of globalization refer to as a 'race to the bottom', where all production will shift to countries which have the lowest environmental and employment standards. The impossibility of competition between workers in Western economies, protected by minimum wage legislation, and those in the poorer nations is clear from the comparison of wage rates illustrated in Figure 9.2. Increasingly this has led to a situation where everything is made in China. While writing this book I discovered that a cousin of mine, who works as a thatcher in Devon, UK, actually imports the thatch he uses for 'sustainable' roofing from China.

Green critics of globalization are very keen to make clear that their objection is not based on narrow xenophobia. Hines draws a distinction between globalization and internationalism, which can be thought of as 'the flow of ideas, technologies, information, culture, money and goods with the end goal of protecting and rebuilding local economics worldwide. Its emphasis is not on competition for the cheapest but on cooperation for the best.'[5] As Jeremy Seabrook writes, 'It is time to rescue what true internationalists have always worked for from the clutches of a rapacious, expansive, colonising globalization,' a task in which he is joined by Doreen Massey.[6] The following opinion

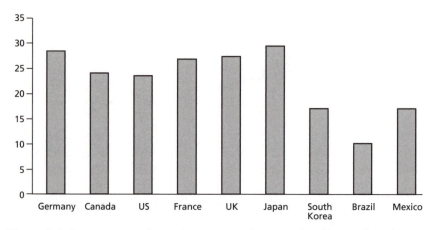

Figure 9.2 *Comparison of wage rates in a selection of countries, based on purchasing power parities, 2005 (Hourly manufacturing wages in US dollars)*

Note: Purchasing power parities are a way of comparing the value of money in different economies in terms of their ability to buy goods, by removing the distortions caused by fluctuations in exchange rates.

Source: Data from the Jus Semper Global Alliance: www.jussemper.org.

from J. M. Keynes is frequently and favourably quoted by greens:

> *I sympathize with those who would minimize, rather than with those who would maximize, economic entanglement among nations. Ideas, knowledge, science, hospitality, travel – these are the things which should of their nature be international. But let goods be homespun whenever it is reasonably and conveniently possible and, above all, let finance be primarily national.*[7]

I hope it is clear throughout this book that a green approach to economics does not distinguish between one prescription for wealthy Western countries and another for those countries that are still 'developing'. As equality is one of the fundamental principles of green economics, so is a clear commitment that if the system we are designing does not work for all then it does not work at all. In fact, the commitment to 'learning from the South' spelled out in Chapter 1 indicates that, in many ways, from a green perspective some people in the countries of the South have a more sustainable approach to using the Earth's resources than the self-styled 'developed' economies of the West.

Political protection for local economies

Among green economists there is a consensus that, in James Robertson's words, 'A revival of more self-reliant local economies must be a key feature of the 21st-century world economy.'[8] However, there is less agreement on the sorts of policies needed to revive those economies. This section looks at some policies that have been suggested. Other greens despair of political solutions and look for home-grown actions that lie within the power of communities: their activities are documented in the next section.

Hines' 2000 'manifesto' includes policies designed to localize production and dismantle TNCs, specifically a 'site-here-to-sell-here' policy. This is a classic example of the protection of a locality's industry for strategic reasons – to ensure security of supply of the essentials of life – as well as in order to protect the environment and provide meaningful employment and social cohesion in the post-industrial communities of Western countries. According to Hines, 'Market access would be dependent on compliance with this policy, ensuring that whatever a country or a geographical grouping of countries could produce themselves they did.'[9] This is similar to France's stated policy of 'economic patriotism', which was demonstrated by former Prime Minister de Villepin's decision to defend the iconic French company Danone against takeover by the US Pepsico corporation in July 2005.[10] Here the emphasis is apparently on strategic interests, although repositories of French national pride (such as Taittinger champagne) are the real focus. In April 2008, French agriculture minister Michel Barnier blamed 'too much liberalism, too much trust in the free market' for world hunger. He said: 'We must not leave the vital issue of feeding people to the mercy of market laws and international specula-tion.'[11] The Minneapolis-based Institute for Local Self-Reliance (ILSR) has called for green taxes to incorporate the full costs of long-distance transport and trade, while the UK Green Party proposes import and export tariffs to reduce and regulate international trade. Various policies discussed in other chapters would also have the effect of supporting local economies, for example any form of taxation that increases the price of transporting goods long distances (see Chapter 10).

Woodin and Lucas go further in their support for local economies by suggesting an end to all subsidies to agricultural exports and the introduction of a food security clause into the World Trade Organization treaty to protect self-sufficiency in poorer countries.[12] The severe need for this in some of the world's poorest countries is becoming clear as the international price of staple grains increases rapidly and countries face political turmoil if they are powerless to either underwrite prices or support domestic production. The Green Group in the European Parliament has called for strong measures to support local food economies, including prohibiting the dumping of subsidized EU production, greater local self-reliance in food production, and 'Rewriting the EU Treaty and the rules of the World Trade Organization. This is necessary to ensure that food security and maximum self-sufficiency, with its inherent reduction in fossil-fuel use, replaces the present emphasis on more open markets and international competitiveness. At the same time, poorer countries which currently depend on their exports to EU markets, must be supported in order to enable them to develop stronger national and regional markets closer to home.'[13]

Photo 9.1 *Stroud farmers' market*

It becomes clear that green economists have a much more hands-on view of how the local economy should be managed than the laissez-faire pro-market economists who presently dominate national and international decision making. This extends to support for specific sectors which are vital in a sustainable economy and to complete bans on others. As an example, the ILSR has proposed the abolition of waste exports and others are calling for a moratorium on trade in biofuels. The Scottish greens have introduced an Organic Targets Bill to provide income support for farmers who are converting from conventional to organic production, as well as support for renewable energy producers. A report by World Wildlife Fund found that there was the potential to create 50,000 jobs in Scotland's green economy.[14]

At the heart of green policy for the local economy is a focus on the small, locally based businesses which create most jobs. The UK Green Party has a policy of banding corporation tax so that the larger the business the higher the rate of tax it pays on profits. This would benefit small businesses financially but also encourage the break-up of the larger corporations – the exact opposite of what is happening now with increasing consolidation. It would also increase competition and improve market efficiency. The party supports the establishment of democratically accountable community banks, which could provide capital for local businesses, as well as local and community currencies.

Pro-localization campaigners in the UK have successfully written and had passed into national legislation a bill to promote sustainable communities. As indicated in Box 9.1, it invites local authorities to draw up a 'sustainable community strategy' which must take account of many of the negative conse-

---

BOX 9.1 PROVISIONS OF THE UK'S SUSTAINABLE COMMUNITIES ACT (2007)

Matters to which local authorities 'must have regard' when drawing up their sustainable community strategy:

(a) the provision of local services;
(b) the extent to which the volume and value of goods and services that are sold or procured by public bodies are produced within 30 miles of the boundary of the public body;
(c) the rate of increase in the growth and marketing of organic forms of food production and the local food economy;
(d) measures to promote reasonable access by all local people to a supply of food that is adequate in terms of both amount and nutritional value;
(e) the number of local jobs;
(f) measures to conserve energy and increase the quantity of energy supplies which are produced from sustainable sources within a 30-mile radius of the region in which they are consumed;
(g) measures taken to reduce the level of road traffic including, but not restricted to, local public transport provision, measures to promote walking and cycling, and measures to decrease the amount of product miles;
(h) the increase in social inclusion, including an increase in involvement in local democracy;
(i) measures to increase mutual aid and other community projects;
(j) measures designed to decrease emissions of greenhouse gases;
(k) measures designed to increase community health and well-being;
(l) planning policies which would assist with the purposes of this Act, including new arrangements for the provision of affordable housing;
(m) measures to increase the use of local waste materials for the benefit of the community.

---

quences of globalization, including increased transport of goods and the threat to local employment.

Self-reliant local economies on the ground

For many greens, waiting for government policies to support local economies is not an option: they believe that we need secure access to our basic resources and are working to develop local systems of production and distribution. Fred Curtis describes such a system of interrelated but independent local economies as 'eco-localism' and argues that it includes: 'local currency systems, food co-ops, micro-enterprise, farmers' markets, permaculture, community-supported agriculture (CSA) farms, car sharing schemes, barter systems, co-housing and eco-villages, mutual aid, home-based production, community corporations and banks, and localist business alliances'.[15]

According to Richard Douthwaite,[16] the four basic steps towards greater local self-reliance are:

• setting up an independent currency system so that the economy can still function no matter what happens in the global financial system;

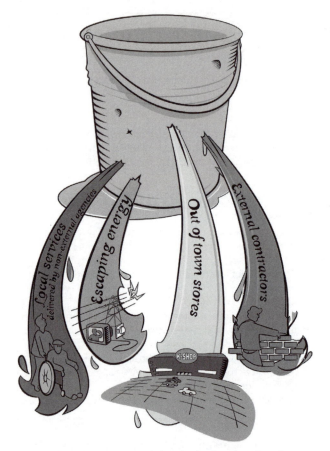

Figure 9.3 *NEF's image of the 'leaky bucket' local economy*

Source: Thanks to **nef** (the New Economics Foundation) for permission to reproduce this figure.

- the establishment of an independent banking system, such as a credit union, again to protect the local economy from international financial pressures;
- the production of enough energy to meet the needs of the local economy;
- meeting people's need for food and clothing from within the local economy.

It is interesting that Douthwaite begins with the economic structure before moving on to energy, food and clothing, which might appear more fundamental. The explanation is that without control of the infrastructure of the economy any attempts to address more basic needs will be distorted by the pressure from the globalized economy. An obvious example is the fact that local craftspeople cannot produce goods more cheaply than those imported from China.

BOX 9.2 ESSENTIAL FEATURES OF A SUSTAINABLE TERRITORY

- It has a stable population.
- It provides the basic necessities of life for its population from renewable resources under its control and expects to be able to continue to do so without overusing or degrading those resources for at least a thousand years.
- It is therefore able to trade with the outside world out of choice rather than necessity.
- It is able to protect its renewable resources and its population both militarily and economically.
- Its collection of economic protection weapons includes an independent currency and banking system.
- It has no debts to lenders outside and there are no net flows of capital across its borders.
- It does not depend on continual economic growth to stave off collapse. Its economy grows very slowly if at all.

Source: Adapted from R. Douthwaite (1996) *Short Circuit: Strengthening Local Economics for Security in an Uncertain World*, Totnes: Green Books.

London's New Economics Foundation asks people to imagine their local economy as a bucket (see Figure 9.3). In the era of globalization most money that comes into any local economy will flow straight out again because it can always obtain a greater rate of return by being invested in the global money markets. The local economy is like a bucket with holes in it. Regeneration policy is focused on attracting inward investment with little thought given to ensuring that local people benefit from that investment. It is not so much the amount of money that comes into a local economy that matters but what happens to it once it enters that economy. If you can plug the leaks you can ensure a better quality of life without endlessly having to find new sources of money. NEF also refers to this as 'increasing the local multiplier', which means an increase in the number of times money is spent within the local economy before it moves outside it. For example, if someone is paid Working Families Tax Credit and they spend it on a weekend break in Majorca, which they buy through a chain of travel agents, the money is immediately lost. If instead they went to a local hotel where they paid for a massage and an expensive meal with local ingredients, they are increasing the links in the chain: a local healer, a restaurant owner, a chef, a local dairy, a farmer, a supplier of local vegetables, and so on. Increasing the size of the local multiplier is one tool for underpinning flourishing local economies.

The campaign for localization has made most headway in the area of food – unsurprising given that this is our most basic need. The objective is not for self-sufficiency but for self-reliance:

> *A system of farming that was truly designed to feed people and to go on doing so for the indefinite future, would be founded primarily on mixed farms and local production. In general, each country ... would contrive to be self-reliant in food. Self-reliant*

*does not mean self-sufficient... Self-reliance does mean, however,
that each country would produce its own basic foods, and be able
to get by in a crisis.*[17]

The most vibrant expression of the determination to relocalize our economic
system is the Transition Towns movement, which began in the UK in 2006. The
Transition Town groups are born of people's awareness of government and
market failure to tackle the problem of climate change. While negative and
critical views are not encouraged within the transition culture, confidence in
'politicians' and traditional politics is fairly limited with a consequent sense
that the priority is to 'do it yourself'. This DIY approach includes the reactiva-
tion of local economic production and distribution: many Transition Towns
have focused on food as a first step here, as in the example of Transition Town
Llandeilo's Afallon Teilo group, which is working to encourage the growing
and eating of more local varieties of apple. Totnes has created its own community currency as a similar gesture in favour of a more localized economy. The
movement has grown outwards from its origin in Totnes, Devon in 2006 and
now embraces 70 or so communities worldwide.

The concept of resilience is central to the ideology of the movement. Rob
Hopkins (the primer mover in publicizing the concept) takes a definition from
the ecologist Brian Walker: 'Resilience is the capacity of a system to absorb

---

BOX 9.3 THE THAMES GATEWAY DEVELOPMENT AS AN EXAMPLE OF A NON-SELF-RELIANT COMMUNITY

Although there are many examples of misguided planning decisions which do not take account
of the climatic and topographical changes likely to be caused by climate change, the Thames
Gateway in the UK has to be one of the most glaring. The Thames Gateway is the biggest
development project in Western Europe and a flagship regeneration project of the UK
Department of Communities and Local Government. It is claimed to be 'a world-class model of
sustainable development', a claim largely based on the inclusion in the plans of some parks and
green spaces. The area now designated as the Thames Gateway (the communities it includes
have no particular cultural, administrative or transport links) stretches from Canary Wharf in
London to Southend in Essex and Sittingbourne in Kent. The area, which is home to 1.45
million people, has suffered the result of industrial restructuring but is to be home to the 2012
Olympics – hence the need for refurbishment. Under plans for the regeneration 160,000 new
homes will be built and 180,000 jobs created by 2016. The Environment Agency reported to
the government that half of the area proposed for development is within the floodplain of the
Thames. A report from independent consultants W. S. Atkins also concluded that a significant
proportion of the area designated for development is in the floodplain and that the risk of
flooding is increasing. Most of the proposed development sites are on the riverside. Atkins
estimated the annual cost of maintaining infrastructure in such a flood-prone setting as £47
million, with an estimate of £4–5 billion in the case of a catastrophic flooding event. The site
has been chosen because it is close to London and because it suits business interests. It does
not fit within the local environment or make much sense to existing local communities.

Source: www.thamesgateway.gov.uk; www.communities.gov.uk; G. Darch (2006) 'The impacts of climate
change on London's transport systems', CIWEM Metropolitan Branch Conference, 22 February.

Box 9.4 A sufficiency economy in Thailand

Thailand has developed an alternative model for measuring progress made by its country and its people, as reported in the latest UN report, entitled *Sufficiency Economy and Human Development*. Rather than using money as a yardstick, or measuring economic activity in terms of GDP, the report focuses on various aspects of a Human Achievement Index. The report owes much to the thinking of Thailand's King Bhumibol Adulyadej:

> *The important message of the theory was the King's conclusions about how to achieve real development with real benefits for ordinary people. Progress had to be achieved in stages. Before moving to another stage, there first had to be a firm foundation of self-reliance or else there was a strong chance of failure and loss of independence. The driving force for development had to come from within, based on accumulation of knowledge. In summary:* Self-reliance. Moderation. Resilience. Inner dynamic. Knowledge.

In agriculture the message is one of self-reliance based around the model of the family farm. This is in stark contrast to the export-led growth model encouraged for smaller economies by international development agencies. The report also prioritizes diversity and security, using a networking and mutual support model to encourage these. The example cited is that of Serm Udomna who took out a loan of 5000 baht in 1979 to become a cassava farmer. By 1986 his debt had increased to 30,000 baht and he decided to switch to replacing the cash crop he was growing with rice, vegetables and fruit, using a permaculture-style forest-garden approach. He now has more than 260 kinds of trees growing in his 'agro-forest' and has paid back most of his debts.

As a tactic for moving towards sustainability the report proposes 'moderately working with nature' and within this framework using the following principles:

- seek solutions offered by nature;
- seek solutions in traditional practice;
- consider the impact on other parts of the eco-system;
- favour solutions which are self-sustaining;
- favour solutions which are economical.

This solution from the South has much in common with the response to the environmental crisis suggested by the Transition Towns movement in the UK.

Source: UNDP (2007) *Sufficiency Economy and Human Development: Thailand Human Development Report 2007*, Bangkok: UNDP.

---

disturbance and reorganize while undergoing change, so as to still retain essentially the same function, structure, identity and feedback.' As well as reducing the use of fossil fuels, Transition Towns aim to build stronger, more coherent and more 'resilient' communities, meaning communities that can absorb shocks and respond to them with positive change, rather than fragmenting. The message of Transition is not a new one; what is new is the style and presentation – often more like a revivalist meeting than a political campaign. In contrast to the 'lean economy'[18] or the 'freedom to be frugal',[19] Transition offers 'a positive vision'. As Hopkins writes,

I like to use the analogy of inviting a reluctant friend to join you on holiday. If you can passionately and poetically paint a mental picture of the beach, the pool, and the candle-lit taverna by the sea, they will be more likely to come. Environmentalists have often been guilty of presenting people with a mental image of the world's least desirable holiday destination – some seedy bed-and-breakfast near Torquay, with nylon sheets, cold tea and soggy toast – and expecting them to get excited about the prospect of NOT going there. The logic and the psychology are all wrong.[20]

The localization message is not limited to countries in the West or more developed countries. In many ways its message is more important for the 'less developed' economies which have not yet become so bereft of subsistence skills or so dependent on fossil fuels: 'The principle of more self-reliant local development, and many practical applications of that principle, are equally valid for people in rich and poor countries alike. To turn any economy which creates local dependency into one that enables self-reliant local development to become the norm calls for similar changes in psycho-social outlook, economic and financial organization, and political and social power structures.'[21] As Box 9.4 makes clear, some countries which have travelled a long distance along the path towards a complex, capitalist economy have had traumatic experiences, persuading them that a different path might suit them better.

The next step: The bioregional economy

Beyond localization, the concept now developing among green economists is that of a bioregional economy – an economy which is embedded within its environment. The crisis we face is essentially an ecological crisis: if we fail to recognize our place within the complex system of interrelationships that life on Earth represents, then the future of humankind as a species is under threat. Bioregionalism represents a culture of living that acknowledges ecological limits (Kirkpatrick Sale's take on what this might mean as principles for building an economy is presented in Box 9.5). From an economic perspective, bioregions are natural social units, determined by ecology rather than economics, and which can be largely self-sufficient in terms of basic resources such as water, food, products and services. The concept of 'bioregionalism' itself assists in interpreting economics in a broadly geographical way, in contrast to the post-globalization economics which revolves around price (usually the price of labour) and downplays the role of geography altogether. Climate change re-emphasizes the importance of transport-related CO_2 emissions and therefore an economic response to climate change requires the re-embedding of space within our understanding of the economy. This new economic paradigm requires us to live consciously and carefully within our ecological niche: 'Bioregionalism recognizes, nurtures, sustains and celebrates our local connections with: land; plants and animals; rivers, lakes and oceans; air; families, friends and neighbors; community; native traditions; and traditional systems of production and trade.'[22]

Bioregional economics is therefore about reconnecting with our local environment and having deeper relationships with the suppliers of our resources, as a substitute for the thin nature of such economic relations within the globalized capitalist economy:

> *Your bioregion is effectively your backyard. It is the part of the planet you are responsible for. Bioregionalism means living a rooted life, being aware of where your resources come from and where your wastes go. It is the opposite of a life lived in the limited knowledge that food comes from Tesco, leaving every-thing to the global corporations, who are only too willing to take on this responsibility in return for their profits. Unlike political boundaries, bioregional boundaries are flexible, but should be guided by the principle of subsidiarity in the case of any individ-*

BOX 9.5 KIRKPATRICK SALE'S ESSENTIAL ELEMENTS TO GUIDE A BIOREGIONAL ECONOMY

1   All production of goods or services would be based primarily on a reverence for life. All systems have limits and they must be learned and adhered to in every economic act, and overuse of a resource or species, or their depletion and exhaustion, would be seen as a criminal act of violence, and overproduction of a resource or a species, such as the human, would be seen as a criminal act of avarice and greed, not to mention stupidity.

2   The primary unit of production would be the self-sufficient community, within a self-regard-ing bioregion, which would strive to produce all its needs, shunning long-distance trade except for non-essential objects of beauty, and essential political and economic decisions would be taken democratically at that level, mindful of the health of the entire bioregion.

3   Consumption would be limited, for it is not a rightful end in itself but merely a means to human well-being, for which only a little is necessary to satisfy vital human needs: the goal of economic life is not the multiplication of wants but the satisfaction of basic needs.

4   Everything produced and the means of its production would embody the four cardinal principles of smaller, simpler, cheaper, safer – that is to say, technology on a human scale, comprehensible, affordable for all, and non-violent.

5   The only jobs would be those that enhance the worker, contribute to the immediate community, and produce nothing but needed goods – and that means goods, not bads.

6   All people who wish to do so would work, for the purpose of work is not to produce things to satisfy wants but rather primarily to nourish and develop the individual soul, aiming at fulfilling the highest nature of the human character, including identification with community and the satisfaction of its needs.

7   All economic decisions would be made in accordance with the Buddhist principle: 'Cease to do evil; try to do good,' and the definition of good would be that which preserves and enhances the integrity, stability, diversity, continuity, and beauty of living species and systems; that which does the contrary is evil.

Source: K. Sale (2006b) 'Economics of scale vs. the scale of economics: Towards basic principles of a biore-gional economy', *Vermont Commons*, February.

> *ual resource or service. Within the bioregional approach begin-*
> *ning with the local is a principle that trumps principles such as*
> *price or choice.*[23]

In a sense there is nothing new about this sort of thinking. Schumacher saw fuel and food as two basic necessities for survival.[24] All communities should strive to be self-sufficient in these as far as possible – otherwise they would become economically and politically vulnerable. Peter Kropotkin, William Morris and Robert Owen all called for the return to small, self-sufficient, land-based communities – largely for social rather than environmental reasons. What is different about bioregionalism is that it is being used as a tool to challenge globalization: a way of fleshing out the ideas of localization into a fully fledged economic alternative.

Elsewhere I have described the bioregional economy as requiring a 'Robinson Crusoe economics'.[25] By this I mean that we need to adopt the perspective of a person washed up on a desert island seeking to meet his or her needs. This is the opposite of what we do in the global economy, where we start out with our desires and then seek to meet them using resources from anywhere on the globe, processed by people in countries with the lowest levels of wages. The inclination would be to begin with what is closest to hand and to improvise solutions to needs using ingenuity and innovation. These talents are not called for in the globalized capitalist economy but will become increasingly vital as oil supplies dwindle and climate change undermines the communication routes we presently rely on. In the words of Theodore Roosevelt it will mean 'Doing what you can, with what you have, where you are.'

These theoretical statements are all very well but might leave us asking, 'But what would it feel like to live in a bioregional economy?' Because the history of the UK since medieval times has been a process of continual dislocation of people from their land, such an economic life feels distant and can be hard to imagine. We can be sure, however, that we will have a closer relationship with our locality, as more of our resources will be drawn from our very local environment. This will also increase our responsibility for our environment, which will come to be our backyard in a positive sense – the piece of the planet we are accountable for and which we protect because it is the source of our well-being. Within a bioregional economy those who share a local environment will need to build closer relationships – these will be genuine economic relationships, where we rely on each other's skills. This will help to restore community: an economic life where workers are skilled, autonomous and genuinely productive may also offers solutions to many of our social ills. Finally, the bioregional economy will not require the wearing of hair shirts, locally produced or otherwise; sociality and conviviality are likely to replace the purchase of energy-intensive goods. We will rely on each other and our personal interactions to provide a sense of well-being and joy, rather than the purchases we make in out-of-town shopping centres.

Photo 9.2 *The Cuban 'camel': Improvised urban public transport in Havana*

Source: Thanks to Megan Quinn for supplying this photo free of charge. Photograph by John M. Morgan. From the documentary *The Power of Community: How Cuba Survived Peak Oil* (2006).

Again we may be able to learn some lessons 'from the South' in moving towards a low-carbon, locally based bioregional economy. In this case an example which has provided much inspiration is that of Cuba, which had to respond rapidly to the end of imports of cheap oil from the Soviet Union following its break-up in 1990. There were a number of make-do-and-mend strategies in the transport sector. The famous remnants of 1950s US cars had long been patched and repaired, but without oil to run them people had to resort to other means of transport. A huge quantity of bicycles were imported from China and large semi-trailers pulled by agricultural vehicles have created a new type of vehicle, nicknamed 'the camel', which can transport 300 passengers. Cuba's main success has been in the growing of vegetables within an urban context. Before 1990 the vast majority of Cuba's basic diet of rice and beans was imported, but without foreign exchange this became impossible. Instead, Cubans created *huertos*, a form of urban vegetable garden which took over urban spaces such as car parks (which were no longer needed!). Larger market gardens, known as *organipónicos*, took over other urban sites, and vegetable growers became some of the best-paid workers. The change in diet has been dramatic, as has the increase in domestic production: Havana now produces 50 per cent of its food within the city and 85–90 per cent of Cuba's vegetables are grown domestically.

Conclusion

This chapter has presented proposals from green economists to replace the globalized capitalist system with a network of self-reliant local economies. As

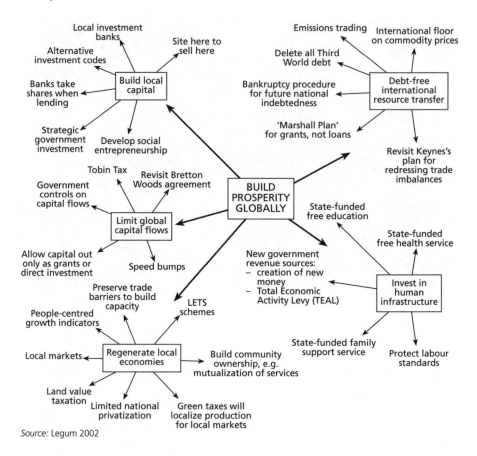

Source: Legum 2002

Figure 9.4 *Margaret Legum's design for building prosperity globally*

made clear in the previous chapter, this will not mean the end of trade, but it will mean that preference is given to local production for goods that can be produced locally. Figure 9.4 gives an indication of how the restructured sustainable economy might look. This will mean a shift in the focus of our economic life: we will need many more people skilled in practical crafts and especially in agriculture. There is no question that within such an economy we will need to become different kinds of people: we will achieve our satisfactions in life in new ways, and we will be called upon to be more creative and ingenious than we presently are. Some aspects of the transition will cause hardship, but others will be more deeply fulfilling than our lives within a capitalist work-and-consumption system can ever be.

Climate change means that some shift along these lines is inevitable: for a green economist this is an exciting and welcome challenge. There are social, as well as environmental benefits, to an economy organized more locally. As Douthwaite argues, such a development is the response to the environmental crisis that is most likely to achieve sustainability:

There is therefore a close link between restoring local economic self-reliance and achieving sustainability. Theoretically it might be possible to develop a world-wide industrial culture that enables all humanity to live sustainably within the limits of the world, but the scale and the complexity of the task are immense. An easier, more feasible alternative is to create a system that would encourage a greater diversity of diet, clothing, building materials, and life-styles. This would take the pressure off over-used resources just as it does in the natural world where each species has it own ecological niche and avoids competing directly with others.[26]

Notes

1   C. Hines (2000) *Localization: A Global Manifesto*, London: Earthscan.
2   M. Woodin and C. Lucas (2004) *Green Alternatives to Globalisation: A Manifesto*, London: Pluto, p. 10.
3   J. Vidal (2006) 'How world's biggest ship is delivering our Christmas – all the way from China', *Guardian*, 30 October.
4   C. Lucas, A. Jones and C. Hines (2006) *Fuelling a Food Crisis: The Impact of Peak Oil on Food Security*, Brussels: Greens in the European Parliament, p. 5.
5   Hines, *Localization*, p. 5.
6   J. Seabrook (2006) *Consuming Cultures: Globalization and Local Lives*, Market Harborough: New Internationalist; D. Massey (2005) *For Space*, London: Sage.
7   J. M. Keynes (1933) 'National self-sufficiency', *Yale Review*, 22/4: 755–69; reprinted in D. Moggeridge (ed) *The Collected Works of J. M. Keynes*, vol. 21, Basingstoke: Macmillan.
8   J. Robertson (1990) *Future Wealth*, London: Cassell, p. 52.
9   Hines, *Localization*, p. 68.
10 J. Thornill and A. Jones (2005) 'De Villepin stands by calls for "economic patriotism"', *Financial Times*, 22 September.
11 Timesonline, 14 April 2008.
12 Woodin and Lucas, *Green Alternatives*.
13 Lucas et al, *Fuelling a Food Crisis*, p. 31.
14 World Wildlife Fund Scotland (2003) *A Smart, Successful, Sustainable Scotland: The Potential for Green Enterprise and Green Jobs*, Aberfeldy: WWF.
15 F. Curtis (2003) 'Eco-localism and sustainability', *Ecological Economics*, 46, 83–102: 83.
16 R. Douthwaite (1996) *Short Circuit: Strengthening Local Economics for Security in an Uncertain World*, Totnes: Green Books.
17 C. Tudge (2003) *So Shall We Reap: What's Gone Wrong with the World's Food – And How to Fix It*, Harmondsworth: Penguin.
18 D. Fleming (2004) 'The lean economy: A vision of civility for a world in trouble', in *Feasta Review 2: Growth: The Celtic Cancer*, Dublin: Feasta, pp. 69–81.
19 M. S. Cato (2004) 'The freedom to be frugal', in *Feasta Review 2: Growth: The Celtic Cancer*, Dublin: Feasta, pp. 48–53.
20 R. Hopkins (2008) *The Transition Handbook*, Totnes: Green Books.
21 J. Robertson, *Future Wealth*, p. 52.

22 K. Sale (2006) *After Eden: The Evolution of Human Domination*, Durham, NC: Duke University Press, p. 133.

23 M. S. Cato (2006) *Market, Schmarket: Building the Post-Capitalist Economy*, Gretton: New Clarion Press, p. 102.

24 Schumacher, D. (1998) 'Introduction', in *This I Believe*, Totnes: Green Books.

25 M. S. Cato (2007) 'Climate change and the bioregional economy', in A. Cumbers and G. Whittam (eds) *Reclaiming the Economy: Alternatives to Market Fundamentalism in Scotland and Beyond*, Glasgow: Scottish Left Review Press.

26 R. Douthwaite (2004) 'Why localisation is essential for sustainability', in *Feasta Review 2: Growth: The Celtic Cancer*, Dublin: Feasta, pp. 114–24, pp. 116–17.

10
Green Taxation

When there is an income tax, the just man will pay more and the unjust less on the same amount of income.

Plato (attrib.)

From being the preserve of a handful of green economists in all but the most progressive of countries just a few years ago, green taxation has now moved to the mainstream of the political debate. Politicians are waking up to the fact that they can use a national taxation system strategically, to achieve goals for the environment much as health-related taxation has always been used to encourage more beneficial lifestyles. Because green taxation used in this way is explicitly a form of social engineering, exactly which kinds of taxes are introduced is the subject of fierce debate since this raises questions about exactly what sorts of lifestyles we should be encouraging as part of our future sustainable economy. Do we wish to encourage airline companies to buy more efficient planes or be careful to fill those they do own to the maximum? Or is our concern rather to discourage passengers from flying so often or from purely hedonistic motives? Or do we wish to use our taxation system for even deeper green ends, such as encouraging smaller, locally based businesses rather than global corporations?

The chapter begins with a theory of green taxation. On what moral and strategic basis are decisions made about taxation within a green view of the economy? The next section addresses the strategy of taxation policy, including concern for the inadvertent or unpredicted consequences of taxation, as human beings find means of evading it or avoiding rendering their income to the common pot. After that we look at a specific group of taxes which are favoured by green economists but are not directly related to pollution: taxes on commons. Finally we explore the ecotaxes that have been proposed, devised and introduced in various countries.

Theory of green taxation

Taxation serves two main functions: first, it raises revenue for governments to spend on public goods and services or to redistribute to bring about a more equal society; second, it offers policy makers a chance to influence behaviour, encouraging what they see as beneficial and discouraging what they consider as destructive.[1] Green economists refer to this as shifting the burden of taxation from 'goods' like useful employment on to 'bads' like pollution.[2] However, these two motives for introducing taxes are often in conflict. For example, taxes on cigarettes raise the price of cigarettes and reduce levels of smoking, and also reduce the level of spending needed to treat people suffering the health consequences of smoking. However, if fewer people smoke there is less revenue for the government for general investment. Similarly, in the case of environmental taxation, aviation taxes may cause an increase in the price of flights and hence a reduction in demand. However, governments may come to rely on this tax and ultimately may face a perverse incentive not to allow air travel to decline too rapidly.

When devising tax strategy policy makers must also consider the likely response by citizens, most of whom are keen to control as much of their income as possible and preserve it for private expenditure. The behavioural consequences resulting from tax changes are notoriously difficult to predict and frequently confound the expectations of policy makers. An example is the plastic bag tax in Ireland, which was intended to generate revenue for an Environment Fund to pay for waste management and anti-littering projects. The tax was introduced at the relatively low rate of 15 cents but it reduced the use of plastic bags by some 94 per cent, yielding very little in terms of revenue, but having a beneficial environmental impact. The success of the tax in changing behaviour has led to discussion in the Scottish Parliament and London Assembly about introducing a similar tax.

The key point for a green economist is that taxation should be used primarily as an important tool to move us towards a sustainable economy. Margaret Legum defines the objectives of a taxation system as follows:

> *Taxes should encourage social inclusion, social equity, economic efficiency and environmental sustainability. They should discourage the use of non-renewable resources, monopoly of common resources, pollution and waste.*[3]

Existing taxes are perverse because they:

- reduce employment by taxing it and value added by it;
- subsidize capital and energy-intensive production;
- encourage pollution and waste, which the state then has to repair through the health service;
- encourage inefficient land use and speculation;
- encourage currency speculation;
- subsidize long-distance transport and hence inefficient use of resources.

The quotation makes it clear that the theory of green taxation is informed by principles of green economics that we have already established, namely sustainability, equity and genuine economic efficiency. Legum identifies some of the key criticisms of a conventional approach to taxation, especially its focus on encouraging the substitution of capital and energy for labour, and its failure to tackle pollution and inefficient land use. As we would expect from preceding chapters, a green taxation system would be focused on the efficient and minimal use of resources and the elimination of wasteful economic activity, whether through transport or speculative activity. Rather than focusing on a marginal argument over the exact rate of income tax, a green critique questions the need for such a high level of government spending. A holistic approach to the economy would suggest tackling pollution as one major source of ill health which would then reduce the need for tax on incomes to pay for treatment of the sick. Similarly, an economic system which reduced the distance freight was transported would have less need to invest in maintaining its road network.

The green economist's aim of greater equity within society is another target of the fiscal regime. James Robertson argues that, just as we should not be taxing incomes to pay for the ill health that our economy is creating, we should avoid the need for taxation to redress the imbalances which that economy creates. In what he refers to as 'predistribution' rather than 'redistribution', he makes a case for asking more searching questions about the sharing of basic resources such as land and housing, which would then reduce the need for later redistribution of incomes:

> This will involve a shift from the idea of redistribution to the idea of predistribution. Whereas redistributive taxes aim to correct the outcomes of economic activity, predistributive taxes and charges will share the value of essential inputs to economic activity. Whereas redistribution is dependency-reinforcing, predistribution will be empowering. It will correct an underlying cause of economic injustice, inequality, exclusion and poverty.[4]

Environmental economists, operating within a more conventional economic paradigm, have argued the case for introducing environmental taxes and reducing employment-related taxes in a way that is 'revenue neutral', i.e. there is no additional money going into the national coffers; the two taxes balance each other out. They have argued this position on the basis of a 'double dividend' because the tax system can be made more efficient, in neoclassical economic terms, while achieving environmental benefits at the same time.[5] However, from the viewpoint of green economics, questions also need to be asked about the quality of the jobs created and the type of economic growth that is stimulated: if it is won at the cost of further pollution and resource depletion, and if the jobs are demoralizing and destructive then there may not be a double dividend or any sort of dividend at all.

Strategic taxation

It is clear that for a green economist one of the key strategic aims of fiscal policy is to ensure that activities beneficial towards the environment are encouraged while those that are detrimental are discouraged. But green economists favour the use of a whole range of strategic taxes to achieve different aims: redistributing income, encouraging the deconsolidation of large corporations into smaller businesses, supporting less polluting forms of agriculture, and so on.

Green economists are deeply concerned about the wide and growing inequality both within developed economies and between them and the poorer economies of the South: 'Questions of equity must be central in designing green tax systems.'[6] In the UK context, the reduction in the top rate of tax to 40 per cent has resulted in a huge shift in both income and asset ownership towards the upper end of the income range: in other words, the rich are growing much richer while the poor are growing much poorer.[7] Figures reproduced in Table 10.1 show a similar trend. Green economists argue that wealth should be redistributed within developed economies through a range of taxes, the most fundamental of which is income tax on higher earners. However, green economists are also concerned with the increasing share of assets owned by a smaller proportion of very wealthy people. Thus a green economy would be likely to involve distribution of assets using enhanced inheritance and capital gains taxes.

The debate over inheritance tax is related to the discussion about commons in the following section. While from the perspective of the individual it may feel natural to pass wealth you have accrued in your lifetime on to your descendants, from the perspective of the 'commonwealth' there is an argument that this money should be shared between all those who share in the wealth of the nation. As an attempt to balance these two perspectives the UK Green Party has proposed an Inheritance Tax with a reasonably low threshold but which allows those making bequests to avoid tax if they share their wealth with a relatively large number of inheritors, whom they can choose. Because the tax relates to the wealth of the inheritor rather than the bequeather the system

Table 10.1 *Share of UK wealth owned by different sectors of the population*

Most wealthy	1976	1986	1996	2001	2002	2003
1%	29	25	26	34	37	34
5%	47	46	49	58	62	58
10%	57	58	63	72	74	71
25%	73	75	81	88	87	85
50%	88	89	94	98	98	99

Note: Percentages represent marketable wealth less the value of dwellings.
Source: P. Sikka (2007) 'Reclaiming the economy: Taming the corporations', in A. Cumbers and G. Whittam (eds) *Reclaiming the Economy: Alternatives to Market Fundamentalism in Scotland and Beyond*, Glasgow: Scottish Left Review Press; data from UK Office for National Statistics.

provides an incentive for those making bequests to choose poorer inheritors, thus ensuring redistribution. A similar policy was adopted by the Fabian Society in the UK.[8]

For green economists the most glaring inequality in today's world is that between the rich nations of the West and the poor nations of the South. They interpret this as an outcome of a historical relationship of exploitation that began with colonization and has since been continued under the guise of multilateral institutions such as the World Bank and World Trade Organization that are, in reality, dominated by the rich nations.[9] Given this analysis, the prescription is that the economic terms of trade between nations should be renegotiated in a democratic manner; this proposal is discussed more fully in Chapter 5 (money) and Chapter 8 (trade). As an interim measure green economists have lent their support to the proposal for a Tobin Tax, first proposed by Nobel-Prize-winning economist James Tobin. This is a percentage tax on speculative financial transactions, imposed at the global level with the revenue invested in projects to improve the lives of those living in poorer nations. Although such an initiative would be supported by most green economists, 'As a panacea itself it would certainly be a failure since it could not deal with the fundamental systemic problems.'[10]

Within a green economy taxes would also be used strategically to influence the power and behaviour of businesses. The neoliberal domination of policy making has resulted in the shift of taxation away from corporations and on to the incomes of private citizens. In the US personal income taxes make up 30 per cent of tax revenues while corporate taxes contribute only 6.3 per cent; in the UK 45 per cent of tax revenue comes from individual incomes (direct income tax and national insurance contributions) with only 8 per cent coming from corporation tax.[11] The tax burden on individual UK citizens has increased rapidly (from £48.8 billion in 1989/90 to £109.5 billion in 2002/3), while that for corporations has not.[12] Meanwhile, despite a large growth in corporate profits during the same period, the tax they paid rose from £21.5 billion to only £29.3 billion. During a period of downward pressure on incomes and upward movement in profits individuals saw their taxes rise by 124 per cent while corporate taxation rose by only 36 per cent.[13] One aim of a green government would be to redress this balance by increasing the rates of taxation of businesses. However, a more strategic aim would be to use banded corporation tax to encourage smaller businesses by relating the rate of tax to the size of the business, as proposed by the UK Green Party. A similar objective might be achieved by reversing the policy of a unified business rate, which relates the level of tax paid to the floor space of the business, to one which related to the turnover of the business. This would help to reverse the relentless consolidation of businesses and the movement of retail outlets out of city centres leading to what the New Economics Foundation refers to as 'ghost town Britain'.

Taxes on commons

According to James Robertson, 'common resources are resources whose value is due to Nature and to the activities and demands of society as a whole, and not to the efforts or skill of individual people or organizations'.[14] Robertson gives as an example the sudden increase in the value of properties located near the Jubilee line on the London Underground after the route was published, an increase which he valued at £13 billion. Although land is the most obvious and important example of a commons there are others, of which the radio spectrum is one that is now the subject of government fees rather than taxation. EU governments raised considerable revenue by auctioning off the right to use various bandwidths, some £22.5 billion in the case of the UK government. For green economists such commons are shared resources, the bounty of nature, whose value should be shared. If it is to be exploited by a few then they should pay for that privilege.

The Land Value Tax, or as Robertson refers to it, the 'Land-Rent Tax':

> *is a tax on the annual rental site value of land. The annual rental site value is the rental value which a particular piece of land would have if there were no buildings or improvements on it. It is the value of a site, as provided by nature and as affected for better or worse by the activities of the community at large. The tax falls on the annual value of land at the point where it enters into economic activity, before the application of capital and labour to it.*[15]

Greens share with libertarian economists a fondness for the land tax because of its extreme simplicity and efficiency. According to classical economists rents were to be eschewed since they encouraged decadence and idleness: increasing the value or quality of a piece of land, or producing something from it was to be encouraged; merely living from its wealth should be discouraged, preferably by high rates of taxation. This simplicity is the object of obfuscation by many writers on economics. Their argument is that economic rent cannot be quantified and hence is not a secure basis for taxation. Richard Bramhall provides an amusing critique of their argument concluding that economists have 'dumped a valuable fiscal tool on the scrap-heap of history, leaving the burden of tax to fall on labour and enterprise, while the landowner grows fat doing nothing'.[16]

In today's planning environment, where local authorities have the legal right to decide what land can be used for, vast quantities of value can be generate by the stroke of a computer keyboard, as when agricultural land undergoes a 'change of use' and becomes development land. Those who argue for a land-value tax claim that this value is democratically created and hence should be shared between all the citizens of the local authority. For many proponents of a land tax it can be a single tax, simply because of the vast sums it can generate.

BOX 10.1 THE LONDON CONGESTION CHARGE

The congestion charge in London was motivated more by irritation at the slow pace of traffic in the city than by environmental concern, but it has none the less been an important example of how traffic can be reduced in one of the world's largest cities. By the 1990s traffic was moving more slowly in the UK's capital than it had been at the beginning of the 20th century before cars had been invented! Following his election as mayor in 2000, Ken Livingstone launched an 18-month period of public consultation and the outcome was a decision to introduce a congestion charge based on area licensing rather than parking levies. Considerable research and modelling were undertaken to predict the correct level of the charge to deter the desired number of people (30 per cent) from continuing to drive into the capital. In February 2003 a daily charge of £5 was introduced between 7.00am and 6.30pm on weekdays; this was increased to £8 in July 2005. Research had predicted that, at a rate of £5, car miles travelled in central London would be reduced by 20–25 per cent and total vehicle miles would be reduced by 10–15 per cent. Car traffic was actually reduced by 33 per cent representing up to 70,000 journeys no longer made by car on a daily basis. Details of changes in road-traffic journeys are given in Table 10.2. Transport for London estimates that about half these journeys are now made by public transport; a quarter divert to avoid the zone; 10 per cent have shifted to other forms of private transport including bicycles; 10 per cent have either stopped travelling or changed their time of travel. There have been sharp rises in journeys by bus, taxi and bicycle. Meanwhile, travel speeds have increased by some 17 per cent. The reduction in vehicle usage within the charging zone was greater than expected, leading to less revenue than had been predicted. The London Congestion Charge appears to have been a political and environmental success. It has encouraged changes in behaviour towards less polluting forms of transport, reducing CO_2 emissions. It is also an example of a tax which is flexible, since the rate can be increased or decreased depending on the relative balance of traffic and public transport desired by the city's residents.

Table 10.2 *Impact of the congestion charge on traffic in London*

Type of vehicle	% change
Cars	-34
Vans	-5
Trucks	-7
Taxis	+22
Buses	+21
Motorcycles	+6
Bicycles	+28
All vehicles	-12

Source: J. Leape (2006) 'The London congestion charge', *Journal of Economic Perspectives*, 20/4: 157–76.

Robertson's calculation for the potential revenue from site-value tax on land in the UK was between £50 billion and £90 billion annually in 1994.[17]

Other taxes in the green economist's knapsack can be justified on the basis of being taxes on commons. For example the streets of a thriving city belong to all; if only a few choose to use them for private transport then that right can be charged for and the proceeds shared with others through a congestion charge. By a similar argument the right to pollute the Earth's atmosphere with greenhouse gases, causing economic disaster for others, should be paid for with a carbon tax.

A carbon tax can be considered a 'commons tax', since it attempts to reduce behaviour that adds to the amount of CO_2 pollution in the atmosphere, which is a shared commons. There are several variants of the scheme, but the basis of the tax is that it should be a unified tax on the carbon content of fuels to replace the complex array of fuel-related taxes that are in effect in many countries. Such a tax would provide a strong incentive for both businesses and individuals to reduce their energy consumption, their driving, and to switch to non-fossil-fuel heating as well as renewable electricity supply. In the mid-1990s the EC considered a proposal to introduce a carbon tax throughout the European Union. This was rejected, although Sweden, Finland, Norway, the Netherlands and Denmark introduced related taxes. The Swedish carbon tax achieved a reduction in CO_2 emissions of 7 per cent, while the Danish energy tax resulted in a 10 per cent reduction in energy use.[18]

Ecotaxes

Ecotaxes have two aims: to discourage pollution and to change behaviour, especially behaviour that leads to the unsustainable use of non-renewable resources. In the case of some ecotaxes, as in the example of the Irish plastic bag tax cited above, a related aim may be to generate revenue, but this is generally then intended to be spent directly on policies to support the central aim of the tax, i.e. for recycling in the case of the plastic bag tax, or to invest in more public transport in the case of the congestion charge in London. A more subtle aim of ecotaxes is to change the relationship between labour and resources within the economy as a whole. During an era of industrialization, and especially since the discovery of fossil fuels, profits can more easily be generated by exploiting natural resources rather than by using labour. While, as pointed out in Chapter 4, green economists are not inclined to create work for its own sake, there is a sometimes a desire to emphasize the contribution of human labour relative to nature's services when considering how production is to be achieved:

> In the industrialized countries, labor is relatively more expensive and more highly taxed; materials are cheap and lightly taxed. Green taxation can level the playing field for eco-material vis-à-vis nonecological products, it can discourage waste, and it can help create an economy that is more people-intensive than capital-intensive.[19]

The Scandinavian countries led the way on ecotaxes, with Norway setting up a Green Tax Commission in 1994 and Sweden following suit the following year.[20] As indicated in Table 10.3, there is a vast range of possible taxes. We have already considered the carbon tax and the congestion charge as an example of a transport tax (which can also be considered as a commons tax).

Table 10.3 *Examples of environmental taxes and charges*

	Upstream charge on resource use or environmental emissions	Downstream charge on resource use	Downstream charge on environmental emissions
Energy	Carbon tax on primary energy	Energy tax	Energy tax differentiated by fuel carbon content
Water	Charges on abstractions or emissions by water companies	Metered water charges	Not possible
Transport	Carbon tax on petroleum producers	Fuel tax	Fuel tax or vehicle excise duty differentiated by emissions
Waste	Landfill tax	Volumetric waste charges	Differentiated waste charges

Source: S. Dresner and P. Ekins (2004) *Green Taxes and Charges: Reducing their Impact on Low-Income Households*, York: Joseph Rowntree Foundation, Table 1.

The other main types of environmentally related taxes are those on pollution, such as the landfill tax cited in the table, or the Swedish pesticides tax considered in Box 10.3, and those on scarce resources, such as the UK Aggregates Levy. While a primary motivation for proponents of a green economy is to shift consumption towards renewable resources, for those which will always be in limited supply there is support for the introduction of taxes. This should encourage the switch to renewable alternatives where these are available, and where they are not it should encourage efficient use of the scarce resource, its retrieval and reuse. Such a policy could be diverse and flexible, with rates of taxation being increased or decreased as particular metals or minerals became more scarce or as new deposits were discovered.

The German experience with taxation represents a deliberate attempt by a red–green coalition to achieve significant environmental goals by using targeted fiscal measures, and one which has been well documented.[21] The programme of measures introduced in Germany on 1 April 1999 represented an attempt to increase the price of energy and resource consumption while simultaneously reducing the cost of labour. Taxes on mineral oils and electricity were raised in a series of steps between 1999 and 2003; on the labour side pension contributions were reduced. According to the German *Umweltbundesamt* (Federal Environmental Bureau) these taxes achieved substantial CO_2 reductions of more than 7 million tonnes by 2002, while leading to the creation of at least 60,000 new jobs. Overall, Germany managed to reduced its CO_2 emissions by 15 per cent between 1990 and 2000, although the economic recession in the former East Germany following reunification accounted for a significant proportion of this reduction.

Box 10.2 Energy tax credit programme in Oregon, US

The Department of Energy of Oregon state in the western US operates a scheme to offer tax reductions to residents who invest in energy-efficient improvements to their homes. The maximum rebate is $1000 annually for appliances and $1500 annually for either renewable energy equipment or an alternative fuel or hybrid vehicle. Eligible appliances include washing machines, dishwashers and fridges, heat-pump systems, CHP installations, high-efficiency boilers, wind turbines, and fuel-cell, geothermal or hydroelectric generation equipment. Table 10.4 shows the uptake for the programme in 2006, and indicates that the overwhelming majority of tax credits were granted for the purchase of energy-efficient appliances.

Table 10.4 *Types of installations resulting in tax credits for Oregon citizens in 2006*

Product/system	Number of installations	Total tax credits annual energy ($)	Savings* ($)
Renewables	489	1,017,830	80,049
Appliances	34,023	4,696,088	871,248
Ducts	993	222,564	78,063
Furnaces and boilers	4,627	1,620,371	294,003
Heat pumps/AC	672	244,021	35,907
Heat/energy recovery ventilators	28	3,008	–
Alternative fuels/hybrid vehicles	2,129	3,178,000	796,615
Total	42,961	10,987,323	2,158,893

Note: * Includes savings values for electricity, natural gas and automobile gasoline.
The cost of the residential and business schemes was $73.8 million in 2006, but this was balanced by an estimated increase in economic activity in the state of $142.7 million during the same year. This included the creation of 1240 new jobs, an increase in wages of $18.6 million, and increased tax revenue of $10 million. Energy costs were reduced by $48 million.
Source: EconNorthwest (2007) *Economic Impacts of Oregon Energy Tax Credit Programs in 2006.*

Table 10.5 *Examples of ecotaxes in a range of EU countries*

Sector	Transport	Waste	Resources	Pollution
Denmark	Petrol, energy	Domestic refuse	Water supply	CO_2
Ireland	Road tax, petrol tax	Domestic refuse, non-domestic water	Plastic bag tax	Effluent levy
The Netherlands	Fuel	Refuse	Energy, groundwater, tap water	
Sweden	Air travel tax	Drinks cans, batteries		Carbon tax, taxes on NOx and SO_2, fertilizer, pesticides
UK	Vehicle excise duty, mineral fuels tax, air passenger duty	Landfill levy	Aggregates levy	Climate change levy (CO_2)

Sources: Netherlands Environmental Assessment Agency, FEASTA (Dublin), ONS (UK).

Box 10.3 Pesticide taxation in Scandinavia

From the mid-1980s onwards, Norway, Sweden and Denmark introduced policies to reduce the levels of pesticides in use by their agricultural sectors in response to concerns about the levels of residues from the pesticides in food and in the groundwater. The policies involved strict regulation of which pesticides could be used, as well as limits on the number of applications, but there was also a taxation element. By the late 1990s, reductions in usage of 47 per cent for Denmark, 54 per cent for Norway, and 67 per cent for Sweden had been achieved. Sweden estimates that the risk to human health was reduced by 77 per cent between 1997 and 2001.

Source: Pesticides Action Network Europe, Briefing No. 6: www.pan-europe.info/publications/PesticideTax.htm.

Table 10.6 *Revenue from environmental taxes in the UK, 1993–2006 (£000s)*

	1993	1996	1999	2002	2003	2004	2005	2006
Duty on hydrocarbon oils	12,497	16,895	22,391	22,070	22,476	23,412	23,346	23,448
Climate change levy	0	0	0	825	828	756	747	711
Vehicle excise duty	3482	4149	4873	4294	4720	4763	4762	5010
Air passenger duty	0	353	884	814	781	856	896	963
Landfill tax	0	113	430	541	607	672	733	808
Total	19,755	25,673	32,635	32,695	33,729	34,924	34,907	35,368

Note: Individual figures do not sum to the total because only a range of taxes have been included.
Source: I. Gazley (2006) 'Review of environmental taxes', *Economic Trends No. 635*; based on data from ONS.

In spite of strong rhetorical support for ecotaxes in the UK, environmental tax receipts fell as a percentage of taxation following a high point reached in 1999. Table 10.6 provides figures for the revenue raised from various environment-related taxes in the UK between 1993 and 2006. An international comparison of the significance of environmentally related taxes to the GDP of a range of developed economies is offered in Figure 10.1. It makes clear that, as expected,

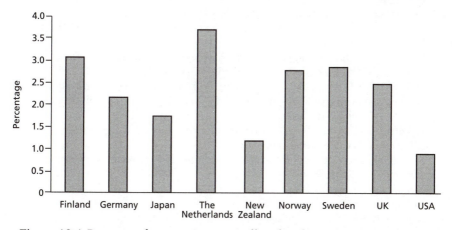

Figure 10.1 *Revenues from environmentally related taxes as a percentage of GDP in various OECD countries*

Source: Data from OECD Statistics Division.

The Netherlands and the Scandinavian countries have some of the highest rates of environmental taxation; it is also worth noting that, in spite of the growing political salience of the environmental crisis, many countries are reducing their rate of ecotaxation as a proportion of their GDP.

At the level of policy, concern has also been expressed by both green and environmental economists about the possible regressive consequences of a range of green taxes, and regimes need to be devised and tested to ensure that they would be fiscally advantageous to those in the lowest income groups before they are introduced. One study found that 'poor households already pay substantially more per unit of energy than rich households' and proposed a scheme that 'would effectively abolish fuel poverty, could achieve carbon savings of four million tonnes of carbon (mtC) over ten years and save households nearly £20 billion net present value'.[22] Other green policies, particularly the introduction of a Citizens' Income, would clearly operate to support the incomes of the poorest in society. The German experience suggests that, when ecotaxes are judiciously combined with tax reductions and other social policies, they can lead to an increase in income for the majority of households.[23]

Notes

1   H. Diefenbacher, V. Teichert and S. Wilhelmy (2004) 'How have ecotaxes worked in Germany?', *Feasta Review 2: Growth: The Celtic Cancer*, Dublin: Feasta. Diefenbacher and colleagues also draw attention to the principles of basing the rate of taxation on objective and transparent criteria and spreading the tax burden equitably.

2   J. Robertson (2004) 'Using common resources to solve common problems', *Feasta Review 2: Growth: The Celtic Cancer*, Dublin: Feasta.

3   M. Legum (2002) *It Doesn't Have to Be Like This*, Glasgow: Wild Goose Publications.

4   Robertson, 'Using common resources', p. 141.

5   A. Leicester (2006) *The UK Tax System and the Environment*, London: Institute for Fiscal Studies.

6   B. Milani (2000) *Designing the Green Economy: The Postindustrial Alternative to Corporate Globalization*, Lanham, MD: Rowman & Littlefield, p. 197.

7   D. Byrne (2001) 'Class, tax and spending: Problems for the left in postindustrial and postdemocratic politics – or why aren't we taxing the fat cats till the pips squeak?', *Capital and Class*, 75: 157.

8   R. Patrick and M. Jacobs (2003) *Wealth's Fair Measure: The Reform of Inheritance Tax*, London: Fabian Society.

9   M. Woodin and C. Lucas (2004) *Green Alternatives to Globalisation: A Manifesto*, London: Pluto.

10 Milani, *Designing*, p. 198.

11 Milani, *Designing*.

12 S. Adam (2004) *A Survey of the UK Tax System*, London: IFS.

13 P. Sikka (2003) 'How about responsible taxes?', *Guardian*, 17 November.

14 J. Robertson, 'A green benefits and taxation system', in M. S. Cato and M. Kennet (eds) *Green Economics: Beyond Supply and Demand to Meeting People's Needs*, Aberystwyth: Green Audit, pp. 65–77.

15 Robertson, 'Using common resources', p. 144.
16 R. Bramhall (1999) 'Land value taxation', in Cato and Kennet, *Green Economics*, p. 96
17 Robertson, 'Using common resources'.
18 D. Fullerton, A. Leicester and S. Smith (2007) *Environmental Taxation*, London: Institute for Fiscal Studies.
19 Milani, *Designing*, p. 195.
20 R. Brannlund and I. M. Gren (1999) *Green Taxes: Economic Theory and Empirical Evidence*, Cheltenham: Edward Elgar.
21 Diefenbacher et al, 'How have ecotaxes'.
22 S. Dresner and P. Ekins (2004) *Green Taxes and Charges: Reducing their Impact on Low-Income Households*, York: Joseph Rowntree Foundation.
23 Diefenbacher et al, 'How have ecotaxes'.

11
Green Welfare

'How do we know that Adam and Eve were Russian?'
'Because they thought they were in paradise although they had no clothes and only one apple to share between them.'

Green approaches to social policy

How is social policy affected by taking a green perspective on economics? The answer is that the way we think about 'welfare' could not be more deeply affected. For most contemporary commentators 'welfare' concerns only the welfare of human beings, and for a neoclassical economist the welfare of people living in the poorer countries of the world is often dismissed in the quest for efficient and profitable business. The commitment to widening the circle of people and species who count when we design our economy, as outlined in Chapter 1, has a fundamental impact on whose interests and welfare we need to take into account.

The other aspect of green economics that has a deep impact on welfare, especially when narrowly defined in terms of material wealth or monetary income, is the idea that what the planet can provide is limited and that we need to create an economy that respects those limits and lives in balance with the natural world:

> *Essentially, environmentalists identify a disjunction between what we demand of the world and what the world is capable of supplying. If the demands we make are infinite, yet the resources upon which we can realistically draw are finite, then ours is an unsustainable existence. Sustainability therefore implies reducing human demands and/or increasing resources so that disjunction between the two becomes less and less significant.*[1]

Green economics has grown out of the need to live sustainably within limits and this makes questions about the distribution of available resources all the more pressing. We saw in Chapter 1 that there is a commitment to social justice inherent within green economics as a discipline. In this chapter we will consider how this affects greens' attitude to social policy.

For some environmentalists, human welfare and a joyful, fulfilled human existence require a deep relationship with nature, and for nature to be unsullied by the pollution that modern society – and especially the growth-focused economy – generates with such alacrity. This leads to an inevitable link between 'human flourishing and the preservation of biosphere integrity'.[2] We may also suggest that showing respect for the planet to enable such flourishing requires material security; that those who struggle daily merely to survive cannot show the necessary standards of environmentally conscious behaviour. This is a strong argument for social justice and a basic level of material well-being, since without these the natural beauty 'fix' required for us to have true human welfare is threatened.

As we have already seen, a commitment to equity is fundamental to a green vision of society, and this extends beyond our own species to a consideration of future generations, animals and plants, and the planet itself: 'Sustainability therefore implies a redistribution from the affluent to the non-affluent, from present to future generations and from humans to non-humans.'[3] So we cannot use the labour of children in the sweatshops of the global South to guarantee for ourselves a higher level of welfare; and we must ensure that the standard of living we define for ourselves does not result in a situation where the planet is damaged, so that our descendants will be faced with a shortage of resources to meet their own needs. Similarly, we need to respect animals' rights and, if we are to eat meat, we should ensure that the animals enjoy the highest standards of welfare themselves before being slaughtered. For greens, welfare cannot be divorced from relationships, whether with others in our community or on the other side of the globe, or with the animals we rely on for meat, milk or leather.

Greens have three main criticisms of existing welfare systems:

- that they are tied in to the expansionist dynamic of the capitalist economy and thus are inherently unsustainable;
- that social policy is based on wage-earning, and assumes an economy where needs are met through exchange of money earned by labour-power for goods produced by others in the same situation;
- that they are centralized and bureaucratic and require loss of autonomy on the part of the citizen.

The first critique is discussed further in the following section, which deals with how we think about poverty. In terms of the basis of the welfare system in an employment economy, we have already seen in Chapter 4 that a green economy would include considerably more scope for self-provisioning and for taking responsibility for meeting many needs outside the workplace or the supermarket. For this reason, greens might be as critical of 'welfare dependency' as some far-right pro-market ideologues, although with considerably more compassion and a quite different range of policy solutions. For example, a green critique of dependency might lead to a policy of land redistribution and enabling the development of self-reliant, low-impact communities in the countryside. This links to the third point to some extent, since the centralization of welfare policy has been the partial cause of disempowerment of the citizen. As will be seen in later sections, green approaches to health care and pensions are both sympathetic to local solutions and closer to pre-1945 mutual aid principles than the state bureaucracy of today.

In 1998 James Robertson proposed a 'new social compact':

> *which does not tax people for what they earn by their useful work and enterprise, by the value they add, and by what they contribute to the common good;*
>
> *in which the amounts that people and organisations pay to the public revenue reflect the value they subtract by their use or monopolisation of common resources; and*
>
> *in which all citizens are equally entitled to share in the annual revenue so raised, partly by way of public services and partly as a Citizen's Income.*[4]

The focus placed on this alternative prospectus for achieving genuine welfare should not distract attention from the very strong calls by greens operating within the existing economic paradigm for a bolder approach to redistribution.[5] Green parties generally favour the use of the tax system to achieve fairer distribution of wealth within society although, as discussed in Chapter 10, this might involve taxation of assets as well as higher rates of income tax.

What is poverty? What is welfare?

Many neoclassical economists will concede that capitalist growth tends to generate inequality, but they will divert attention towards distribution. In a sense this is the distinction between a relative and an absolute definition of poverty. An absolute definition is concerned with the basic necessities of life that allow survival; hence somebody who is absolutely poor finds their very subsistence threatened by this condition. By contrast, somebody who is relatively poor measures their own condition by comparison with others in their society. It is the gap or the inequality that is problematic. Henry Wallich, a former governor of the Federal Reserve and professor of economics at Yale said that: 'Growth is a substitute for equality of income. So long as there is growth there is hope, and that makes large income differentials tolerable.' Green economists would be more likely to agree with the counter-argument that 'this relation holds both ways round. It is not simply that growth is a substitute for equality, it is that equality makes growth unnecessary. It is a precondition for a steady-state economy.'[6]

This distinction between absolute and relative poverty has a particular salience for green economists because of their theoretical assumption of the limited nature of the Earth's resources and the consequent need for limits to growth. This debate is often discussed in terms of a pie. For a conventional economist the fact that the more privileged members of society always have a larger slice of the pie is not important, because economic growth can always increase the size of the pie, so that those who receive a smaller slice are still enjoying more pie. In reality, of course, even if we do not meet technological limits to our ability to increase the size of the pie we will reach certainly reach planetary limits – in fact green economists would argue that we already have.

So we can reverse the argument of neoclassical economics and suggest that, rather than economic growth being able to solve the problem of poverty, poverty may be deliberately created in order to create a need for the economic growth that sustains capitalism as an economic system. As Robertson has argued, 'Money is the scoring system for the game of life';[7] in other words if you don't earn that much you are judged to be a social failure, a loser. Whether it is in terms of consumption or money, the feeling of inferiority is what drives us to greater economic effort. Evidence from the UK for the link between health and inequality shows that this status treadmill is destructive to human health as well as to the planet.[8]

> *The relative definition of poverty and the growth dynamic of a capitalist society enjoy a symbiotic relationship, catalysed by the advertising industry. These major forces combine to impose consumptive pressure on people and the planet and in themselves increase perceived inequality and hence unhappiness. Such definitions actually reduce human freedom, by setting a standard of consumption that we feel pressured to achieve. The role of the advertising industry in driving the onward advance of that standard is clear: its purpose is to manipulate the market for consumer goods against the interest of both people and planet. The limits of planetary capacity must be recognised as a brake on this accelerating movement towards greater consumption.[9]*

John Barry links consumption and the power of the marketing industry to the imperative in late capitalist consumer societies to instil a pervasive sense of 'insecurity', the solution to which is the 'right kind' of consumption. Hence brands are created to make people feel safe and also to generate greater consumption and economic growth.[10]

Professor Michael Marmot, famous for the Whitehall studies exploring why those further up the hierarchy live longer than their status inferiors, found that control over our lives and opportunities for social participation were the key factors in determining our health, based on more than 25 years of research from a multitude of societies around the world. Commenting on his work a colleague wrote that: 'Despite the widespread belief that molecular biology will

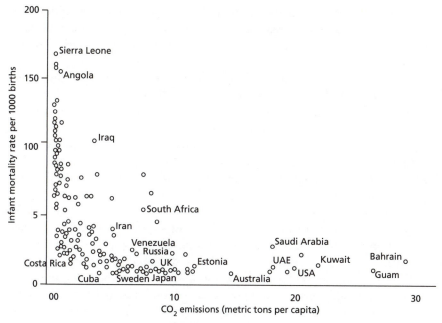

Figure 11.1 *Relationship between infant mortality and carbon dioxide emissions*

Source: Wilkinson and Pickett, 2009, forthcoming.

soon vanquish disease, there remains the discomfiting fact that health can be predicted to an astonishing extent by being poor, *feeling* poor, and being *made* to feel poor.'[11]

On the one hand we can challenge the suggestion that being a wealthy society is good for the health of the individual; but in these carbon-conscious times we can also question the relationship between energy use (a key marker of a more 'developed' society) and public health. Figure 11.1 indicates that low rates of infant mortality can be achieved in a low-carbon economy – in other words good health is not an energy-intensive process. In fact many greens would argue that the post-carbon society will be considerably healthier than the one we are living in now.

Clearly, then, we need a more sophisticated approach to defining poverty. We may start with the definition advanced by Amartya Sen: his 'capability approach' to poverty.[12] Sen argues that the inability to function in society is the best marker of poverty, and that this can be related to different levels of actual income in different societies at different times. 'Poverty', he says, 'must be seen as the deprivation of basic capabilities rather than merely as lowness of incomes.' He goes on: 'Being relatively poor in a rich country can be a great capability handicap, even when one's absolute income is high in terms of world standards. In a generally opulent country, more income is needed to buy enough commodities to achieve the same social functioning.' Sen's argument is for a relative rather than an absolute definition of poverty, but identifies what it is about being poor that is really detrimental to human functioning. He fails, however, to connect the idea of a poverty standard to the growth dynamic inherent in a capitalist economy.

At a deeper level still, anthropologists have asked questions about where the idea of poverty first emerged from. Marshall Sahlins has characterized hunter-gatherer society as the 'original affluent society'.[13] According to Sahlins, societies we like to think of as primitive accepted a lower standard of living not with reluctance but because of a deeper sense of the value of life. This he refers to as 'the Zen road to affluence', based on the assumption that 'human material wants are finite and few, and technical means unchanging but on the whole adequate. Adopting the Zen strategy, a people can enjoy an unparalleled material plenty – with a low standard of living.' Today's green economists would share this perspective and suggest that the unbridled consumption which is the central driver of our economy displays a failure of imagination and a regression from the understanding of less complex societies. Since there was no comparison with other societies and their complex and varied consumption goods, there could be no sense of poverty: 'Poverty is not a certain small amount of goods, nor is it just a relation between means and ends; above all it is a relation between people. Poverty is a social status. As such it is the invention of civilization.' Kirkpatrick Sale quotes a similar sentiment expressed by a member of the Irokwa tribes of eastern North America:

> *Before the colonists came, we had no consciousness about a concept of commodities. Everything, even the things we make, belong to the Creators of Life and are to be returned ceremonially, and in reality, to the owners. Our people live a simple life, one unencumbered by the need of endless material commodities. The fact that their needs are few means that all the people's needs are easily met... Ours was a wealthy society. No one suffered from want'.*[14]

Sharing the wealth; sharing the poverty

In contrast to early human societies, which focused on subsistence and sufficiency, a capitalist economy is based around accumulation and investment. Depending on population size and the abundance of the local environment, successful human communities are likely to generate a surplus, and how to manage this is a social problem:

> *Early human societies, faced with excess, regarded this excess as a curse: la part maudite, in Claude Bataille's words. The accursed share. They then set about wasting it: potlatches, sacrifices, parties. Tibetan monks, in our own day, make immensely*

> *complex sand mandalas, months of painstaking work and a huge*
> *quantity of embodied human capital: a magnificent investment –*
> *and then they chuck it all in the river for the dedication of the*
> *river god. Problem solved.*[15]

The potlatch is an interesting phenomenon which baffled anthropologists schooled in capitalist ways of frugality and accumulation. The potlatch is a ritual feast with excessive eating, drinking, dancing and singing, but it was also a huge gift-giving ceremony when those who had more than they needed gave it to others, or rather exchanged it for prestige. Giving a potlatch was a way of enhancing your status, which increased according to how much you could give away. The Puritanical missionaries were appalled and urged the authorities to illegalize the practice, which they did in the late 19th century. Anthropologists could interpret the ceremonies as ways of managing the potential for social tension that material inequality gives rise to.

The potlatch story illustrates that welfare cannot be defined absolutely and depends on the culture of the given society. German development economist Manfred Max-Neef tells a cautionary tale of the dangers of taking our judgements about welfare across cultural boundaries.[16] He made a visit to Mexico City shortly after the 1985 earthquake and saw 'a proud neighbourly spirit, vigorous activity with small building co-operatives everywhere; we saw a flourishing shadow economy.' However, he commiserated with one of his companions about the general level of poverty. 'Promptly, one of our companions stiffened: "*No somos pobres, somos Tepitanos*" [We are not poor people, we are Tepitans] ... I had to admit to myself in embarrassment that, quite involuntarily, the clichés of development philosophy had triggered my reaction.' Sachs concludes, 'The stereotyped talk of "poverty" fails to distinguish, for example, between frugality, destitution and scarcity ... Frugality is the mark of cultures free from the frenzy of accumulation ... Poverty here is a way of life maintained by a culture which recognizes and cultivates a state of sufficiency; sufficiency only turns into demeaning poverty when pressurized by an accumulating society.' In a similar vein a friend told of a visit to India when her companion expressed horror at the sight of old people living in hovels or on the street. The companion replied with equal horror that she had heard that in the West old people were forced to live shut away from society and never saw their grandchildren.

We should eschew making judgements about the living standards of others, but similarly we should avoid romanticizing the poverty that many are forced to endure in the global South. Those commentators who observe it with such rose-tinted spectacles are unlikely to have endured such conditions themselves. For this reason 'sufficiency' is a term preferred by green economists to the earlier term 'subsistence', which has come to sound patronizing.[17]

Much as we argued in Chapter 7 that GDP is not a very useful measure of human well-being, so we can question to what extent economic activity, especially fossil-fuelled economic activity, contributes to human well-being.

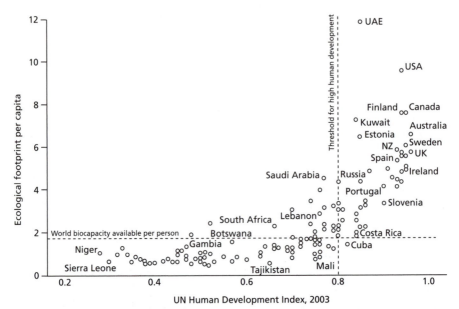

Figure 11.2 *Human well-being and sustainability: Ecological footprint and Human Development Index compared, 2003*

Source: Wilkinson and Pickett, 2008.

Figure 11.2 compares countries' ecological footprints with their scores on the UN Human Development Index. It indicates that there is no correlation between the two: countries manage to achieve a high HDI score based on consumption of the Earth's resources ranging from less than 2 to 10, in the case of the US, and even 12 in the case of the United Arab Emirates.

When considering well-being on a global basis we also need to remember that the consequences of many environmental pressures are borne most immediately and most heavily by those in poorer societies. Whether we think of the consequences for Bangladesh and the low-lying Pacific islands of climate change, the failing of the glacier-fed rivers that water the Indian subcontinent, or the droughts caused by changing climate in the Horn of Africa, it is clear that the costs of the environmental crisis are shared as unequally as the consumption that gave rise to it. A similar case can be made for developed economies, where the poor tend to bear the brunt of the environmental crisis. In most countries, low-income communities have traditionally found themselves closer to incinerators, motorways and waste dumps. In the US this has led to the growth of the environmental justice movement and calls for an end to 'environmental discrimination'.[18] In the UK this is now explicit government policy, with financial incentives being offered to local authorities who agree to accept the site of a proposed nuclear-waste repository. At the personal level, too, wealthy car drivers are subsidized through road-building schemes while the minority who do not own cars (many because they are too poor – a

---

BOX 11.1 ENDURING TERRORS: THE WAR AGAINST TERROR IN GLOBAL CONTEXT

- Number of people who died in attacks on the Twin Towers, 11 September 2001: 3000
- Number of people who died of hunger on 11 September 2001: 24,000
- Number of children killed by diarrhoea on 11 September 2001: 6020
- Number of children killed by measles on 11 September 2001: 2700
- Number of malnourished children in developing countries: 149 million
- Number of people without access to safe drinking water: 1100 million
- Number of people without access to adequate sanitation: 2400 million
- Number of people living on less than $1 a day: 1200 million
- Number of African children under 15 living with HIV: 1.1 million
- Number of children without access to basic education: 100 million
- Number of illiterate adults: 875 million
- Number of women who die each year in pregnancy and childbirth: 515,000
- Annual average number of people killed by drought and famine, 1972–1996: 73,606
- Annual average number of children killed in conflict, 1990–2000: 200,000
- Annual average number of children made homeless by conflict, 1990–2000: 1.2 million

Source: J. Porritt, (2007) *Capitalism as if the World Matters* (London: Earthscan) based on data from *New Internationalist*.

---

third of households in the UK) pay the health costs including asthma, heart disease and cancer. Box 11.1 draws attention to some of these 'enduring terrors' that attract considerably less attention than terrorist threats to the comfortable Western consumer lifestyle.

What is the welfare state?

The first theorist of the green approach to social theory, John Barry, offers three main reasons for greens' negative attitude towards the state.[19] The first is the strong influence on green thinking of anarchism, so that even relatively mainstream green thinkers such as Jonathon Porritt can view the state as the embodiment of 'materialism, institutionalized violence, centralization, hierarchy'.[20] Second, greens are wary of being identified with authoritarian state-sponsored solutions to the ecological crisis. Third, there is a cultural resistance among many greens to the technocratic and bureaucratic solutions offered by the state in a hierarchical structure, which contrast with favoured solutions emerging from the community in a democratic manner. According to Barry, many greens thus conclude that 'talk of a "green state" is an oxymoron at best, or a betrayal of the radical promise of green politics, at worst'. While in modern developed economies the state has taken on supporting human welfare, it is also responsible for the 'welfare' of the environment. When these two are in conflict, because the resources of the latter are consumed to provide the former, it is the state's role to mediate this contest, so that 'the welfare state helps to regulate the depletion of the very resources, and the degradation of the very environment, upon which it itself depends'.[21]

The anarchist strand within green thinking is best represented by the writings about welfare of Peter Kropotkin, who used the term 'mutual aid' to describe a system of informal, reciprocal support between people, which he suggested was the natural state of being. His historical account is one of the alienation of people one from another as a result of central state interference, with the suggestion that small, self-sufficient communities could better provide for the needs of the vulnerable. Such thinking is clearly evident in the following extract from the *Manifesto for a Sustainable Society* from the UK Green Party, 'A return to smaller, more caring communities would reduce the need for both volunteers and social workers. The current role of welfare agencies would change and diminish; they would no longer carry the main responsibility for those in need.' This is clearly an aspirational statement, but indicates the difference in approach from the statist welfare system that UK citizens struggle with in 2008.

Cahill traces the history of the centralization of welfare provision in the UK, away from the multiplicity of trade-union benefits schemes, cooperatives, friendly societies and savings schemes that typified the 19th-century municipality to the monolithic welfare state of the late 20th century onwards. He is clear about the advantages brought by the post-war welfare state but notes that:

> It did eclipse a variegated and substantial social policy culture in the locality where it was more amenable to local and democratic influence. Power was transferred not only from local associations and local government to central government but also from volunteers to professionals.

Aside from the focus on the importance of relationships and locality in ensuring welfare, greens are also concerned to take a holistic approach when considering the welfare state. In an argument that undercuts the stale political debate about public spending, they ask questions about what caused the problems that are so expensive to solve. Much of this spending is 'defensive' – 'negative costs of the organization of the economy aimed at securing increases in economic growth'.[22] This holistic approach informs the whole of green policy making, of which health and social policies are seen as an integral part, so that greens see social policy: 'Not as a set of discrete policies or policy areas but as interrelated and mutually determining. For example, housing policy is related to transport and health (including mental health) policies, since housing affects health.'

Paul Hoggett offers a view of the welfare state he calls 'ecowelfarism', distinguishing it from consumerism, where goods to ensure well-being are bought in the market, and welfare-statism, which locates well-being in the quality of public services received by right.[23] His criticism of the monolithic welfare state is its focus on 'normality', excluding those who refuse to conform to an ideal type (probably a fit and healthy worker), leaving the sick, the weak, the old, the frail, the disabled and the mad disempowered. By contrast:

Green welfare would promote the utmost respect for human dependency and would champion the development of a new generation of human-scale institutions and integrated, community-based models of support in which holistic models of health, social care and education would flourish.[24]

Citizens' Income and people's pensions

One policy is most significant in the proposals for welfare in a green society: the idea of a basic income paid to all citizens as of right. This Citizens' Income (CI) policy is distinct from the redistributivist policies of conventional left-wing ideologies, however much distribution they might require. CI does not require anything from the recipient; its justification is based on natural human rights, and especially on the understanding outlined earlier that our welfare requires a healthy planet and that leaving people without basic necessities will force them into plundering its resources to meet their needs. In contrast to CI, conventional systems of welfare payments tend to be based on the norms of reciprocity and efficiency.[25] An efficiency argument can be made for the Citizens' Income (and indeed has been made by Sam Brittan, among others), since it is a single tax policy that incentivizes work and simplifies the benefits system. Social democratic welfare regimes, which were once based in a social contract of protecting the vulnerable, have always included a requirement to work in exchange for benefits, so long as one was still physically capable of work. The Citizens' Income scheme explicitly does not. It is sometimes called the 'social dividend', making explicit the fact that one's entitlement is based on citizenship rather than any sort of contribution. It is considered to be a fair share of the value of a nation's wealth, which was once common property but has been enclosed and is now enjoyed exclusively by certain groups. The Citizens' Income would universalize this entitlement.

It is thus a universal benefit of the type favoured by greens for a number of reasons.[26] Targeted benefits cause people to adjust their behaviour to maintain eligibility and also require intrusive means-testing: both these aspects undermine a green commitment to autonomy and freedom. They can also be argued to be socially divisive, sowing discord between those who are and are not eligible, as well as being administratively complex in requiring the establishment of a distinction between these two groups. Arguments against CI focus on the risk of 'scrounging', to which supporters would reply that the enclosure of resources by a minority has undermined the ability of others to meet their own needs directly, and might also point to the parallel something-for-nothing attitude of those who live from rents on assets or property. While CI might be thought to be an expensive policy, it would be funded from new taxes on commons (see Chapter 10) and is unlikely to cost more than the various in-work benefits which now exist in many societies to supplement low wages. Overall it is a key policy for achieving the ambition for equity within a green society:

The result will be doubly progressive. The CI will be progressive because the same amount of money is worth relatively more to poor people than rich. The taxes will be progressive because they will impact richer people both in terms of their spending and in terms of their incomes and wealth. Their higher spending as consumers will mean they will pay more than poorer people, for example for the energy that has been used in producing the goods and services they buy. The larger proportion of their incomes and wealth (salaries, dividends, capital growth, etc.) derived directly or indirectly from land ownership and the use of other common resources like energy, will mean they pay proportionately more tax (indirectly) on their incomes.[27]

A survey carried out in 2002 found a generally supportive attitude towards CI among European Green parties.[28] Support was based, first, on the expectation that it would encourage 'a greater degree of communal self-reliance', and second, that 'it would help to shift social activity in an environmentally benign direction'.

Similar arguments are made among green social policy theorists about pensions policies. There is a felt need for a democratization and localization of pension provision and a call for the investors in pension schemes to be able to wrest control of such a large proportion of the global economy from the fund managers.[29] The so-called 'people's pension' is a proposal from the UK that has attracted interest in green circles because it solves two problems simultaneously: addressing the shortage of cash for public investments and the insecurity of pensions saving in the global financial system.[30] Such funds would also be primarily local and thus respond to the inherent tendency among greens to favour the smaller scale. Each pension fund would be linked to a local authority, public-sector organization (such as a school or hospital), social enterprise or government department. Working people would use their savings to buy bonds in the organization they chose. Their money would then be invested in infrastructural improvements. The return on this investment would be in the form of rents on the buildings or other facilities. The scheme thus entails risks, but only in a similar way to investments in existing pension schemes, and it has the advantage of local control and therefore, arguably, a greater degree of accountability. It also fits well with green commitments to self-help, mutual aid and ethical investment. So far this proposal has not been implemented, but as a plan it contains many aspects of a green approach to pension provision.

The Swedish JAK bank takes a mutual approach to the need to borrow money that is reminiscent of early building societies and savings schemes that people in poor communities continue to use, such as the tontines of West Africa. This sort of framework could be applied to pensions policy. In the JAK system saving and borrowing is seen as a way of balancing your needs across your own life, with support from other members. This is illustrated in Figure 11.3, which centres around a single person's lifetime income generation, illus-

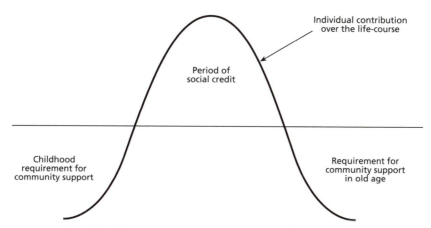

Figure 11.3 *Illustration of the ability to provide for one's individual needs over the productive life-course*

Source: Thanks to Chris and Tracey Bessant of New Clarion Press for permission to use this figure.

trated as an inverted U-shaped curve. As a child you are below the self-suffi-ciency line, reliant on others' earnings, and you return to this state in old age. During the middle phase, when you are healthy and productive, you have more income than you need and this needs to be saved for later use. In the JAK system you need to imagine other curves overlapping horizontally with this basic curve, since these represent people at other stages of their lives who can supplement your income, and whose income you supplement during your middle years. These schemes have the enormous advantage that no money is lost from the system; in contrast, interest-based systems rely on the lure of a certain percentage per year to attract depositors, who are people who have spare money. This interest must be paid by the borrowers, and often amounts to more than the value of the initial loan. In effect, therefore, any lending scheme that applies interest involves the transfer of money from the poor to the rich. The UK teachers' pension scheme follows an approach similar to the JAK bank model: rather than investing the savings of present workers, today's teachers pay the pensions of those who have already retired, and can expect to have their retirement supported by the teachers of tomorrow. So long as children need teachers the system is stable. Such a system could work for any trade or profession which is likely to be needed by society in the long term.

A health service, not an illness service

The current political rhetoric favouring the localization and personalization of health services responds very closely to a green agenda for health. Even the age-old green slogan that gives this section its title has been taken up by UK policy makers in the health field. However, when mainstream politicians talk about preventative health care they tend to mean screening and public-health education; greens have a much deeper understanding of health which may best be encapsulated in another popular slogan: 'Heal self, heal planet.' This indicates a deeper view of sickness, a sickness of the spirit which results from the alienation of people from the ecosystem they are part of, the 'disembedding' which feminist economists explain as resulting from a patriarchal arrangement of social relationships. This breakdown of our connection with the Earth is expressed at the personal level by a loss of connection with our own bodies. For some green economists this also relates to the nature of work and the absolute necessity in a capitalist production system of selling one's bodily effort as labour for survival.

An obvious example of how the economy is detrimental to human health is pollution. There is not space here to cover the huge and growing range of pollutants that can damage human and animal health. To quote one of many studies linking pollution to illness and death, a US study of particulate pollution in urban air (the result of vehicle exhaust emissions) found that it was responsible for 5 per cent of all infant deaths, 12 per cent of cot deaths, and 19 per cent of deaths from respiratory disease among babies. Work-related stress is another example of the huge health costs that are being created by the way our economy is organized.[31] For the UK, the Health and Safety Executive found that in 2006/7 around half a million people were experiencing work-related stress so severe that it was making them ill, while 14 per cent of those in work thought their job was very stressful. Depression or anxiety relating to workplace stress resulted in 13.8 million days of sickness leave in the same year. There is also non-work-related stress and mental illness caused by the way the economy demands success and measures this in terms of consumption, and the way work pressures lead to family and community breakdown.

From an economic point of view, many greens would bring into the health field their familiar critique of the scale and profitability of many of the pharmaceutical corporations which dominate global health-care provision. The manufacturers of drugs have an incentive in hyping – or even, it is suggested, inventing – syndromes or conditions for which they have a treatment available. Such 'disease mongering' leads to a sudden huge rise in conditions such as restless legs, irritable bowel syndrome, attention deficit disorder and sexual dysfunction being publicized through media interest and online surveys, resulting in the prescription and profitable sale of drugs to treat them.[32] A similar argument can be made in the case of the manufacturers of costly medical equipment and the supplies used in the burgeoning health-screening industry. The green critique is that it is profitability rather than good health which is driving this process. Ivan Illich long ago argued that it is public sanitation and primary health care that have been the underlying causes of increased length and quality of life,[33] and the Cuban primary health-care system is a contemporary example of a system which efficiently achieves high standards of care without high technology.

So from a green perspective we need to consider health holistically, rather than as something that only arises when somebody suffers symptoms or makes an appointment at the doctor's surgery. Thus questions about the cost of health care miss the point – we are paying the price of our inability to live comfortably within our environment. If we solved this problem first health-care costs would be minimized. Another saying popular among greens who take an interest in health matters is, 'Let your food be your medicine and your medicine be your food' – an aphorism attributed to the Greek father of medicine Hippocrates. This suggests taking responsibility for the care of one's own health rather than living an unhealthy lifestyle and then expecting an expert to sort out the problems this inevitably causes.

The organization of the residual 'illness service', which citizens of a green society might require, would be locally based and responsive to personal and community priorities. Communities might invest in their own hospitals, following the proposal for a 'people's pension' outlined in the last section, and there is an interest in the idea of 'the mutual state', although subject to national basic requirements about standards and availability for users, and terms and conditions for health workers. In the area of health, as in consideration of welfare generally:

> *The community focus of green social policy integrates its decentralist, democratic, local and self-reliant aims in that a green social policy agenda would seek to allow people in communities to decide themselves how and in what way 'their' welfare ought to be provided, with the explicit goal of enabling and encouraging as many people as possible to become less reliant on either formally paid employment or welfare benefits and services.*[34]

Notes

1   T. Fitzpatrick and M. Cahill (2002) 'The new environment of welfare', in T. Fitzpatrick and M. Cahill (eds) *Environment and Welfare: Towards a Green Social Policy*, Basingstoke: Palgrave, pp. 1–20, p. 2.
2   M. Humphrey (2002) 'The ideologies of green welfare', in Fitzpatrick and Cahill (eds) *Environment and Welfare*, pp. 43–60, p. 51.
3   Fitzpatrick and Cahill, *Environment and Welfare*, p. 3.
4   J. Robertson (1998) *Beyond the Dependency Culture: People, Power and Responsibility*, London: Praeger.
5   D. Byrne (2001) 'Class, tax and spending: Problems for the Left in postindustrial and postdemocratic politics – or why aren't we taxing the fat cats till the pips squeak?', *Capital and Class*, 75: 157–66.
6   Quotation and interpretation from R. G. Wilkinson and K. E. Pickett (2009, forthcoming) *The Spirit Level: Why More Equal Societies Almost Always Do Better* (Harmondsworth, Penguin)
7   J. Robertson (2004) 'Using common resources to solve common problems', *Feasta Review 2: Growth: The Celtic Cancer*, Dublin: Feasta.
8   Wilkinson and Pickett *Spirit Level*.
9   M. S. Cato (2004) 'The freedom to be frugal', *Feasta Review 2: Growth: The Celtic Cancer*, Dublin: Feasta.
10 J. Barry (2007) 'Towards a model of green political economy: From ecological modernisation to economic security', *International Journal of Green Economics*, 1/3: 446–64.

11 R. Sapolsky (2004) author of *Why Zebras Don't Get Ulcers*, reviewing M. Marmot (2004) *Status Syndrome: How Our Position on the Social Gradient Affects Longevity and Health*, London: Bloomsbury.

12 A. Sen (1999) *Development as Freedom*, Oxford: Oxford University Press.

13 M. D. Sahlins (1972) *Stone Age Economics*, Chicago: Aldine.

14 Quoted in K. Sale (2006) *After Eden: The Evolution of Human Domination*, Durham, NC: Duke University Press, p. 131.

15 D. Fleming (2004) 'The lean economy: A vision of civility for a world in trouble', *Feasta Review 2: Growth: The Celtic Cancer*, Dublin: Feasta, p. 76.

16 W. Sachs (1992) 'Poor, not different', in Paul Ekins and Manfred Max-Neef (eds) *Real Life Economics: Understanding Wealth Creation*, London: Routledge, p. 161.

17 P. Singh (2006) 'North–South inequality, global capitalism and sustainability: transcending Marxian and Green perspectives or synthesizing the two?', paper presented at the Annual Conference of the Association of Heterodox Economics, London School of Economics, July.

18 See, for example, the work of Susan L. Cutter (1995) 'Race, class and environmental justice', *Progress in Human Geography*, 19/1: pp. 107–18.

19 J. Barry (1999) *Environment and Social Theory*, London: Routledge, ch. 4.

20 J. Porritt (1984) *Seeing Green: The Politics of Ecology Explained*, Oxford: Blackwell, pp. 216–17.

21 T. Fitzpatrick (2002) 'Green democracy and ecosocial welfare', in T. Fitzpatrick and M. Cahill (eds) *Environment and Welfare: Towards a Green Social Policy*, Basingstoke: Palgrave, pp. 61–81, pp. 64–5.

22 J. Barry and B. Doherty (2001) 'The greens and social policy: Movements, politics and practice?', *Social Policy and Administration*, 35/5: 587–607, pp. 594, 595.

23 P. Hoggett (2001) 'Democracy, social relations and ecowelfare', *Social Policy and Administration*, 35/5: 608–26, p. 615.

24 J. Jain and J. Guiver (2001) 'Turning the car inside out: Transport, equity and environment', *Social Policy and Administration*, 35/5: 569–86.

25 M. Humphrey (2002) 'The ideologies of green welfare', in Fitzpatrick and Cahill, *Environment and Welfare*, pp. 43–60.

26 J. Robertson (1998) *Transforming Economic Life*, Schumacher Briefing no. 1, Totnes: Green Books; C. Lord (2003) *Citizen's Income: A Foundation for a Sustainable World* (Charlbury: Jim Carpenter).

27 J. Robertson (1998) 'Resource taxes and green dividends: A combined package?', paper presented at a conference Sharing Our Common Heritage: Resource Taxes and Green Dividends, organized by the Oxford Centre for the Environment, Ethics and Society at Rhodes House, Oxford, 14 May; available online at: www.jamesrobertson.com/book/sharingourcommonheritage.pdf.

28 T. Fitzpatrick (2002) 'With no strings attached?', in Fitzpatrick and Cahill, *Environment and Welfare*, pp. 138–54.

20 Fitzpatrick, 'No strings'.

30 R. Murphy, C. Hines and A. Simpson (2003) *People's Pensions: New Thinking for the 21st Century*, Ely: Fulcrum Publishing.

31 R. Kaiser, I. Romieu, S. Medina, J. Schwartz, M. Kryzanowski and N. Kunzli (2004) 'Air pollution attributable postneonatal infant mortality in U.S. metropolitan areas: A risk assessment study', *Environmental Health*, 3: 4.

32 S. Cox (2008) *Sick Planet: Corporate Food and Medicine*, London: Pluto.

33 I. Illich (1975) *Medical Nemesis: The Expropriation of Health*, London: Calder and Boyars.

34 Barry and Doherty, 'The greens', p. 600.

12
Land and the Built Environment

Buy land: they're not making it any more

Mark Twain

As discussed in Chapter 3, within the green economics perspective land is a vital part of human and community identity. The view of the land is quite distinct from the reductionist conception of a 'factor of production' held by classical and neoclassical economists. For many green economists, the breakdown of our relationship with the natural world, what Mellor (2006) refers to as 'disembedding', is the fundamental source of the ecological crisis.[1] The bulk of this chapter is concerned with policies favoured by greens to manage land. However, first we need to establish the principles which provide the framework for these policies. We will begin by contrasting the green view of the role and meaning of land with that of classical economics, and move on to consider the various strands of thought that have influenced green thinking about land including the indigenous perspective; the Levellers and Diggers of 17th-century Britain; and contemporary land-rights movements. The following sections detail green policy prescriptions for sharing the value of land through a system of land taxation; planning informed by a bioregional perspective; building dwellings on land; and managing the process of growing food on land.

Land and economics

According to the classical economists, 'land' is an overarching term that stands for 'natural resources as factors of production' (*Oxford Dictionary of Economics*), thus including productive land that can be used for agriculture or development, as well as the minerals it contains. The classical economics view of land, and the justification for its private ownership, begins with John Locke, who argued that private ownership was more efficient, since it encouraged the owner to invest in and improve the land.[2] Such a view was an inherent part of Enlightenment thinking, imbued with values such as human dominion over nature, Christian virtue as related to improvement and hard work, and the dominant notion of progress.[3]

In agreement with Mark Twain, mainstream economists concede that 'the distinguishing feature of land is that it is essentially in fixed supply to the whole economy even in the long run'.[4] However, it is not considered to be inherently different from capital, and can be discussed as an equivalent 'factor of production' and considered appropriate for sale in a market which determines prices on a supply-and-demand basis. The classical economists were concerned about the ability of landowners to live from rents, which they considered led to an inefficient use of land and a failure to innovate, but this concern has declined over time among mainstream and neoclassical economists. In strong contrast to the position of green economics, classical and neoclassical economists consider land to include all the resources that the land provides, such as minerals; these are not considered in this chapter but rather in Chapter 10, which discusses ecotaxes to manage the use of such resources.

In contrast to the conventional economist's view, for the green economist land has a life of its own, rather than being an inert resource to be exploited for human ends:

> *In societies whose very existence depended upon knowing the earth and how to hunt its animals and forage for its foods – the way of life for 99 percent of human history – respect for the natural world and an appreciation of the land itself as sacred and inviolable was surely inevitable. That sensibility was literally so vital that it was embedded in some central place in each culture's myths and traditions and was embodied in each culture's supreme spirits and deities.*[5]

The green understanding of land has been deeply influenced by the approach of indigenous peoples, which one native American describes as follows:

> *All land is sacred. It is their bible. Indigenous people do not see the land as a commodity which can be sold or bought. They do not see themselves as possessors but as guardians of land. A fundamental difference between the indigenous concept of land and the western idea is that indigenous peoples belong to the land rather than the land belonging to them.*[6]

While there is no single view among green economists about whether or not land ownership is just and appropriate, the fact that this question is debated indicates in itself how powerful has been the influence of indigenous thinking. For Aldo Leopold, the intimate relationship with land, which he termed 'land ethic', was necessary to underpin both human relationships and ecological respect: 'when we see land as a *community* to which we belong, we may begin to use it with love and respect. There is no other way for land to survive the impact of mechanized man.'[7] Other commentators suggest that giving indigenous peoples the rights to their own land is a better guarantee of their protection than leaving them open to exploitation by corporations.[8] The

---

Box 12.1 MST: The land rights campaign in Brazil

One of the most prominent movements for land reform is the MST in Brazil (*Movimento dos Trabalhadores Rurais Sem Terra*, or Movement of Landless Rural Workers). The movement began in October 1983, when a large group of landless peasants from across the state of Rio Grande do Sul in southern Brazil occupied a 9200ha cattle ranch which was owned by an absentee landlord. Over the following eight years the movement staged 36 more occupations alongside protest rallies, marches and hunger strikes. They were supported by local radical priests and eventually succeeded in settling 1250 families on their own land. This campaign took place in one of the most unequal societies in the world, an inequality exacerbated by the pattern of land use in which 1 per cent of the population who are landowners control nearly half the nation's farmland. This unequal distribution pattern is a legacy of the colonial era and the MST has been a vanguard for progressive forces in both political and religious circles in Brazil to challenge the historic oligarchs. The campaign has been enormously successful, leading to the redistribution of nearly 30 million hectares of land; today some 45 per cent of Brazil's agrarian settlements are connected to the MST.

Source: M. Carter (2005) 'The MST and democracy in Brazil', Working Paper CBS–60–05, Centre for Brazilian Studies, University of Oxford.

---

example cited is that of the Chipko movement in the Himalayas, where local people were refused permission to fell their own trees, a right which was being granted to a foreign corporation. These are the famous 'tree-huggers' ('chipko' means 'to hug' in Hindi), who joined hands around their trees to protect them; their campaign eventually led to the protection of their rights to their own land.

The argument over land rights is now being made in developed Western societies, where most people migrated from the land to the urban centres several generations ago. In the UK, for example, The Land is Ours is a land rights campaign 'by and for people who believe that the roots of justice, freedom, social security and democracy lie not so much in access to money, or to the ballot box, as in access to land and its resources'.[9] As in the example of the Chipko movement, it believes that protection of the land depends on those who are reliant on the land and depend on it for their own future, hence their emphasis on low-impact development (as discussed in a later section).

There are more practical reasons for challenging the nature of land ownership that have been a constant strand in radical thinking and have been woven into green economics. In the UK context one prominent example is the Diggers, a group of men and women who carried out an early piece of non-violent direct action by climbing St George's Hill in London on April Fool's Day 1649 and proceeding to plant vegetables there. Their aim was:

> *That we may work in righteousness, and lay the Foundation of Making the Earth a Common Treasury for All, both Rich and Poor, That every one that is born in the Land, may be fed by the Earth his Mother that brought him forth, according to the Reason that rules in the Creation.*'[10]

This quotation provides a fascinating link with the indigenous wisdom already explored. The reference to 'working in righteousness' is used to draw a contrast with the process of enclosure, already under way in the UK at this time, preventing self-provisioning – a theme that has been covered in more detail in Chapter 4.

This discussion takes us on to consider how the wealth of the land would be used within a sustainable economy. The position adopted by greens can be seen as a reaction against the attitude of domination of nature that has prevailed since the Enlightenment, characterized as follows:

> *The natural world is essentially there for our benefit, our use, our comfort. The Colorado River is there to provide water for the people and farms of Southern California, needing only the technology of a Boulder Dam to complete what nature forgot to do; the Northwestern forests are there to provide lumber that the growing populations of the carelessly sprawling suburbs need to build their rightful houses; the Hudson River flows purposefully to the Atlantic so that human wastes and industrial poisons such as PCBs can be carried away, out of sight and mind, to the sea.*[11]

This stance of exploitation, a word used with no sense of moral qualm by neoclassical economists, needs to be replaced by one of respect. Here the insights of ecology are brought to bear, particularly the concepts of 'carrying capacity' and 'regenerative capacity'. Every species within its ecological niche must respect the limits of that niche if it is to survive and flourish.[12] This means keeping the level of population and consumption within the limits of that ecosystem's regenerative capacity, and not exceeding what it can support or 'carry'. These are the key ecological principles that should guide our use of the land.

So we arrive at three principles that inform the relationship between humans and land in a green economist's perspective:

- Land ownership is conceptually dubious, with a preference for stewardship. In fact, for many greens, rather than land belonging to people, people belong to the land.
- Rather than exploiting the Earth and its resources we should adopt a posture based on respect for the land, perhaps as an entity in its own right.
- Since land is a 'common treasury' or 'common wealth' it follows that it should be shared fairly between those who have a need for it, and according to that need.

Taxing land

The concept of the 'common treasury' continues to be popular among radical economists and was translated into a powerful policy prescription that has been adopted by greens in many countries: the land value tax. The idea of 'the single tax' was made popular by Henry George, whose book *Progress and Poverty* (1880) became an international best-seller and who achieved the unlikely feat of interesting millions the world over in both economics and taxation![13] The arguments made by George chimed well with the third principle outlined above, namely that the value gained from land should be shared between all members of the community.

A point made strongly by the Henry George Institute to this day is that land, while in fact providing all the value within an economy, is marginalized within economic theory:

> *Land is a distinctive factor of production, which must be considered separately from the other two factors, capital and labor. This is a point that modern-day economics de-emphasizes, or even denies outright... Land is needed for all production, for all human life and activity of any kind. When most people think of 'land', their mental picture is of farm land: crops, orchards, pastures. But in fact, our most valuable natural resource, by a very large margin, is urban land. In cities, activities take less land area per head, but more land value, because the price of city land is hundreds, sometimes thousands of times higher than the price of rural land, per unit area.* (Henry George Institute website)

The idea of a land tax is taken into policy circles under a number of different names, including Site Rental Tax and Land Value Tax, but the basic underlying principle is the same: land is the most valuable resource available to the human community and thus the value derived from it should be shared between all members of that community. This is the argument based on fairness, but it is matched by an argument based on economic efficiency, with which some green economists would be more uneasy:

> *The arguments for a land-rent tax are to do with fairness and economic efficiency. Most of the reward from rising land values goes to those who own land, while most of the cost of the activities that create rising land values does not. This is because rising land values – for example in prosperous city centres or prime agricultural areas – are largely created by the activities of the community as a whole and by government regulations and subsidies, while the higher value of each particular site is enjoyed by its owner.*[14]

The economic efficiency argument relates to the fact that there should be no incentive to keep land idle while awaiting a rise in its value or to prevent others from using it productively, or simply to live from rental incomes rather than maximizing the use of the land. It is clear that there may be something of a

Table 12.1 *Experiences with LVT in various countries*

Country	Experience
Australia	Some form of LVT in every federal state
Russia	Following privatization of land in 2001 land tax was set at fixed rate per hectare
Denmark	Land tax levied on all private property, at a rate that varies between municipalities
USA	Two-rate property and land tax used in Pennsylvania; two-rate system used in Pittsburgh between 1913 and 2001
Canada	Some cities and provinces tax land values at higher rates than improvements – a commitment to the principle of land value tax

paradox when considering the introduction of a land tax from a green perspective. Certainly, proponents of the land tax, including Henry George, saw the rentier class, those who lived from the income their land ownership generated, as holding back economic progress. They could merely sit on their land and live a comfortable life without having to engage in useful economic activity. A similar argument is made today against the holding of land for speculative reasons, including by supermarkets with their so-called 'land banks'.[15] A land tax would require the tax to be paid on the land whether it was put to productive use or not, thus increasing the pressure for using land for economic activity. This might run counter to green thinking about limits to growth and the need for 'de-growth' or a reduction in levels of economic activity as measured by GDP (for more see Chapter 7).

BOX 12.2 LAND TAX IN AUSTRALIA

Henry George made a lecture tour of Australia in 1890 and his ideas found fertile ground. His first speech, in Sydney in May and shortly after his arrival, was called 'The Land for the People'. Many towns and administrations were newly established and the prospect of taxing land, which was far easier to pin down than people and far easier to assess for value than their incomes, had immediate appeal. There was also considerable resentment about the accumulation of land in a new colony in the hands of the few. In one lecture George questioned whether 'If the first people were to parcel out heaven as men parcelled out this world, would there not be poverty in heaven itself?', and is also famously quoted as saying that the landowners of Australia were 'more destructive than the rabbit or the kangaroo'. As a result of his lecture tour many towns and states instituted forms of land value tax, including New South Wales in 1905, and a federal land tax was introduced in 1910. Australia is a federation consisting of six states, all of which have a state land tax, but with variations in implementation. At the level of local government, property rates are permitted to be based on the value of the site, a continuing commitment to the Georgist principle. From 1910 Australia had a federal land tax, whose stated intention was to break up large estates, although this was abolished in 1952. The principle of land value taxation has also been eroded by increasing levels of exemption, i.e. increasingly large amounts of land on which no land tax is payable.

Sources: G. A. Forster (2000) 'Australia: land and property tax system', *American Journal of Economics and Sociology* 59/5: 399–416; J. Pullen (2005) 'Henry George in Australia', *American Journal of Economics and Sociology* 64/2: 683–713.

There is a third, less pressing, argument in favour of a tax on land and that is to reduce the concentrated nature of land ownership. This is based on both fairness and efficiency criteria. Landholdings tend to pass from generation to generation, especially in societies like the UK's, where a lengthy historical continuity in ownership has led to increased concentration of wealth. In the UK context, 157,000 landowners hold 70 per cent of the country,[16] and 10 per cent of the land still belongs to descendants of the Plantagenets, who acquired it during land grabs following the Norman invasion of 1066! The critique of this lasting inequity in the distribution of the major source of wealth is not restricted to the more radical among green commentators. In 1984 Jonathon Porritt wrote that 'the Liberals have given up trying to get across the ideas of Henry George. And that's a pity ... the only way to break the monopoly of landownership is some form of land tax.'[17]

Building on land

The paradox identified in green economics between concern about increased economic activity and the importance of taxing land is resolved to some extent by the interaction of planning and land tax systems. A Land Value Tax could be flexible, with different rates charged to encourage particular forms of land use. For example, supermarket developments could be charged a high rate, whereas organic farmers could be charged a correspondingly low rate. Another example might be the creation of incentives to build on brownfield sites in urban areas rather than greenfield sites or greenbelt land by imposing a low rate of land tax on the former.

More widely, green planning would respond to ecology rather than to business priorities. This would mean 'the melding of ecosystem management, regenerative resource use and conservation, regional planning, regenerative systems, and sustainable community design';[18] it would be an essentially holistic process. Thayer recognizes, as all green economists must, that green planning is itself something of a paradox, since the process is intended to work from the bottom up, respecting the needs of the ecosystem and of local communities, in contrast to their present obligation to fit into hierarchical planning structures. Thayer suggests that New Zealand has moved furthest towards an ecologically responsive planning system through its Local Government Reform Act and Resource Management Act, which passed responsibility for strategic planning to the local regions, which were themselves based on hydrological basins.

The green critique of existing planning is that it responds to market priorities rather than the needs of local people or the environment. Powerful players within the existing economy can ensure that decisions that meet their needs are made, without account being taken of the negative impacts. An example might be the granting of planning permission to an out-of-town supermarket development. The costs in terms of loss of biodiversity for a greenfield site, or the increased traffic generated by the development, may not be considered when permission is given. A green economics perspective on land would suggest planning lives so that environmental impact is minimized, for example by encouraging people to live close to their place of work and to have thriving communities including shops and leisure facilities near where people live to reduce the pressure on transport.

However, the commitment to the greenbelt is not absolute, and for many greens using the land respectfully is more important than condemning the natural world to the status of a museum piece. Some greens have been at the forefront of attempts to challenge restrictive planning decisions; they argue in favour, rather, of low-impact development. Brithdir Mawr in Pembrokeshire is an example of such a development. The homes are self-built and the inhabitants meet many of their needs from the local environment. The community has been refused planning permission, but their discussions with Pembrokeshire County Council appear to have resulted in a change of policy. In 2006 the County published new planning guidance that 'provides a context for permitting development in the countryside as an exception to normal planning policy ... exemplars of sustainable living may be permitted... Proposals need to be tied to the land and provide sufficient livelihood for the occupants.'[19] Proposals for such developments need to include a 'Sustainable Livelihood' section, indicating how 75 per cent of basic household needs can be met 'by means of activities centred around the use of resources grown or occurring naturally on the site'. The permission is also dependent on minimal and sustainable travel and that if more than one family is involved 'the proposal will be managed and controlled by a trust, co-operative or other similar mechanism in which the occupiers have an interest'. In effect, the County Council is accepting that building may take place on land not available for development, when that building is for the benefit of a community who will maintain a sustainable livelihood. Questions remain about connection to services such as electricity and water, about vehicle access and about the possibility of requiring future generations or future owners to commit to the same low-impact lifestyles, but this is an interesting legal development.

These experimental low-impact communities are sometimes referred to as 'ecovillages'. At present they are spearheading a distinct view of 'sustainable development' which may mean allowing more people on to the land yet requiring a commitment from them to meet their needs locally and produce minimal pollution. So far planning guidance has not been supportive:

The tightening regulatory framework together with lack of access to official financing have acted as a significant brake on new and existing ecovillage developments. The first step in addressing this is for government at national and local level to recognize the value of ecovillages as social and technological pioneers and as catalysts for regeneration.[20]

Dawson emphasizes the regeneration potential of this form of community development; this is particularly important since many of those who live in ecovillages exist within an alternative cultural paradigm.[21]

In terms of individual dwellings, the broadly defined 'green movement' has made considerable contributions to social and technical innovation. In the UK, sustainable construction has largely taken place outside the construction industry, based on the work of committed self-builders working with organizations such as the Centre for Alternative Technology, itself an intentional community based in Machynlleth, Mid Wales. There is evidence of market failure in this sector, with demand outstripping supply and consumers being better informed and more sympathetic to sustainable building than construction 'experts'. The research makes clear that the initiators of low-energy housing development in the UK have been registered social landlords, self-builders and local authorities, with the private sector accounting for only 6 per cent of such developments.[22] The explanation is that the strong values and uniting ideology of the green movement have provided support for sustainable construction developments.

Greens also ask questions about the ownership of housing and of the land, as we have already seen. When applied to housing this is translated into novel forms of ownership, such as the Community Land Trust and co-housing. The most democratic form of shared housing is arguably the Mutual Home Ownership Model developed by David Rodgers and Pat Conaty of CDS (Co-operative Development Society) Co-operatives in the UK. As they describe it, it is a 'market-equity form of tenure in which residents have an equity stake in residential property'.[23] However, it is distinct from private ownership and a conventional market involvement in the housing market because 'The residents interested and eligible for the housing are admitted into membership of a Mutual Home Ownership Trust (MHOT), a registered Industrial and Provident Society. This enables variation on statutory tenancy provisions and allows flexibility between equity and lease-holding; it also allows increase in equity value to be tax exempt as in conventional home ownership.' In other words owners can keep in step with the housing market in spite of not fully owning their homes, and not owning the land their houses are built on. The process of equity creation by CLTS is illustrated in Figure 12.1.

The MHOT model is based on joint ownership and a shared mortgage which is taken out against a portfolio of property. This is then divided up into units which residents 'buy' and pay for with monthly mortgage payments. They can increase or reduce the number of units they own as their individual circumstances dictate. Monthly charges are set at 35 per cent of net income, which is considered an affordable level and is related to the individual's ability to pay in a way that market housing purchase is not. There are two levels of ownership within the CLT: one common and the other private. Some people will own many shares in the CLT and gain an income from them; others will only own a few. This is distinct from the amount of space people occupy in the houses themselves. Hence, according to Conaty, 'CLTs are best viewed as a

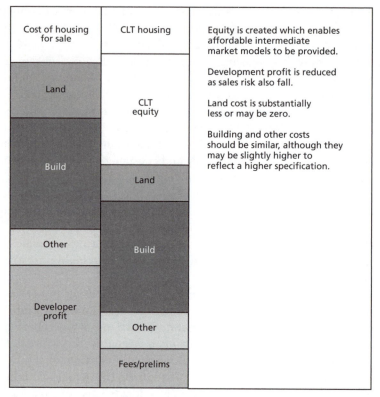

Figure 12.1 *Equity creation through a CLT*

Source: Community Finance Solutions.

form of dynamic property rights that seeks to find a mutual modus vivendi between individualism and collectivism.'

Co-housing is another innovative approach to home ownership that is favoured by greens. Co-housing is based around notions of 'shared space' and a concern that individualized lifestyles in contemporary society are not only socially divisive and pernicious at the community level, but also require an increased level of resources per person and are thus environmentally inefficient. A survey of 14 shared-living projects in Germany (a system similar to co-housing) found that the inability to share space communally and the felt need to own to the exclusion of others is leading to overconsumption of space and resources.[24] For this reason 'Building a sustainable community one neighbourhood at a time' is the mission statement of the US Co-housing movement. Co-housing developments often require residents to meet other ecological criteria, such as low-energy designs or the exclusion of cars within the area of the project. Co-housing is popular in Scandinavia and the US. It represents an important step towards breaking down the individualism created by market solutions to housing need and can help to rebuild community and thus offer support to more vulnerable members of society.

Photo 12.1 *Springhill Co-housing, Stroud*

BOX 12.3 CO-HOUSING IN DENMARK

The idea of co-housing began in Denmark in the early 1960s and is generally considered to have been initiated by Jan Gudmund-Hoyer, an architect, and Bodil Graae, who wrote an article called 'Children should have one hundred parents'. This title makes clear the commitment in the co-housing movement to community. Building was begun in 1968 and two communities – Saettedammen and Skraplanet – were ready for habitation by the end of 1973. In 1971 the Danish Building Research Institute sponsored a national design competition for low-rise, clustered housing: the winning proposal focused on the importance of residents being involved in the design of their homes and the sharing of facilities. This supported the spread of the co-housing movement in Denmark, and the first rental co-housing community – Tinggarden – was built in 1976. By 1982 there were 22 owner-occupied co-housing communities in Denmark. Co-housing is now a popular and common form of home building in Denmark and its innovative design aspects, including shared facilities such as gardens and community houses and a range of housing units of different sizes and ownership types, has spread into the mainstream home development sector.

Source: D. Milman (1994) 'Where it all began: Co-housing in Denmark' (Co-housing company) www.getriil.org/cgiwrap/getriil/details.php?anum=1505.

Growing on the land

The most fundamental role played by land in any human community is as a provider of food and for the past 10,000 years or so that has been increasingly through agricultural systems. However, the systems of farming that have developed have been increasingly intensive and have not been within the bounds of

Figure 12.2 *Agriculture and economic systems of sustainable agriculture*

Note: All systems are organic.
Source: Drawings by Imogen Shaw.

ecology. Whether we think of the highly water-intensive agriculture of California[25] or the monocultural production systems that underlie most of our staple food crops such as rice and maize, modern agriculture does not live in balance with nature.[26] Green economists' criticism of this industrial form of agriculture has three main strands: the failure to function in balance with nature (what ecologists would call 'draw down'); the loss of cultural and species diversity as a result of the development of global agricultural monocultures; and the threat to human health from unnatural farming practices.

Jules Pretty suggests that, although farming has been in existence for 600 generations, during which time it was 'intimately connected to cultural and social systems',[27] in the past two or three generations these connections have been lost, resulting in damage to biodiversity, water quality and human health. He details how food crises such as BSE ('mad cow disease') and the lack of trust in genetically modified crops have undermined faith in conventional, large-scale farming methods. What is more, in an era of climate change and

---

BOX 12.4 THE PRINCIPLES OF PERMACULTURE

- Working with nature saves energy.
- The problem is the solution.
- Make the least change for the greatest possible effect.
- The yield of a system is theoretically unlimited (or only limited by the imagination and information of the designer).
- Everything gardens (or modifies its environment).

Source: W. Mollison (1998) *Permaculture: A Designer's Manual*, Sister's Creek, Tasmania: Tagari.

---

peak oil, where energy must be used to achieve the maximum in terms of human well-being, the agro-industrial system is seen to be grossly inefficient, requiring 10 calories of energy to produce 1 calorie of food.[28] Tudge sketches the green alternative:

> *A system of farming that was truly designed to feed people and to go on doing so for the indefinite future would be founded primarily on mixed farms and local production. In general, each country ... would contrive to be self-reliant in food. Self-reliant does not mean self-sufficient... Self-reliance does mean, however, that each country would produce its own basic foods, and be able to get by in a crisis.*[29]

Such a system of local production for local consumption, working within the existing ecosystem would owe much to a system of farming known as 'perma-

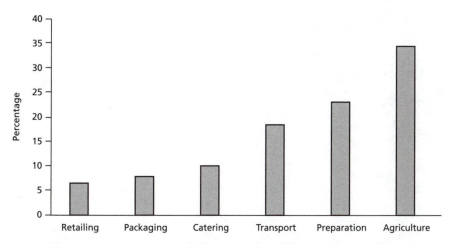

Figure 12.3 *Percentage of energy used in different aspects of food production and distribution*

Source: Data from C. Lucas, A. Jones and C. Hines (2006) *Fuelling a Food Crisis: The Impact of Peak Oil on Food Security*, Brussels: Green Group in the European Parliament.

Box 12.5 Stroud Community Agriculture

Stroud Community Agriculture is a community-supported farm on two sites between Stroud and Gloucester in the West Country, UK. The farm sites are both owned by educational institutions and make up about 45 acres of farmland in total. The sites are both mixed farms with vegetable-growing and animals, plus hay, grassland and green manures, all farmed according to biodynamic principles (a system based on the theories of Rudolf Steiner). One of the sites belongs to Wynstones Steiner School and was formally called Kolisko Farm – a pioneering Steiner venture. By 2007 the SCA was supplying vegetables to 150 families on a share system, i.e. people paid a monthly sum to be members of the farm, in return for which they received a share of what was produced each month. The farm owns a certain amount of equipment but the major costs are farmers' wages and land rental. The farm is managed by a core group of members elected each year at the AGM. Connecting with the land is a key theme of the farm's activity, with a cycle of festivals reflecting the turning of the year. Seasonality is obviously also built into the provision of vegetables as is a near elimination of 'food miles'. Members of the farm are encouraged to participate in monthly farmdays, and many also contribute extra time; for labour-intensive activities such as haymaking as many members as possible are involved. The farm spreads farming skills among members and has an apprentice with whom these skills are shared.

culture', first developed by Australian ecologists. The principles of permaculture are outlined in Box 12.4. As well as working positively with ecological systems, permaculture makes use of indigenous knowledge. An example is the traditional Zuni farming practices in what is now New Mexico;[30] these were sustainable and productive, but were undermined by US assimilation policies that resulted in the degradation of natural resources. The Zuni people are now

Photo 12.2 *Stroud Community Agriculture: Weeding in the cabbage patch*

Source: Photograph courtesy of Nick Weir.

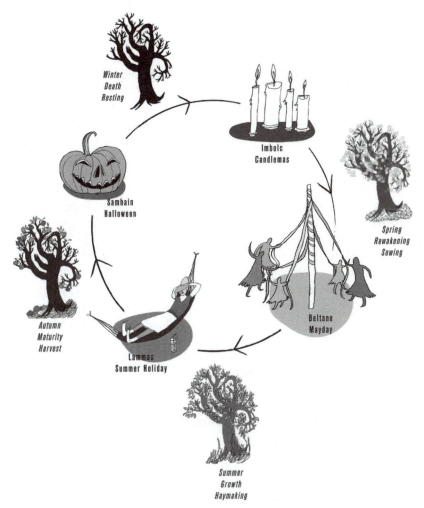

Figure 12.4 *The turning of the year: The annual cycle of growing and celebration on the land source*

Source: Drawings by Imogen Shaw.

working to combine their traditional values, knowledge and technology with other forms of scientifically based knowledge to develop a sustainable form of agriculture.

During the economic crisis in Cuba after the ending of Soviet economic support, Australian permaculturalists used the country as a test bed for their ideas about small-scale, urban, pro-ecology agriculture, and with very impressive results. The Cubans extended their existing system of *huertos* (urban vegetable gardens), spreading them to rooftops and verges, and created *organopónicos*, a kind of organic allotment system. By the mid-1990s there were over 28,000 *huertos* in Havana city province, run by 50–100,000 individuals. Cuba was producing between 80 and 90 per cent of its own vegetables, and Havana produced enough to meet 50 per cent of its own needs within the city boundary.[31]

Green agriculture would be almost exclusively organic in nature. There are two major reasons for this: first that organic agriculture follows the principles of permaculture by working with nature rather than against it, thereby preserving the environment, and second that, as shown in Figure 12.3, the greatest proportion of oil used in food manufacture is actually used on the farm (to produce fertilizer, for farm machinery and to produce pesticides). Greens would use subsidy systems to encourage the transition towards sustainable agriculture. Scotland's Organic Action Plan is a case in point. It began as the Organic Farming Bill, put forward by Robin Harper MSP on behalf of the Scottish Green Party. Having been amended it gained the support of a majority of Scotland's elected members and now provides support for organic farmers as a sustainable sector. The target for the plan was to have 30 per cent of Scotland's arable or grassland in organic production by 2007.

Linking concerns with ownership and with sharing and reconnecting with the land brings us to a system of farming known as community-supported agriculture (CSA). As in the example of Stroud Community Agriculture (Box 12.5), such schemes change the relationship between farmer and consumer, who now enjoy a much closer link than that typical in the market. Participants in a CSA pay an annual or monthly amount to support the farmer in her/his vital role and then receive a share of the produce. The advantage for the farmer is the removal of anxiety over her/his income and finding an automatic market for the produce; the advantage for the customer is a closer relationship with the land and knowledge about how her/his food is produced.

Notes

1   M. Mellor (2006) 'Ecofeminist political economy', *International Journal of Green Economics*, 1/1–2: pp. 139–50.
2   J. Locke [1690] (1980) *Second Treatise of Government*, ed. C. B. Macpherson, Indianapolis, IN: Hackett; D. Russell (2004) 'Locke on land and labor', *Philosophical Studies*, 117/1–2: 303–25.
3   J. Barry (1999) *Environment and Social Theory*, London: Routledge, ch. 8.
4   D. Begg, S. Fischer and R. Dornbusch (1991) *Economics*, London: McGraw-Hill, p. 228.
5   K. Sale (2000) *Dwellers in the Land: The Bioregional Vision*, Athens, GA: University of Georgia Press, p. 5.
6   D. Zapata and S. Schielmann (1999) 'Indigenous peoples, globalisation, and transnational corporations', in M. S. Cato and M. Kennet (eds) *Green Economics: Beyond Supply and Demand to Meeting People's Needs*, Aberystwyth: Green Audit, pp. 234–43, p. 236.
7   A. Leopold (1949) *A Sand County Almanac and Sketches Here and There*, New York: Oxford University Press.

8   J. Pretty (2002) *Agri-culture: Reconnecting People, Land and Nature*, London: Earthscan.

9   www.tlio.org.uk; see also G. Monbiot (1996) 'The Land is Ours', Schumacher Lecture, Bristol, October.

10 G. Winstanley (1989) *Selected Writings*, ed. Andrew Hopton, Nepean, Ont: Aporia Press, p. 15

11 Sale, *Dwellers*, p. 22.

12 R. Thayer (2003) *LifePlace: Bioregional Thought and Practice*, Berkeley, CA: University of California Press.

13 H. George (1880) *Progress and Poverty: An Inquiry into the Cause of Industrial Depressions and of Increase of Want*, New York: Appleton & Co.

14 J. Robertson (1999) 'A green taxation and benefits system', in Cato and Kennet, *Green Economics*, pp. 65–86, pp. 67–8.

15 A. Simms (2007) *Tescopoly: Why One Shop Came Out on Top And Why It Matters*, London: Constable.

16 K. Cahill (2005) *Who Owns Britain: The Hidden Facts Behind Landownership in the UK and Ireland*, Edinburgh: Canongate, p. 209.

17 J. Porritt (1984) *Seeing Green: The Politics of Ecology Explained*, Oxford: Blackwell, p. 181.

18 Thayer, *LifePlace*, p. 163.

19 Pembrokeshire County Council (2006) Supplementary Planning Guidance: Low Impact Development Making a Positive Contribution, Haverfordwest: PCC, p. 1.

20 J. Dawson (2006) *Ecovillages: New Frontiers for Sustainability*, Schumacher Briefings no. 12, Totnes: Green Books, p. 84.

21 H. Lovell (2004) 'Framing sustainable housing as a solution to climate change', *Journal of Environmental Policy & Planning*, 6/1: 35–55.

22 H. Lovell (2005) 'Supply and demand for low energy housing in the UK: Insights from a science and technology studies approach', *Housing Studies*, 20/5: 815–29.

23 Community Finance Solutions (2006) 'Community Land Trusts: Affordable Homes, in Sustainable Communities', Salford: Community Finance Solutions.

24 A. Sennlaub (2005) 'Living with commons – between strain and opportunity: The sustainability of habitation through communal ownership', *GAIA: Ecological Perspectives for Science and Society*, 14/4: 323–32.

25 B. Joyce, S. Vicuna, L. Dale, J. Dracup, M. Hanemann, D. Purkey and D. Yates (2006) *Climate Change Impacts on Water for Agriculture in California: A Case Study in the Sacramento Valley*, Berkeley, CA: California Climate Change Center.

26 V. Shiva (1999) *Stolen Harvest: The Hijacking of the Global Food Supply*, Cambridge, MA: South End Press.

27 Pretty, *Agri-culture*, p. xii.

28 R. Heinberg (2006) 'Threats of peak oil to the global food supply', paper presented at the FEASTA Conference, 'What Will We Eat as the Oil Runs Out?, 23–25 June, Dublin, Ireland: www.richardheinberg.com/museletter/159.

29 C. Tudge (2003) *So Shall We Reap: What's Gone Wrong with the World's Food – And How to Fix It*, Harmondsworth: Penguin.

30 D. A. Cleveland, F. Bowannie, D. F. Eriacho, A. Laahty and E. Perramond (1995) 'Zuni farming and United States government policy: The politics of biological and cultural diversity in agriculture', *Agriculture and Human Values*, 12/3: 2–18.

31 Heinberg, 'Threats of Peak Oil'.

13
Summary and Further Resources

Chapter 1: Green Economics: Economics for People and the Planet

Green economics broadens the perspective of 'economics' beyond the concerns of the 'rational economic man'. It seeks to include the perspectives of those who are marginalized within the present economic structure – primarily women and the poor of the world – as well as taking seriously the needs of the planet itself.

Green economics has not grown up as an academic discipline but from the grassroots. It is distinct from environmental economics, which uses conventional economics but brings the environment into the equation, and ecological economics, which is still an academically focused discipline. Green economics is rather about people and the planet.

Green economics seeks to move the target of our economy away from economic growth and towards flourishing, convivial human communities which do not threaten other species or the planet itself. In place of economic growth we should move towards a steady-state economy.

Green economics is the first significant alternative to capitalism that is not communism. It offers a different economic paradigm to challenge neoliberalism.

Chapter 2: Where Did It All Start?

Aristotle's distinction between a household economy (*oikonomia*) and an economy dominated by money and property (*chrematistics*) is a good starting point for a green consideration of economics.

Greens are also happy to take lessons from Marx, although their attitude to socialism in practice varies. They are likely to have more sympathy with the worldview of the utopian socialists such as Peter Kropotkin and Robert Owen.

Many green economists acknowledge a spiritual inspiration and grounding, although this source emerges as an eclectic range of organized and disorganized religions.

James Robertson (1928–) has made a vast contribution to the development of green economics, covering areas such as the reorganization of work, the design of just money systems, and taxation and welfare policy.

E. F. Schumacher (1911–1977) gave the green economist the slogan 'small is beautiful', summarizing his concern with scale in economics. His other major contributions were in terms of intermediate technology and his Buddhist economics.

Kenneth Boulding (1910–1993) invented the field of 'evolutionary economics' – an attempt to combine economics with ecology. He proposed a circular rather than a linear economy and invented the analogy of the spaceship Earth as a symbol for the way we should care for our planet.

Nicolas Georgescu-Roegen (1910–1994) made his major contribution by applying the second law of thermodynamics ('the entropy law') to economics, thus making clear that economics must respond to the limited nature of the planet and its energy.

Hazel Henderson (1933–) is an evolutionary economist who has written widely on green economics themes. She is most famous for her model of the global economy as a cake, of which conventional economics only considers the highest layer.

Richard Douthwaite (1942–) began by critiquing the concept of economic growth but now works mainly on energy and climate issues. He has also worked practically in local economic development and the creation of alternative currencies.

Green economists are sceptical of the role of academic economics, which they see as providing a fig leaf for the operation of the neoclassical economy and the politicians who support it. Alternatives are now arising in the form of the Heterodox Economists Association and the Post-Autistic Economics Network.

Chapter 3: Economics and Identity

A green economy will be guided by sustainability values rather than monetary value.

The central change will be from considering economy, environment and society as intersecting but separate to recognizing that the economy is located within society, which is in turn embedded within the environment.

A green economy will abandon the present addiction to economic growth and become a steady-state economy.

A green economy will be a convivial economy where relationships and communities substitute for consumption and technology.

More aspects of our economic lives will take place outside the market, which will itself change to become concerned with human interactions rather than monetary transactions.

Patriarchy has led to the denial of our dependence on nature and our disconnection with our physical selves: as the key cause of environmental crisis this must be reversed, with a re-embedding into the environment economically and socially.

Permaculture principles are useful in guiding economic developments; for example, we will have more examples of closed-loop economics, where the consequences of our economic decisions impinge on us directly rather than being exported to other distant communities.

Chapter 4: Work

There is a tension among green economists between those who would reclaim the control of work-based production and make it more sustainable and those who would move towards a future of self-reliant communities with a greater role for self-provisioning.

There is agreement that the use of resources to make items which are unnecessary and merely generate profits is wasteful, and that in the short term we will experience a Green Industrial Revolution which will involve a large input of labour to make the shift towards sustainable systems.

Greens favour a system of 'ownwork' where people are more in control of their own time and reject the alienating form of work that has developed under industrial capitalism.

The move towards a sustainable economy will also require a considerable degree of reskilling and more labour-intensive forms of skilled employment such as in mending and repairing.

A green economy would have a wider role for the informal economy and for cooperative and community-based systems of mutual support; this is in contrast to sucking ever more areas of our lives into the market.

Several green economists have been inspired by medieval economics, including the concept of the 'just price' and the organization of production through craft-based guilds.

Chapter 5: Money

Green economists are critical of the capitalist money system because: it is undemocratic with banks holding the power over a crucial economic institution; it channels energy in other directions than those which would achieve maximum human well-being; it leads to inequality within and between countries; the nature of money creation by debt leads to pressure on the planet's resources.

The reserve currency system that was set up at Bretton Woods following the end of the Second World War has led to massive global inequalities and is in urgent need of revision.

Money is not linked to economic value, and its growth through the creation of debts creates pressure to work to earn money to repay those debts – hence it inherently creates a strong motivation towards economic growth and growth in financially profitable activity.

Environmentalists have been well represented in the growth of alternative currencies around the world, which they see as more humane currency schemes that will support the development of local economies, and maybe substitute for them if the unstable money system collapses.

There is disagreement among green economists about whether we need a wholesale democratization of money creation or just a strengthened system of local currencies to complement national bank money.

Chapter 6: Green Business: From Maximizing Profits to a Vision of Conviviality

Greens reject the idea that 'business-as-usual' can lead to a sustainable future and consider 'sustainable development' to be an oxymoron.

For green economists the issue of scale is key to accountability and environmental responsibility; hence businesses will be inherently limited to a certain optimum size.

Much can be achieved by 'learning to switch the lights off' and using energy as efficiently as possible, as well as by tracing the environmental impact of production processes and supply chains, the so-called 'ecological rucksack' approach.

In a sustainable economy businesses will lead the way in learning from nature; hence the importance of closed-loop production systems and biomimicry – products such as Velcro that follow nature's design.

The green economy will be a convivial economy where relationships and self-generated jobs will substitute for the high-energy, unsustainable lifestyles of today.

Chapter 7: The Policy Context

Green economists reject the 'ecological modernization' discourse which suggests that we can achieve sustainability without significant changes to our social and economic structures.

Green policies are unlikely to be based on market solutions and will involve an enhanced role for mutual and community-based economic activity, widely defined, within a framework of strict international regulation of environmental and social standards.

In the case of climate change, for example, green economists would favour a system of sharing CO_2 emissions equally between the world's citizens; hence support for the Contraction and Convergence model.

There is debate among green economists about whether a system of rationing, such as the TEQs proposed by David Fleming, or a system of tradable permits, such as the cap-and-share proposal from Richard Douthwaite, would be more effective at curbing CO_2 emissions.

Greens reject GDP as a useful measure of economic life, suggesting instead simple human-scale measures such as the ecological footprint, and keeping in mind that some of the most import aspects of life simply cannot be measured.

Chapter 8: Globalization and Trade

Greens are sceptical about the benefits of the vast increase in global trade that has occurred since the Second World War and challenge the 'theory of comparative advantage' on the basis of which it is justified.

The terms of global trade are controlled by political focus and this, combined with the system of reserve currencies, allows the wealthy nations to take an unfair share of the world's commodities.

Trade is not the solution to global poverty: the countries of the South would be better placed if they focused on self-sufficiency rather than export-led growth.

The recognition that climate change is caused by CO_2 emissions is a major threat to the global trade system, which relies on extended supply chains to generate profits.

Green economists propose a system of 'trade subsidiarity' where we trade for luxuries rather than necessities and begin our search for goods at the local level, only moving further afield when we have exhausted more local options.

At the global level, greens propose a General Agreement on Sustainable Trade (GAST) to replace the World Trade Organization. It would allow governments to protect their domestic industries for reasons of resource security, environmental protection or social benefit.

Chapter 9: Relocalizing Economic Relationships

The system of globalization has left local communities vulnerable and in an era of dwindling oil supplies there should be more focus on resource security and especially food security.

The focus of policy should be sustainable communities, with policies to support them including site-here-to-sell-here clauses, import and export tariffs, and encouragement of mutual aid and community projects.

A sustainable territory will also need to take control of its financial system, replacing its reliance on a global currency that responds to the demands of the international financial system with local currencies and banking systems.

Beyond this, green economists propose moving towards a system of inter-related bioregional economies, each rooted within its own environmental and cultural niche – bioregions will be self-sufficient in their basic resources.

While the transition towards localization will inevitably result in some hardship, the future of small, self-reliant communities that green economists envisage will require us to use our creativity and ingenuity as more fully rounded human beings.

Chapter 10: Green Taxation

A green taxation system would be used strategically to achieve three objectives: a fair distribution of resources, efficient use of non-renewable resources and the elimination of wasteful economic activity, whether through production or consumption.

To achieve equality within nations, greens would support changes to inheritance tax and higher rates of income tax; to begin to redress international inequalities, greens support the introduction of a Tobin Tax on international speculation in currency values.

Greens argue for taxes on commons, whose value should be shared between all citizens: the primary example is a Land Value Tax, but another example is a carbon tax on the right to pollute the global atmosphere.

Taxes on resources and pollution can be used strategically as resources become more or less in demand and more or less scarce. Scandinavian experience with resource taxes and the German experience with taxes on mineral oils and electricity were the consequence of political activity by green parties.

Because environmental taxes can be regressive, i.e. hitting the poorer members of society hardest, they need to be combined with welfare measures such as a Citizens' Income scheme which can be funded from the tax yield.

Chapter 11: Green Welfare

Greens are deeply aware of the relationship between human needs and what the planet can supply and question the assumption of the modern economy that more will make us happier.

Because of the need for limits to economic growth the issue of sharing the Earth's resources fairly is particularly salient.

Greens favour autonomy and small-scale solutions and are thus sceptical about the state in general and the welfare state in particular.

Beyond a basic level of sufficiency, the appropriate standard of living for a human community is socially and culturally determined.

Greens favour the introduction of a Citizens' Income – a universal welfare payment made to all citizens as a basic right of citizenship and without any reciprocal demands.

In a green economy the health system would focus on fostering good health and providing primary care, on a local basis, rather than on high-tech medicine and pervasive pharmaceutical corporations.

Chapter 12: Land and the Built Environment

Rather than a 'factor of production' greens see land as a common treasury which should be respected and shared fairly; for some the concept of land ownership is itself problematic.

Green economists favour a land tax both for reasons of equity (a way of sharing the proceeds of a common resource) and to enable better and more efficient management of land by local communities.

While green planning would prioritize fitting human development within ecological systems, there might be less strict enforcement of greenbelt restrictions and permission to live on the land for those who would be prepared to live sustainably from the land.

Sustainable construction has largely emerged from the work of green activists; green home building also favours shared living space and co-housing schemes, as well as cooperative approaches to home ownership.

In terms of growing food on the land, a green economy would replace the current fossil-fuel and intensive agriculture systems with organic agriculture, and systems such as community-supported agriculture, where people are much more closely linked to the sources of their food.

Further Resources

Websites

James Robertson's personal website that provides an excellent showcase for his work: www.jamesrobertson.com

FEASTA, Foundation for the Economics of Sustainability, a Dublin-based think tank co-founded by Richard Douthwaite: www.feasta.org

E. F. Schumacher Society: www.schumachersociety.org

Lean Economy Connection – research centre founded by David Fleming: www.theleaneconomyconnection.net

New Economics Foundation: www.neweconomics.org/gen

The website of the radical economics journal *Sustainable Economics*: www.sustecweb.co.uk

My blog on radical economics: http://gaianeconomics.blogspot.com/

Gaian Economics – a showcase for some work on radical green economics: www.gaianeconomics.org/

Hazel Henderson's work on ethical markets can be found at: www.EthicalMarkets.com and www.EthicalMarkets.tv. Her quality-of-life indicators can be found at: www.Calvert-Henderson.com. Her personal website is: www.hazelhenderson.com

Association of Heterodox Economists: www.open.ac.uk/socialsciences/hetecon

Post-Autistic Economics Network: www.paecon.net

The Transition Towns wiki provides information about the towns which are part of the movement: www.transitiontowns.org

Rob Hopkins' personal blog: http://transitionculture.org

Community Land Trusts: www.communitylandtrust.org.uk

Co-housing in the UK: www.cohousing.org.uk/ and in the US: www.cohousing.org

The Land is Ours, the UK land rights campaign: www.tlio.org.uk

Henry George Institute, with information on land taxation: www.henrygeorge.org

Time banking: www.timebanking.org

International Journal of Community Currency Research: www.le.ac.uk/ulmc/ijccr

Forum for Stable Currencies: www.monies.cc

Green Economics Enterprise in Toronto, Canada: www.greeneconomics.net

Green Economics Institute which publishes the *International Journal of Green Economics*: www.greeneconomics.org.uk

Growth Madness: http://growthmadness.org

The French anti-growth movement: www.decroissance.info

Workgroup on Solidarity Socio-Economy: www.socioeco.org/en

Intermediate Technology Development Group: www.socioeco.org/en

Books

Barry, J. (1999) *Rethinking Green Politics: Nature, Virtue and Progress*, London: Sage

Barry, J. (2007) 'Towards a model of green political economy: From ecological modernisation to economic security', *International Journal of Green Economics*, 1/3: 446–64

Boulding, K. E. (1966) 'The economics of the coming spaceship earth', in H. Jarrett (ed) *Environmental Quality in a Growing Economy*, Washington, DC: Johns Hopkins University Press; available online at: www.panarchy.org/boulding/spaceship.1966.html

Cato, M. S. (2006) *Market, Schmarket: Building the Post-Capitalist Economy*, Gretton: New Clarion Press

Cato, M. S. and Kennet, M. (eds) (1999) *Green Economics: Beyond Supply and Demand to Meeting People's Needs*, Aberystwyth: Green Audit

Chambers, N., Simmons, C. and Wackernagel, M. (2000) *Sharing Nature's Interest: Ecological Footprints as an Indicator of Sustainability*, London: Earthscan

Coates, C. (2001) *Utopia Britannica: British Utopian Experiments: 1325–1945*, Lancaster: Diggers and Dreamers Publications

Daly, H. (1977) *Steady State Economics*, San Francisco: W. H. Freeman

Douthwaite, R. (1992) *The Growth Illusion: How Economic Growth Has Enriched the Few, Impoverished the Many and Endangered the Planet*, Totnes: Green Books

Douthwaite, R. (1996) *Short Circuit: Strengthening Local Economies for Security in an Unstable World*, Totnes: Green Books

Douthwaite, R. (1999) *The Ecology of Money*, Schumacher Briefing no. 4, Totnes: Green Books

Dresner, S. and Ekins, P. (2004) *Green Taxes and Charges: Reducing their Impact on Low-Income Households*, York: Joseph Rowntree Foundation

Ekins, P., Hillman, M. and Hutchinson, R. (1992) *Wealth Beyond Measure: An Atlas of New Economics*, London: Gaia Books

Hawken, P., Lovins, A., and Lovins, L. H. (1999) *Natural Capitalism: Creating the Next Industrial Revolution*, Snowmass, CO: Rocky Mountain Institute

Henderson, H. (1981/1988) *The Politics of the Solar Age: Alternatives to Economics*, first published by Doubleday, New York and republished by Knowledge Systems, Indianapolis, IN

Henderson, H. (2007) *Ethical Markets: Growing the Green Economy*, White River Junction, VT: Chelsea Green

Hines, C. (2000) *Localization: A Global Manifesto*, London: Earthscan

Hutchinson, F. (1998) *What Everybody Really Wants to Know About Money*,

Charlbury: Jon Carpenter

Hutchinson, F., Mellor, M. and Olsen, W. (2002) *The Politics of Money: Towards Sustainability and Economic Democracy*, London: Pluto

Jackson, T. (2002) *Chasing Progress: Beyond Measuring Economic Growth*, London: New Economics Foundation

Legum, M. (2002) *It Doesn't Have to be Like This*, Cape Town: Ampersand

McIntosh, A. (2001) *Soil and Soul: People Versus Corporate Power*, London: Aurum

Milani, B. (2000) *Designing the Green Economy: The Postindustrial Alternative to Corporate Globalization*, Lanham, MD: Rowman & Littlefield

North, P. (2007) *Money and Liberation: The Micropolitics of Alternative Currency Movements*, Minneapolis: University of Minnesota Press

Porritt, J. (2006) *Capitalism as if the World Matters*, London: Earthscan

Pretty, J. (2002) *Agri-culture: Reconnecting People, Land and Nature*, London: Earthscan

Robertson, J. (1985) *Future Work: Jobs, Self-employment and Leisure after the Industrial Age*, London: Temple Smith/Gower

Robertson, J. (1989) *Future Wealth: New Economics for the 21st Century*, London: Cassell

Rowbotham, M. (1998) *The Grip of Death: A Study of the Modern Money, Debt Slavery and Destructive Economics*, Charlbury: Jon Carpenter

Rowbotham, M. (2000) *Goodbye America! Globalisation, Debt and the Dollar Empire*, Charlbury: Jon Carpenter

Sale, K. (2000) *Dwellers in the Land: The Bioregional Vision*, Athens, GA: University of Georgia Press

Schumacher, E. F. (1973) *Small is Beautiful: A Study of Economics as if People Mattered*, London: Abacus

Thayer, R. (2003) *LifePlace: Bioregional Thought and Practice*, Berkeley, CA: University of California Press

Tudge, C. (2003) *So Shall We Reap: What's Gone Wrong with the World's Food – And How to Fix It*, Harmondsworth: Penguin

Waring, M. (1989) *If Women Counted: A New Feminist Economics*, London: Harper Collins

Woodin, M. and Lucas, C. (2004) *Green Alternatives to Globalisation: A Manifesto*, London: Pluto

Abbreviations and Glossary

business-as-usual	a phrase applied by sceptics to the view that the ecological crisis can be solved by technological means and without significant change to the economic system
biomimicry	product design that is inspired by nature, e.g. Velcro
C&C	Contraction and Convergence: a proposed system of reducing global greenhouse gas emissions on the basis of an equal share for every global citizen
cap-and-share	a scheme for allocating the right to produce CO_2 between citizens of a nation state
carbon trading	a system allowing countries or organizations to exchange the right to produce CO_2 so that those who can more efficiently reduce emissions reduce more and are paid money in compensation

carrying capacity	the size of population of species that an ecosystem can support within its natural resource limits and without degrading natural capital for future generations
CI	Citizens' Income: a payment made to every citizen of a state as a right and without reciprocal demands or duties
CLT	Community Land Trust: a system of mutual land ownership by the community
community currencies	alternative forms of money issued by local communities to help strengthen their local economies
CSA	community-supported agriculture
CSR	corporate social responsibility
Defra	Department for Environment, Food and Rural Affairs (UK)
ecological footprint	a way of measuring human demand on the planet in terms of productive land
ecological rucksack	the total weight of material flow carried by an item of consumption in the course of its life cycle
ecological modernization	academic and policy discourse which suggests that sustainability is possible without systemic social and environmental changes
ecotaxes	taxes designed to achieve environmental benefits
embodied energy	the amount of fossil-fuel energy required to make a product that is directly related to the climate change impact of that product
ETS	Emissions Trading System: EU system of carbon trading
Gaia hypothesis	the perception of planet Earth as a single, self-regulating living organism
GAST	General Agreement on Sustainable Trade: a proposed sustainable alternative to the present world trading system
GDP	Gross Domestic Product: a key measure of a country's economic activity within the conventional economic paradigm
Green Industrial Revolution	the idea that moving to a sustainable economy will require an upsurge of ingenuity and activity analogous that which occurred at the dawn of industrialism
greenwash	attempt by a company, generally a large corporation with a significant PR budget, to paint its activities as greener than they are
IMF	International Monetary Fund
intermediate technology	a means of transferring sophisticated technologies to poorer countries using resources available there
ISEW	Index of Sustainable Economic Welfare: a proposed alternative to GDP as a measure of economic activity
Kyoto Protocol	an international agreement adopted in 1997 with the aim of reducing the signatories' greenhouse gas emissions
LDCs	less-developed countries
LVT	Land Value Taxation
NEF	New Economics Foundation
Passivhaus	home designed so that it can be naturally warmed and ventilated without the need for energy inputs
peak oil	the idea that oil production will reach a peak and then decline, with a severe impact on global economic activity

permaculture	a system for designing human settlements so that they mimic the interrelated structure of natural systems
reskilling	the idea that to make possible the sustainable self-reliant communities of the future we will need to learn more practical skills
Right Livelihood Award	the alternative green version of the Nobel Prize, awarded annually by the Swedish Parliament
self-provisioning	providing for more individual or community needs oneself and without resorting to the market
social economy	the part of the economy that is outside the market and the state and responds to human needs rather than the profit motive – a new way of describing 'mutual aid'
solidarity economy	an approach to the global economy that foregrounds social justice in economic relationships
TEQs	a system for rationing the right to produce CO_2 on an individual basis
TNCs	transnational corporations
triple-bottom-line	a way of measuring a company or organization that includes accounting consideration of social and environmental consequences rather than focusing exclusively on the economic
UNCTAD	United Nations Conference on Trade and Development
UNFPA	United Nations Population Fund
UNSNA	United Nations System of National Accounts: the international standard for measuring economic activity within the conventional economic paradigm
WTO	World Trade Organization
zero-carbon house	a home that is neutral in terms of its CO_2 emissions because its fossil-fuel use is offset by the energy it generates via renewable technologies

Index